横浜

Yokohama
Yankee

横浜
Yokohama
Yankee

MY FAMILY'S FIVE GENERATIONS
AS OUTSIDERS IN JAPAN

2 錢貳 Sᴺ

LESLIE HELM
飛行郵便

CHIN MUSIC
PRESS

SPRING 2013
CHIN MUSIC PRESS
SEATTLE

横浜
Yokohama
Yankee

Contents

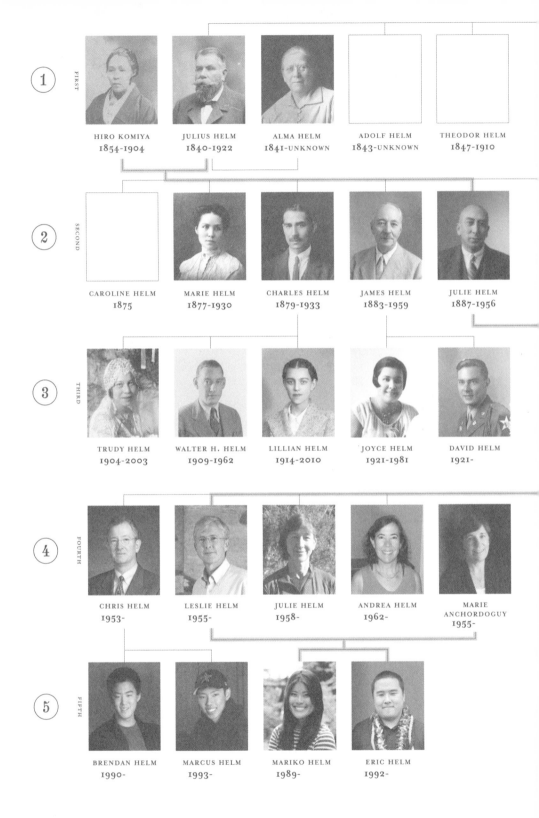

FIRST

1

HIRO KOMIYA
1854-1904

JULIUS HELM
1840-1922

ALMA HELM
1841-UNKNOWN

ADOLF HELM
1843-UNKNOWN

THEODOR HELM
1847-1910

SECOND

2

CAROLINE HELM
1875

MARIE HELM
1877-1930

CHARLES HELM
1879-1933

JAMES HELM
1883-1959

JULIE HELM
1887-1956

THIRD

3

TRUDY HELM
1904-2003

WALTER H. HELM
1909-1962

LILLIAN HELM
1914-2010

JOYCE HELM
1921-1981

DAVID HELM
1921-

FOURTH

4

CHRIS HELM
1953-

LESLIE HELM
1955-

JULIE HELM
1958-

ANDREA HELM
1962-

MARIE
ANCHORDOGUY
1955-

FIFTH

5

BRENDAN HELM
1990-

MARCUS HELM
1993-

MARIKO HELM
1989-

ERIC HELM
1992-

PAUL HELM
1856-UNKNOWN

ANNA HELM
1851-1934

EDMUND STUCKEN
1850-1920

MASU KAWAHARA
1857-1934

FUKU KOSHIRO
1877-1901

ADOLPH
SCHINZINGER
1855-1926

WILLIE HELM
1891-1951

LOUISA HELM
1894-1980

BETTY STUCKEN
1899-1959

ROBERT SCHINZINGER
1898-1988

ANNELISE SCHINZINGER
1897-1946

SHIZUKA TAGUCHI
1930-

DONALD HELM
1926-1991

RAYMOND HELM
1929-

LAWRENCE HELM
1932-2006

BARBARA SCHINZINGER
1924-

ROLAND SCHINZINGER
1926-2004

TOSHIKO HONDO
1936-

ATSUSHI
TSUNEMOCHI
1924-2011

MY FAMILY'S FIVE
GENERATIONS IN JAPAN

South Pier

Yokohama Archives
of History •

Helm House •
(1938-2005)

• Hotel New
Grand

KANNAI
STATION

FOREIGN SETTLEMENT

Julius Helm's
First House (1875)
 • ←

• Helm Yamate Residence

Site of Double
Murder & Suicide → •

Foreign Cemetery
Donald Helm Home → • • ← Yokohama Int'l
Christ Church → •   School
Bluff Hospital → •

ISHIKAWACHO
STATION

BLUFF AREA

•

Julius Helm Home
(1902-1932)

Helm Dairy •

YAMATE
STATION

Yokohama
Country &
Athletic Club
•

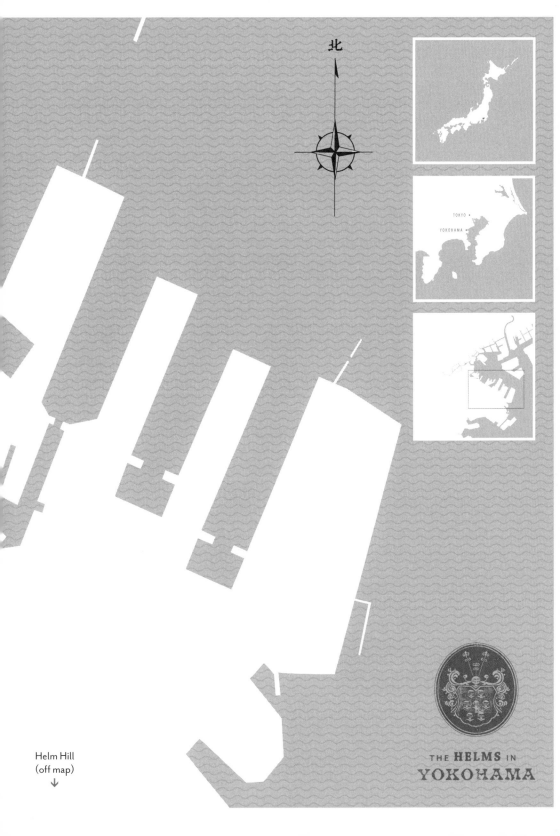

北

TOKYO •
YOKOHAMA •

Helm Hill
(off map)
↓

THE **HELMS** IN
YOKOHAMA

Donald Julius Helm 1926-1991.

01

THE END OF A DYNASTY

A COOL AUTUMN WIND was blowing in from the sea when I reached the Christ Church in Yokohama. At a reception table by the wrought-iron gate, a lady in kimono smiled tentatively as she held down the flapping pages of the guest book while I signed my name. The other receptionist, in a Western dress, opened envelopes filled with ten-thousand-yen bills, and recorded in a separate book the amount contributed by each guest. I hesitated, momentarily ashamed that I had no envelope to give. But I wasn't expected to contribute. This was a memorial for my father.

September 23, 1991. I had taken the day off from work as Tokyo correspondent for the *Los Angeles Times*. At the time, my wife, Marie, was in Seattle teaching at the University of Washington, as she had done every other quarter since we had moved to Japan the year before. So I came to the funeral by myself, bringing a pen and notebook as if this were just another assignment.

"The memorial of Donald Julius Helm was testimonial to the fading presence in Yokohama of a family that witnessed Japan's transformation from a feudal nation ruled by samurai into one of the world's great industrial powers," I might have begun the article. As the owner of the largest foreign-owned stevedoring and forwarding company in Japan, the Helm family had once managed or operated office buildings, apartment complexes, warehouses, cranes, tugboats and barges in every major Japanese port. Helm Brothers was

one of a small handful of foreign companies in Japan that had been continuously owned and operated since Japan's opening to the West in the mid-nineteenth century. It had survived two world wars and a devastating earthquake. The company was founded by my great-grandfather; my father was its last president.

Toshiko, who married Dad soon after my parents divorced in 1973, was dressed in a trim black dress and wore a short string of pearls. She gave me a quick hug and asked me to help greet the guests. I was thirty-five, but as I stood by the gate, I felt like a lost child. I didn't recognize the people streaming into the church courtyard, so I simply bowed my head as I quietly accepted their condolences. I was mystified by the number of people who came to pay their respects: Dad, only sixty-four when he died, had seen so few people in the final years of his life.

After a while, I left my post and wandered through the heavy doors of the church into the still-empty sanctuary, slipping into the front pew. Below the altar, chrysanthemums and lilies surrounded a large framed photograph of my father taken in Hawaii. His balding head was tan and reflected the light of the flash. He wore a pastel pink and blue Hawaiian shirt and, on his face, the look of mild amusement he often had after a few drinks. That familiar look hinted at inside knowledge of some cosmic joke. *You think you've got one over on me, but I'm smarter than that,* he seemed to suggest.

When I was a young child, Dad seemed like a god to me, both frightening and infallible. Once, a Japanese policeman visited our house and began scolding my friend and me for setting a fire to the grass in an empty lot nearby. Dad, awoken from his Saturday morning slumber, slid open the double-hung window to his second-floor bedroom and stuck his head out. *"Urusai!"* (Shut up!), he boomed in a voice so authoritative and contemptuous that the policeman turned pale, gave a quick bow and left.

One day, after settling into his recliner with his glass of Scotch, he exclaimed with a soulful sigh: "The goddamned Japanese!" He believed that you could never really understand the Japanese so you might as well give up trying. It was an odd sentiment since Dad was half-Japanese.

Growing up in Japan, I never thought Dad looked Japanese in the least. But as I looked at his photograph in the church, I noticed the peaked eyebrows, the almond eyes and the smooth bronze skin. A good-looking man, he could be a real charmer with his wry smile, his graceful manner and his hypnotic voice. I had recently found a photo of him as a twenty-year-old lieutenant standing erect with one hand resting lightly on his left hip. There was something about his posture—shoulders pulled back, head held high—that projected a shy, yet alluring self-confidence. His nose, with a slight bump from a childhood accident, gave him a rakish air. When he took over the family firm at age twenty-seven, with no previous business experience, he might have learned to carry the responsibilities of power. Instead, when business didn't go as he expected, he became bitter and turned to drink. He retired early and sought affirmation in the daily gyrations of the stock market.

Looking back today, I have some sense of that combination of self-satisfaction and insecurity that Dad must have felt in those early years. When I first came to Tokyo in 1982 as a correspondent for *Business Week*, I was twenty-six. Frequently invited to speak on Japanese television, I would smugly discuss world affairs as if I were some pundit instead of just a curiosity—a white-faced journalist who happened to speak Japanese.

My Dad and I were similar in another respect. Neither of us had ever been comfortable with our Japanese heritage. When I was eighteen, my brother Chris, two years older than me, told me about an encounter he had had with a great-uncle and aunt. "Growing a beard?" the aunt had asked Chris, pointing to the peach fuzz on his chin. "I can't really grow a beard," said Chris. "Must be my Japanese blood." When the aunt left the room, the uncle turned to Chris with quiet fury: "We don't talk about such things." Our mixed-race uncle who passed for white had never told his Caucasian wife or their children about his Japanese heritage.

When Chris told me the story, I felt as if my eyes had opened for the first time. Of course I was part Japanese! I wear a 6 ½ EEEE shoe, a size I can find in any Japanese shoe store but not in the largest American outlet. Like my brother, I cannot grow a beard. And, now as I thought about it, I was sure I had heard relatives talk about my two Japanese great-grandmothers. I had simply found it convenient to forget.

Later, I would learn my father had a good reason for denying his Japanese blood. Living in California during World War II, his whole family barely escaped being sent to an internment camp. If I had considered this as I sat in the church pew that September day, I might have felt sympathy for Dad. Instead, I was full of anger and resentment.

When I was a child, Dad had a life force that both attracted and repelled me. He could be generous, even gentle, one minute, but then explode unpredictably, like a faulty firecracker. I kept my distance from him. When Dad left my mother to marry Toshiko halfway through my senior year of high school, I was relieved that my parents' incessant squabbling would finally come to an end. When I returned to Japan in 1982 to work for *Business Week,* my wife Marie and I lived just an hour away from Dad and Toshiko, and yet we seldom visited. Dad was still drinking, and I was still afraid of him. On those few occasions we did meet, we played mahjong for money. Mixing, stacking and playing with the bamboo-backed ivory tiles eased the tension. Dad didn't mind losing to me. He seemed pleased when he could settle his account simply by slipping me a couple of one-thousand-yen notes.

When I returned to Japan for the *Los Angeles Times* in 1990, just a year before Dad died, he was drinking less and wanted to see me more, but I had little time for him. When I rushed to his bedside after he had a stroke in early 1991, I was shocked to find him in a dilapidated neighborhood hospital. He was babbling, so I leaned in close and heard him say, "My sons have no time for me." Even as he lay there barely conscious, I wanted to grab his shoulders and shake him.

Dad needed double bypass heart surgery, but I considered the whole Japanese medical system to be an abomination. I had one friend who had almost died because of a mistaken diagnosis and another who nearly had an unnecessary mastectomy. I arranged to have Dad sent to the Stanford University hospital in Palo Alto, California. The surgeon assured us that Dad's odds of surviving were excellent—ninety-six percent—so I saw no need to accompany him to California for the surgery. The last time I saw Dad alive was at the Tokyo airport sitting in a wheelchair as Toshiko pushed him through the gate toward passport control. I was already thinking of the work that awaited me back at the office. When Dad died on the operating table a week later, I wondered if my distrust of Japanese doctors, indeed of *everything* Japanese, had contributed to his death.

NOW, THREE WEEKS LATER, FROM my pew in the Christ Church, I watched as the guests began to spill into the sanctuary. My brother Chris, an attorney in Tokyo, and my sister Andrea, who worked for a Japanese travel agency in Portland, sat next to me. My other sister, Julie, a veterinarian in Colorado, couldn't make it, but we had all been to a memorial in California a week before for Dad's American friends. The church was now full. Reverend John Berg, who had come from Britain to become pastor while I was still a child, took his place at the pulpit. I had always been fascinated by the way he would lean his head back so that his large Adam's apple was exposed and would explode into spasms of laughter. He used to take a group of us foreigners Christmas caroling in a tugboat on Yokohama Harbor. We would board a ship at anchor, sing a few songs, have a few drinks and then head for the next ship.

Reverend Berg sniffled and rubbed his big red nose with a handkerchief. "It's the lilies," he explained to the assemblage. "I'm allergic." Then he began with a story.

"I remember how Don was bringing in some stuff to give to the annual church bazaar when he fell headlong down the steps to the basement. You see," said Berg, looking at the audience with a twinkle in his eye, "Don was not very familiar with the geography of the church."

Laughter rippled through the chapel. There must have been two hundred people packed into the church. Dad would have been surprised at the size of the crowd.

"The name Helm is synonymous with Yokohama," the reverend went on. "The Helm dynasty began when Julius Helm came to Yokohama in 1869. The family played a large part in building up this international city." Berg stopped occasionally during his address to allow the white-robed Japanese pastor at his side to translate his words. "We have in the church today Christians, Buddhists and Muslims representing the international nature of Yokohama ..."

Like my father, I am not a religious person. So when the reverend said it was time for Dad to "go to God and whisper his story in His ear," I grimaced. But when he added, "Maybe *others* won't understand, but God will understand when Don opens up his soul to Him," it was as if Berg were talking directly to me, scolding me for closing my heart. I felt a deep, hollow aching and then tears. I was *kuyashii*. There is no English word for the despair that I felt—that strange combination of resentment, frustration and anger intensified by an immobilizing sense of helplessness.

I was *kuyashii* about the way Dad acted so defeated toward the end of his life. He was smart and rich. What right did he have to be unhappy? I hated his weakness when things got tough. I thought then of a snapshot I had uncovered of Dad as a teenager, his bony ribs thrust out, wearing a winning grin on his face as he proudly held out a small trout. How did this boy, who seemed to have the world in his hand, become the shrunken soul I had come to know who was happiest after his first couple of drinks in the evening? In that twilight between sobriety and drunkenness, Dad would look up, smile and say, "*Ahhh*, I feel no pain."

Reverend Berg asked us to stand and sing "Nearer, My God, to Thee." The Japanese in the church sang the same hymn in *their* language. *I am climbing the road, God, to be by your side.* The two languages melded into a single hum that was comforting in its jumbled incoherence.

Walking through the churchyard afterward, I felt a hand on my arm and turned to find Tsuru-*san*, my father's childhood nanny, at my side. She wore a black silk kimono with autumn flowers splashed across the front. Her gray hair was knotted in a bun at the back of her head and it bobbed as she smiled at me mischievously.

"I spanked your father's bare bottom when he was three years old," she told me as she clutched my jacket sleeve in one wrinkled hand and gave it a tug. "He was always so naughty. I can't believe I outlived him." With her other hand, Tsuru-*san* pulled a handkerchief from her kimono sleeve and dabbed tears from the deep creases around her suddenly reddening eyes. She was more than ninety years old, yet she still maintained the poise that seemed so appropriate to her name, Tsuru, "crane," given her as a young girl because of her long white neck.

I recalled Tsuru-*san* coming to our house in Yokohama once a week to do the sewing. Always dressed in kimono, she spooked me with her stories of the haunted world of old Japan. Once, when a friend and I dug a deep hole in the backyard, Tsuru-*san* stuck her face out of the doorway. "If you keep digging, the *oni* will grab your leg and pull you underground," she screamed, quickly ducking back behind the door. We laughed at her nonsense. Who believed in ogres? But we quickly filled in that hole.

Growing up in Yokohama in the 1960s was like that. I seemed forever to be shifting from one dimension to another, like the hero in a science-fiction movie who travels back and forth through space and time. One minute I was in the Western world of logic: If you pushed the spade into the ground, you would get a shovel full of soil. The next minute, I was considering the possibility that the same spade might break through a thin layer of earth to reveal the gleaming eyes of a wicked ogre waiting to pull me into the dark Japanese netherworld.

From the churchyard, I could see the beer garden across the alley, not twenty yards away, where our house had once stood. My parents would throw lavish parties in our large garden. Paper lanterns strung across the yard would sway in the summer breeze, casting wavering light on the well-dressed men and women. Half a dozen Japanese maids in uniform would weave through the crowd serving men their Scotch and women their gin and tonics. All that remained of that compound now was a low wall made of a much-prized yellow volcanic stone called *oyaishi*. There was never a nameplate outside our house as there were on other foreign residences because Dad feared the Helm name would tempt someone to kidnap his children for ransom.

Our house had been at the center of the Yokohama foreign enclave called The Bluff, where weathered Victorian homes lined the streets along with the occasional two-story townhouse built during the US Occupation as military housing. Within two blocks of our home there were three schools, a hospital, a fire station, a church and a cemetery, all built for foreign residents. I used to joke that you could be born, christened, schooled, rescued from a fire, hospitalized, memorialized and buried without ever going more than a block from our house.

That was the way it was supposed to be. When Japan's shogun, under pressure from Commodore Mathew Perry and the cannons on his massive black ships, had ended Japan's two and a half centuries of isolation in 1854, Japan had sought to limit foreign influence by restricting foreigners to this special settlement, once a tiny fishing village.

Over the next century, a port city of several million grew up around that foreign enclave. Japanese visitors would come to The Bluff in big buses like tourists to a foreign land. Giggling Japanese school girls on class trips would point at me with my blond hair and exclaim: "*Ah, gaijin da!* Look, there's a foreigner!" Japanese boys in their black school uniforms would stick their heads out of bus windows and yell out: "Hey you! You Yankee boy! Disu izu a pen!"

Growing up in Japan as a foreigner, a *gaijin*, that outsider status became a central part of my identity. Everywhere I went, strangers would pull me into their group pictures, like the fake geisha who are paid to walk the streets in Kyoto so tourists can photograph scenes of "old Japan." Only now do I realize how odd it was to grow up like that, always on display, separated from the society around me. For the first time,

I understood that the foreign settlement in which I grew up, the place I had called home, was an anomaly destined to fade away. Dad's death had cut the last strand linking me to that world of my youth. And for the first time, I realized that for all its strangeness, it was a world I had loved deeply, and its absence left me aching.

Across from the church, facing the harbor, was a large park where I played as a child. Waves of nostalgia rocked me. Every spring, clouds of cherry blossoms burst forth, drawing large groups who, ostensibly there to view the blossoms, seemed more intent on drinking and singing late into the night. The *min min min meeeeeeeeeee* of cicadas filled the woods in summer, and I used to capture the insects with bits of well-chewed gum stuck to the end of a bamboo pole. How strange that these insects lay dormant underground for seventeen years before casting off their shells to live in the world for a few short weeks. I have since learned the cicada is a Buddhist symbol of rebirth. One poet compares their cast-off shells to "the hollow shell of human greatness."

I was still standing in the church courtyard when Toshiko interrupted my reverie to introduce me to three men whose deeply tanned faces and hands seemed at odds with their white shirts and black suits. One of the men had been a carpenter at Helm Brothers. He remembered fondly how Dad had taken the time to teach him proper manners so he could play golf without embarrassment at the fanciest courses. These men had lost their jobs at Helm Brothers when Dad's relatives forced the sale of the company in 1973.

The men were there to pay their last respects to Dad, but also to Helm Brothers, a family business that had sustained their families for generations. Helm House, a block of apartments and offices my grandfather built, had, at various times, been Helm Brothers' headquarters, the home of foreign diplomats, the headquarters of the German navy, the home of US Eighth Army officers during the Occupation and the home of the Yokohama Police Department. Now it was just a nameless office building. There were a half dozen real-estate companies that still used the Helm name, but none had anything to do with us. The new Taiwanese owners of Helm Brothers, I was told, had been involved in shady dealings. In the opening scene of a Japanese thriller I read, a corpse is found in an apartment managed by the *Heim (sic) Brothers,* which is described as a seedy international company.

As dusk descended and the courtyard emptied, family and friends gathered a couple of miles away at the modest house where Dad had moved with Toshiko after my parents' divorce. The house sat several feet below the level of the street and it felt like an earthquake every time a bus passed. Before land prices began to plummet in 1990, this little house, the last remaining piece of the family's once extensive real estate holdings, was itself worth a substantial fortune.

As I slipped off my shoes in an entryway already crowded with black leather shoes, I could hear laughter. "I remember the time he shot a hole in one," said one of Dad's former employees. "That cost him plenty!" According to Japanese tradition, a golfer who got a hole in one was obligated to buy gifts for all his golf partners. Dad had not skimped on the gifts. Insurance companies would later offer hole-in-one insurance to cover such rare occurrences.

I poured myself a glass of Kirin and sat down in the dining room. Before long Itoh-*san*, a former employee of Dad's, stood next to me. I remembered him as a thin, confused young man who seemed to tremble before my father. Now he was a sizable man with a protruding belly and a smug, knowing look.

Itoh began to reminisce about the early 1960s, when Dad broke away from Helm Brothers to launch his own business. "He helped me buy my first piece of property," Itoh recalled. "Don said we should know what it was like to be a landlord if we were going to be in the real-estate business."

As Itoh continued to drink, his face darkened. "I was completely against the divorce," he said. "Your relatives liked your mother. Your father lost the support he needed to keep Helm Brothers in the family when he left her."

It felt like Itoh wielded a poker and was messing around among Dad's dead ashes to see if there were any live embers, to see if he could get a rise out of the man who had frequently humiliated him.

Perhaps Itoh spotted my unease because he suddenly changed his tone. "Don was just too honest. He didn't like doing things in an underhanded way," Itoh said. "It's just too bad; you could have all been rich."

A FEW WEEKS LATER, MY brother Chris and I went with Toshiko to the Yokohama Foreign General Cemetery to visit Dad's new grave. The tombstone, a flat block of polished black granite, was tucked against the shrubbery that lined the northern border of the cemetery. At a nearby water tap, Toshiko filled a blue plastic bucket with water and grabbed a couple of the scrub brushes available for visitors to use. While we watched, she squatted down and scrubbed Dad's gravestone. After a few minutes, she handed each of us a brush. I thought it was pointless cleaning the shiny surface of this spotless new stone, but I went through the motions. Meanwhile, Toshiko arranged the flowers she had brought and placed them in the stainless steel vase at the foot of the gravestone.

"See, Don? Your children are here," she said, looking adoringly at the gravestone. "Isn't it nice? They are scrubbing your back."

I cringed. I had never been that close to Dad when he was alive. After putting away the bucket and scrub brushes, we stood in front of the grave to pray. My palms felt awkward pressed together like that—two parts of me that were unaccustomed to each other. What was I supposed to do? Pray to God? Talk to Dad's spirit? I was relieved when Toshiko raised her head and it was time to go.

In the weeks that followed, I spent much of my time dealing with my father's estate. I was discussing business with the man who had become the president of Helm Brothers after my father left. I took the opportunity to ask him if he was aware of any Helm Brothers records.

The man looked at me stiffly. "I used to worship every day before the picture of your great-grandfather, but your family betrayed us," the man replied with a bitterness that startled me. "Sure, there were documents. Helm House was filled with documents when your father sold the company. We had them all sent to the dump."

JUST
ANOTHER
GAIJIN?

ONE EVENING ABOUT A MONTH after the funeral, I was browsing the magazines on display at a train platform kiosk when I saw the banner headline on a copy of the *Bungei Shunju,* an intellectual journal. *"Kenbei,"* it read—contempt for America. I bought it and flipped to the special report. My heart quickened as I began reading the essays. This was incredible! Here were Japan's leading industrialists and intellectuals declaring that the United States was a nation in decline. The chief executive of a giant electronics company said he wouldn't buy American semiconductors because they were shoddy. A Japanese novelist said the noble America she had once admired had turned into a self-centered bully. An economist advised the United States to focus on its one true expertise: farming.

I thought of what Miyazawa Kiichi, the newly appointed prime minister, had told me in an interview just a few weeks before. His greatest fear, he had said, was that America, incapable of competing fairly with Japan, would start a trade war by blocking the import of Japanese products. Miyazawa's low regard for American industry, I realized, was another symptom of this growing disdain for America.

Japan's attitude toward the West had always swung like a pendulum. Western merchants and priests were welcomed into the country from Portugal in about 1543, only to be thrown out a century later. When

Christian converts in Japan refused to renounce their faith, they were massacred by a newly isolationist government fearful of outside interference. In the mid-1800s, the rallying cry of "drive out the barbarians" that followed Commodore Perry's arrival was supplanted by the wholesale importation of Western institutions and technology a few decades later under the Meiji emperor. In the militarist Japan of the 1930s, Westerners were reviled, but following the nation's humiliating defeat in World War II, everything American was worshipped. My family's fortunes in Japan had risen and fallen with those tides.

In those first two decades after World War II, when I was growing up in Japan, the Japanese rushed wholeheartedly toward everything American, but they were a cowed people. In "A Nation of Sheep," a short story by Nobel Prize winner Oe Kenzaburo published in 1958, Japanese men seated in a bus are too intimidated to stop American soldiers from taunting a Japanese college student. Reading the story for the first time in a Japanese literature class in college, I remember identifying with the student. I hated the American soldiers for being such bullies, and I felt contempt for the Japanese men on the bus who refused to defend the boy.

As someone with deep roots in Japan, I was glad to see the Japanese finally stand up for themselves. America *was* a bully. Yet, at the same time I felt defensive as I always did when I heard non-Americans criticize the United States. Perhaps that was what made me uneasy about this notion of *kenbei*: it revealed a gulf between America and Japan that did not allow a place for people caught in between, like the student in the story—like me.

The next day, I began reporting for an article about this growing disdain for America. I talked to dozens of executives, reporters and bureaucrats. "There is certainly something wrong with American society," a vice minister for foreign affairs told me. His office was decorated with costumed dolls, intricately carved daggers and other exotic gifts he had received from foreign dignitaries during his long career as a diplomat. "How can the United States be a model for us when they have to ask us to pay for their war [the Gulf War]?" asked the vice minister. Japan, he felt, could no longer depend on its "older brother," the United States. In hierarchical Japan, few strong relationships are among equals. If America were no longer Japan's superior, then it must now be its inferior.

My article, *In Japan: Scorn for America,* appeared in late October on the front page of the *Los Angeles Times* and was picked up by newspapers around the world. My editors loved it. A friend at the State Department said President Clinton, who was preparing for his upcoming trip to Japan, had commented on it. I loved the attention.

A few days later, the vice minister I had interviewed invited me to an expensive restaurant. Over tender Kobe beef, he expressed concern that my story would not contribute to better relations between Japan and the United States. I didn't fully understand what he was getting at until two weeks later when, sitting at my desk, I received a packet of letters from readers that had been forwarded to me by my editor. The letters were all about my *kenbei* story. The first few were complimentary and I smiled, but as I read on, the blood drained from my face.

"How dare you mock (Americans) ... you spit at those who not only befriended you but taught you how to live," wrote one man in a letter addressed: "To Every Japanese who hates Americans."

A man who claimed to be the founder of "The Great American Majority Association" called my article "America-bashing by Jap scum" and accused me of turning on my country "like a poisonous weasel."

One letter suggested my article be enlarged and placed on billboards near Japanese auto and electronics dealers.

My heart pounded as I continued to read the letters. The raw anger and hatred they expressed frightened me. Later I heard that anti-Japanese graffiti had popped up in parts of Los Angeles following publication of the article. I felt like a child playing with matches who had started a fire he could not control.

Had I been fooling myself? I knew Americans regarded their country as the greatest nation on earth. Of course they would be upset. Wasn't that what made *kenbei* such a good story? Ever since the end of World War II, Japan had played the role of obedient disciple to its American teacher. Now, it seemed, Japan was coming into its own. It was a legitimate story. And yet, I had a nagging feeling. Was I simply reporting a trend or was I venting some deeper personal hostility toward Japan?

I pulled out one of a series of binders from the shelf behind me. These binders were my pride. They contained all the articles I had written during my decade-long career as a reporter. My research assistant had already pasted in the newspaper clip of the *kenbei* story and I re-read it. It was a fine story. Well, perhaps I didn't need the part at the end about the sushi chef who insisted I eat whale meat so I would understand Japan and its whale-hunting culture. The scene was an unnecessary dig at the *you-don't-understand-us-we-are-an-island-nation-with-few-natural-resources* refrain Japanese so often repeated.

I began flipping through earlier stories I had written. Then I pulled out other scrapbooks and went through them as well. Most of the articles I had written over the course of my career were critical of Japan in some way. I looked for genuinely positive articles I had written during my two separate stints as a foreign correspondent in Tokyo. I was embarrassed to discover that there were only a few. In part, I was merely reflecting the dogma of the time. When I graduated from journalism school in 1982, Japan was at the height of its economic power. Japanese companies had conquered one American industry after another, resulting in massive unemployment in many US cities. In my first job interview, a *Business Week* editor had asked me what I thought was key to Japan's economic success. "Protectionism," I answered, sensing this was a litmus test. The editor liked that answer. It showed I was not a sympathizer, that I would not "go native." This was an economic war, and I would be reporting for the American side.

Even so, when I arrived in Japan in the fall of 1982 for my first journalism job, I tried to do everything the Japanese way. I wanted to be different from the typical expatriate. *Business Week* offered me a generous housing allowance. Instead of living in a modern, Western-style apartment, as we did later, Marie and I rented a large, traditional Japanese house from a retired geisha. The house had all the elements I considered most beautiful about Japanese architecture. There were two large tatami-floored rooms with sliding shoji doors that opened onto a stunning Japanese garden of massive boulders and meticulously pruned trees. The doors and the room dividers had exquisitely carved designs. The *tokonoma*, or alcove, had a private altar and a pillar made of a natural tree trunk.

A few weeks after moving into the house, I walked down to the local *senbei* shop to buy a dozen boxes of salty rice crackers wrapped in seaweed, a traditional favorite.

"What are you going to do with all this *senbei*?" the grizzled old man at the shop asked.

"I just moved in around the corner. These are gifts for my neighbors," I replied. Then I bowed to the old man: "*Yoroshiku onegaishimasu* (I look forward to your kind favor)."

"That's very nice. It is a proper gesture," the man said with a smile that revealed glinting steel crowns. "But don't expect to be treated like a Japanese person. You will always be a foreigner, you know."

Not long afterward, I went drinking with a Japanese executive from a large electronics company. We were well into the evening when he asked: "So, how come you speak such good Japanese; do you have a Japanese wife?"

"No. My wife is from Los Angeles. She's Caucasian. I was born in Japan," I said. "My great-grandfather came at the beginning of the Meiji Period and married a Japanese woman."

"Hmmm. Really? I never would have taken you for being part Japanese."

The man looked at me strangely. I asked him where his family came from, but the conversation soon petered out. It was as if, in one instant, he reassessed me and concluded I was not worthy of his time. I was not a *real* foreigner, but some kind of half-breed. Perhaps I was being oversensitive, but after that I stopped talking about my Japanese blood. "I was born in Japan," I would tell people, but leave it at that.

Something unpleasant like this would happen every time I returned to live in Japan. At first, I would feel a deep sense of belonging: the warm press of bodies on a crowded subway; the hot steam rising from a bowl of noodles; even the pungent smell of car exhaust made me feel at home. Every sensation would tap a memory bank that brought me pleasure. Then something would turn sour.

Once I took an American friend who was visiting to a small yakitori bar near my apartment. I loved introducing Western visitors to the small eateries where the best Japanese cuisine is served. When I slid open the glass door to enter, the man standing behind the bar crossed his arms in an "X" to indicate I wasn't welcome.

This tendency to exclude foreigners was not unusual at the time. Owners of small restaurants and bath houses frequently objected to having their regulars disturbed by foreigners. "We can't really relax when we are around outsiders. They don't understand us," a man once confided to me. There is even an ideology called *Nihonjinron,* "the theory of Japaneseness," to describe this sense that the Japanese are a special race of people. Japanese uniqueness was often used as a reason for blocking the import of foreign products. French skis weren't appropriate for Japanese slopes because Japanese snow was different. American beef shouldn't be imported because Japanese intestines couldn't digest it.

The chasm the Japanese deliberately created between *us* and *them* irritated and frustrated many Westerners. But other foreigners had their own identities as Americans or Germans. They were rooted in their own cultures. I had never lived in America as a child and had never really felt like an American. Perhaps that was why I took it personally when I was excluded from a Japanese restaurant. It was a reminder that I had no identity except as a *gaijin*. Although my family had lived in Japan for four generations and I spoke Japanese fluently, to the Japanese I was just another foreigner.

Sometimes there would be an almost surreal disconnect when people saw my Caucasian face and spoke to me in Japanese. Once, about five minutes into a conversation in Japanese with an executive I had just met at a reception, the man asked: "So, do you speak Japanese?"

For a moment, I was disoriented. "We are speaking Japanese now, aren't we?" I said finally, continuing in Japanese.

He cocked his head and chuckled. "Ahhh, that explains it. I didn't think my English was this good." I laughed at the time, but the remark reminded me yet again that while I might occasionally fool myself into thinking I fit into Japan, nobody else would ever make that mistake.

Now, as I went through my old newspaper clips, I realized that my frustration with Japan had found expression in my work as a journalist. I had seen it as my mission to rip off the veil of secrecy with which Japan tried to shroud itself.

The Japanese often claimed that they didn't need lawyers because they were one harmonious family, but I wanted to show how false that was. I traveled to a remote mountain region where villagers had once scraped the arsenic off kilns used to burn arsenic ore so the powder could be sold for rat poison. When villagers started dying of cancer in the 1960s, they filed a lawsuit against the mining company. Most of the plaintiffs were dead by the time I wrote the story in the spring of 1991 and the remaining ones had just agreed to settle with the company to avoid further litigation. In my eyes, this was not harmony, but oppression.

I was also cynical about the many Japanese customs I grew up with that other visitors seemed to find so charming. How generous the Japanese were with their constant exchange of gifts. Hah! This was no quaint custom. They were imposing on each other a complex web of mutual obligations that was the source of much of their misery. *I am not getting caught in that trap*, I told myself.

The Japanese claim they don't need words to communicate their thoughts. They say they understand each other using *haragei*, gut intuition. *Nonsense*, I thought. *Japanese are constantly misreading each other's feelings.* As a young man, I was filled with righteous indignation about the Japanese culture I knew so intimately. Today, looking back on my younger self, I don't necessarily disagree with what I wrote. There is so much about Japan worthy of outrage. But as I sat at my desk with the pile of scrapbooks on my lap, I wondered how much of my critique of Japan was heightened by my own personal reaction to Japan's insularity.

If they are going to exclude me, then I am going to exclude them, I may have reasoned. My expertise on Japan was valuable precisely because Westerners regarded the Japanese as so inscrutable. Wasn't it in my own interest to exaggerate the chasm that separated East from West? The broader the gulf, the more I was needed as an intermediary, the more my life as a *gaijin* had meaning. But there was something achingly unfulfilling in defining myself by what I was not. A *gaijin*, after all, was anybody who was not Japanese. So what was I? Two decades later, I would discover that there are hundreds of thousands of us around the world who academics now refer to as members of "third cultures" because we don't belong entirely to any one culture.

Distracted for the rest of that day, I left work early. Since Marie was still in Seattle, I took the subway three stops to the Foreign Correspondents' Club to grab dinner. The club was on the twentieth floor of an office building on the edge of Ginza, a popular shopping district. Visiting dignitaries gave press conferences at the club. Reporters met with sources for dinner or drinks.

I walked to the bar and sat at the "correspondents' table" where a few regulars gathered. Sipping our beers, we discussed the latest news: perhaps it was the story about the latest politician to deny Japanese soldiers had ever massacred civilians in Nanjing, China, I can't remember. What I do remember about that night was a distinct shift in how I looked at myself and my role as a reporter. I had always felt a sense of esprit de corps among these foreign correspondents—a feeling that we were a special breed reporting an important story. Now I felt disengaged. Weren't we just cycling through variations on the same tired story about Japan's insular ways? The intimacy I felt toward my fellow reporters was real, but the sense of community was not. We were like members of a packaged tour. We enjoyed being together, but when the tour ended, we might never see each other again. So if this wasn't my true community, what was? Lodged uncomfortably at the back of my mind, like a tiny pebble caught in a shoe, was the reality that my father had died at sixty-four without ever finding a place where he belonged.

After dinner, I took a detour home through Shibuya, the heart of Tokyo's busy entertainment district. I followed the crowd off the train, down the stairs and out the turnstiles. I stopped at the pedestrian crossing, but more people kept coming from behind, and soon I was packed as tightly on the sidewalk as I had been on the train. I gazed up to see a teen idol dance across a fifty-foot screen that dangled on the other side of the street somewhere between heaven and earth.

When the light turned green, we surged forward, and for a moment, as a wall of people moved toward us from the opposite side, we looked like two armies converging in battle. I slipped away from the crowd down a narrow lane. I walked past restaurants and bars whose kitchens pumped out smoke that smelled of grilled fish and burnt soy sauce. An old fortune teller who always placed her small table in the middle of the lane, split the flow of pedestrian traffic like a rock in a stream. Her wrinkled face, bowed low over the table, reflected the yellow light of her square paper lantern.

At an electronics store, I stopped to look at a long row of television screens where a boyish-looking man with a blue blazer, scruffy brown hair and goggle-eyed glasses stood frozen, staring out from a passing stream of grey-suited salarymen. It took a moment for me to realize that it was my face being captured by the store's camcorder.

"Irasshai, Irasshai (Welcome)" shouted a young salesman. He put his back to me as he tried to lure passersby into the store. I walked on to an area where every surface—telephone booths, utility poles, walls and ground—was plastered with small flyers advertising prostitutes. If I had been of another generation, I might have called one of those phone numbers. If I climbed a low hill to the left, I would have found myself on one of the quiet, dimly lit streets that surrounded this entertainment district. There, in a love hotel that charged hourly rates, I could have had a private rendering of Shibuya's flashing, thumping sensory sea.

Shibuya was the mecca for Japan's youth, but I was neither Japanese nor young. Perhaps it was the unexpected reaction to the *kenbei* article. Or perhaps it was Dad's recent death. Whatever the reason, I felt as if I had been let loose from my mooring and was drifting rudderless.

PERMISSION
TO ADOPT

ONE MORNING IN EARLY NOVEMBER 1991, about six weeks after my father's funeral, my wife and I found ourselves dressed in our Sunday best, sitting nervously in a drab cubicle in the Shibuya ward office. My only previous visit here had been to get my alien registration card, an identity card every foreign resident in Japan must carry. I had registered at a ward office in Yokohama for the first time when I turned fourteen, and I had always found it daunting to have my fingerprints taken as if I were an outlaw.

On this particular day, however, I felt even more uneasy. A city official would soon decide whether Marie and I were worthy of becoming parents. We had requested permission to adopt a Japanese child.

Although I was the one who first pushed to have children, it was Marie, who, after it became clear we couldn't conceive children, decided we should consider adopting in Japan. Marie had made all the adoption arrangements.

Marie and I had first met in the summer of 1977 when we both worked part-time for a Japanese company based in Berkeley, California, that managed programs for international exchange students. We had both been guides on a tour of San Francisco nightlife. Although we shared an interest in Japan, we could not have been more different. Marie was intensely focused, taking a heavy course load at UC Berkeley as a double major in music and Japanese. The first time I spent the night at her apartment, I woke up at six o'clock in the morning to find her in the living room listening to the same passage from Wagner's *Ring Cycle* again and again. She was studying for a test with a discipline I had never seen before. I was the drifter. In the previous two years I had worked in a French vineyard, studied communism in Paris, worked in an Israeli kibbutz and taught English in Tokyo. Marie focused on Japan with an intensity I found both surprising and refreshing.

When I stood up at the front of the tour bus and spoke to the students about our plans for the evening, Marie thought I was showing off. Born and raised in Japan, I had learned the language naturally. Marie had learned Japanese the hard way, through long hours of study. Unable to find a dorm room in her freshman year, she had taken a job as a manager in a women's dormitory for Japanese students. Entranced by the culture, she had gone to the International Christian University near Tokyo for a year as an exchange student. When I met Marie, her spoken Japanese was still halting, but she was already far better than me in writing and reading Japanese.

As we sat waiting for our interview, I grew increasingly nervous. I agreed with Marie that we should adopt in Japan. It made sense. Since every mother in Japan receives good prenatal care under the country's national health-care system, children relinquished for adoption are typically very healthy. But if the logic was clear, my heart remained uncertain. I wasn't sure why. Perhaps it was the incongruity of the idea of launching a family from this cold, bureaucratic office.

For Marie, there might have been an element of destiny. After all, it was the lack of a dorm room in her freshman year that had gotten her interested in Japan. And decades later, while cleaning out her parents' house, Marie would come across an oil painting she had painted in high school, long before she had any interest in Japan. She had completely forgotten about the painting, and yet, what Marie had painted from her imagination, was a young Asian girl with short bangs and big cheeks—someone who looked hauntingly similar to the girl who would change our lives.

After half an hour of waiting, we were finally ushered into a tiny cubicle. The grim looking, middle-aged woman with her hair tied tightly in a bun was slowly flipping through our file.

"I am Maruoka Kazuko and I will be your representative," she said in Japanese, looking at us with stern eyes. "So, you are thirty-six and you want to adopt a child?"

Marie and I nodded. I imagined Maruoka-*san* mentally ticking off all the reasons we were not competent to be parents. Perhaps she had already found a negative—we were too old.

"Have there been any divorces in your family?"

"Yes, my parents," I said. Mark two against us.

Maruoka-*san* then wanted to know if our families had "a history of physical abuse." I wondered if she saw me flushing, for in that moment something surfaced in my mind that had long been buried. I remained silent.

Marie had not entirely understood Maruoka-*san*'s question and looked questioningly at me. I translated for her.

"No," Marie said quickly. She didn't know about how abusive my father had been, and I wasn't about to bring it up.

"Would you take a child of any race?"

"Yes, of course." Marie and I had talked about this. We knew that many of the children put up for adoption were the mixed-race children of American soldiers or immigrant workers.

"How about a handicapped child?" she asked.

I hesitated, shifting uncomfortably in my seat.

"It depends on the situation," said Marie, standing her ground.

"Hmm," Maruoka-*san* replied.

When she then asked us how we felt about adopting a Japanese child, I finally felt ready to make my case. "I am part Japanese and Marie is a professor of Japanese studies. We both speak Japanese. We plan to raise our children to speak Japanese and understand Japanese culture."

Maruoka-*san* never cracked a smile throughout the interview. When we walked out of that office an hour later, we had no sense of what her evaluation had been.

As our application wended its way through the bureaucracy, Marie never wavered, but I vacillated between fear that we would be turned down and anxiety about what would happen if we were approved. With a biological child, there is inevitability to the process. Nature programs parents to accept and love their biological children, it seemed to me. With adoption, it was far more complicated. If we were approved, and a child became available, Maruoka-*san* would send us a picture. If we were agreeable, we would begin to visit the child at the orphanage over a six-month probationary period. During that time, we, or the city, could decide whether the child was a good fit for us. Once the child grew accustomed to us, we would bring him or her home. At the time, it seemed as if the process involved too much uncertainty, too many decisions.

When I told Maruoka-*san* that race was not an issue, I had not been completely honest. I had read a great deal of research that suggested interracial adoptions resulted in far more complications than same-race adoptions. Our child, looking nothing like us, would get sick and tired of explaining to everyone that she was adopted. As a teenager, the research suggested, she would face a serious identity crisis and might even reject us as parents.

When we received word that we had been approved to adopt, I felt both relief and trepidation. Our next step was to attend a special orientation. In January 1992, Marie and I made our way to the fifty-fifth floor of the newly completed Tokyo City Hall, a one-billion-dollar, twin-towered high rise that was architect Kenzo Tange's idea of a modern Notre Dame Cathedral. The orientation took place in a small nondescript classroom high above a city blanketed in smog.

Marie and I were the only foreigners among a group of twenty prospective parents who all sat behind rows of desks. It is odd how our competitive spirits pop up at the most inappropriate times. And yet, there it was. I felt as if we were in a competition and that if Marie and I were judged worthy, we would go home with a prize: a child of our own. As I sat there, I immediately began weighing our chances. Our biggest weakness, clearly, was that we were foreigners, but we had plenty of other things going for us. We were a good ten years younger than most of the other couples, and our motives were pretty straightforward. In our introduction, we said simply that we wanted children to love. We wanted a family. Everybody else seemed to have some agenda. One single woman had already adopted three children and wanted to "save" another. Several elderly couples said they wanted a child to take care of them in their old age. They didn't speak of family. And love didn't appear to be part of the equation.

After the introductions, a city official gave us the basic facts. There were only a few dozen babies available for adoption each month in Tokyo, a city of nearly thirteen million people. About four-hundred children are legally available for adoption nationwide each year, although there are more than thirty-thousand children in orphanages and other institutions. (I would later learn that only a few dozen of the children went to foreign families. By comparison, Americans adopted 7,900 children from China alone in the peak year of 2005.)

More boys were available, the official said, because Japanese parents preferred to adopt girls who would be more likely to take care of them in their old age.

I assumed there were so few children available for adoption because of the widespread use of abortion as a means of birth control, a result of policies discouraging the use of birth-control pills. Later I learned the story was far more complicated. Many Japanese mothers didn't want to relinquish their parental rights to allow their children to be adopted because, even though their children were now cared for in an orphanage, they wanted their children to take care of them later in life.

At the same time, there were also few Japanese parents interested in adopting children. The adoption system in Japan had evolved not to care for the needs of children without parents, but to ensure family continuity. It was common for Japanese families without sons, for example, to legally adopt an adult son-in-law into the family. The son would take the wife's name, providing continuity. It was also common for a couple to give up one of their children for adoption by a childless relative.

Although there were cases of children out of wedlock being given up for adoption, they were typically done secretly to avoid having to record the transaction in the family registry, as law required. The "special adoption" system we were using had only been in place since 1988. The hope for this new adoption system was to encourage legal adoptions by allowing mothers to take the child out of their family registry so there was no record of the birth, and allowing adoptive families to record an adopted child in their family registry as if the child were a biological child. The special adoption system had not caught on in part because the Japanese were reluctant to adopt a child whose parentage was unknown and who might, therefore, not be of "good blood."

After we had all introduced ourselves, a professor who specialized in adoption rose to speak. He said many Japanese parents moved after adopting a child, hoping they could hide from their neighbors and from their own child the truth about the adoption. He instructed us to tell our children they were adopted before they reached junior high school, at which time they were bound to discover the truth anyway. While nearly two-thirds of adoptive parents believe it is important to tell their children they are adopted, he warned, less than a third actually do so.

These lectures and the shell-shocked look on the faces of the adoptive parents, I am ashamed to admit, pleased me. I wasn't thinking about the many unfortunate children who wouldn't be adopted. I was thinking of my own selfish concerns: For the first time, I felt we had a good shot at being chosen to adopt a child.

In May 1992, two months after our orientation to prepare for adoption, Marie and I still had not heard from the authorities about whether there was a child available to adopt. We were growing impatient. Hoping to prod the system, we visited a Catholic orphanage we had heard about. We were shown to the nursery where about a dozen infants, most of them less than a year old, sat on the floor largely unattended. We sat on the floor among them. I picked up a rattler and caught the attention of the boy closest to me. I was surprised when, without hesitation, the boy crawled onto my lap. He had thick black hair and attentive eyes. I cradled him in my arms, and he lay back against my chest deeply content. A calm came over me as I sat there on the floor with this child in my arms.

I do not find it easy, by nature, to empathize with strangers. As a college student, I once spent several weeks working at Mother Teresa's Home for the Destitute and the Dying in Calcutta. One morning, the nun in charge asked me to shave the head of one of the residents. Afterward, when I picked him up to return him to his bed, I was stunned to find he weighed little more than a newborn baby. Cradling him in my arms, I found it difficult to feel pity for this young man who had only days left to live. I simply could not see the world through his dying eyes.

But as I sat in that nursery cuddling this little boy, it seemed to me that the adoption calculus was far simpler: This boy was starved for affection, while Marie and I wanted a child to love. As we left the orphanage, the director told us the boy was available for adoption and we would soon hear from the city's welfare agency, which had jurisdiction over adoptions at all orphanages.

We did not wait to hear from the welfare agency. Immediately, we bought a crib from an American couple leaving Japan and set it up in the living room. When we didn't hear from the city for several weeks, Marie called Maruoka-*san*, our social worker. The orphanage director had spoken out of turn, Maruoka-*san* told her. The boy was not available. Now, every day when I returned from the office, the empty crib seemed to reflect my inner emptiness.

ONCE THE ADOPTION SEED WAS planted inside me, it grew into an obsession. How could I raise a Japanese child when I continued to be so ambivalent toward Japan? How had my family's long presence in Japan affected my father's attitude toward Japan as well as my own? While waiting to hear from the adoption agency, I often pulled out the cardboard box of old photographs I had brought home from Dad's. The box was soft and tired with age, but the black-and-white family photographs were crisp and sharp. They brought to life my relatives decked out in sharp suits, beautiful dresses and kimonos.

One evening, I came upon a photograph that was different from the rest. Great-Grandfather Julius sat relaxed among a group of stiff Japanese soldiers. It seemed impossible to me that this big husky German with the bushy beard could possibly be my great-grandfather. And the thin soldiers in their jackets, ribbed with braided rope and pinned with medals, seemed as unreal as the painted fireplace in the photo's studio backdrop.

For many Helms, I would later learn, this photograph had become a touchstone, evidence that the Helms had played some important role in Japan's history. But who were these people? I flipped over the picture, which was a copy of the original photograph. Written on the back was an inscription dating the photograph to the seventh year of the

1874
MEIJI 7 KEN
RIKUGUNSHO

乃木希典　　大山　巌.

STANDING: NOGI MARESUKE。 OYAMA IWAO。

SAIGO TAKAMORI。 YAMAGATA ARITOMO。
西郷　隆盛　　山県　有朋

SITTING: 川村 KAWAMURA SUMIYOSHI。 KATSU AWA。勝安房

JULIUS HELM。　SAIGO JUDO。
西郷従道

Meiji emperor's reign, 1874. There was also a list of names identifying the people in the photograph.

One Saturday, not long afterward, I found myself sitting in a library before an encyclopedia set on Japanese history. What I read stunned me. According to the photo's inscriptions, great-grandfather was sitting amid half a dozen of the founding fathers and greatest heroes of modern Japan.

On the top left was Nogi Maresuke. He was responsible for Japan's victory over Russia in 1905, the first time that a modern Asian power had defeated a Western power. Nogi rose from national hero to a godlike figure in 1912 when, following the death of Emperor Meiji, he and his wife committed ritual suicide to atone for a disgrace thirty-five years earlier and for leading the horrific siege of Port Arthur, which resulted in 58,000 Japanese casualties.

To Nogi's left was Oyama Iwao, who selected the poem still used today as the lyrics for Japan's national anthem: *May my Lord's reign continue for a thousand, eight thousand generations, until pebbles grow into boulders, covered in moss.* Yamagata Aritomo, standing on the right, introduced universal conscription and became the architect of Japan's modern army, modeling it on Prussia's military. Right behind Julius was Saigo Takamori, modern Japan's greatest hero. He led the military forces supporting the young Meiji Emperor to defeat the shogunate, thus ending two-and-a-half centuries of Tokugawa shogunate rule in Japan. When Japan abandoned samurai privileges and began adopting Western customs, Saigo would later lead a doomed samurai rebellion against the new government, a story dramatized in the movie *The Last Samurai*.

I was skeptical of what I had found. For one thing, the young Saigo in my photograph looked a lot different than the man pictured in the history books. Despite this discrepancy, I wanted it to be true. I wanted to believe that our family was special—that I was not just another *gaijin*. If my ancestors had made some important contribution to Japan, perhaps I would feel more pride in my family's long ties to the country.

To unravel the Helm story, I began with Great-Grandfather Julius's memoir, as recorded by his brother in 1916 and written in German. The English translation, which is forty-two pages long, begins with a long account of how Julius was pulled out of school at fourteen and sent to apprentice at one farm estate after another, often laboring from three in the morning until eleven at night. He worked the fields and learned to keep accounts. He learned that "rapeseed, peas and potatoes had to be manured, while white oats and rye crops were raised without manure. Each cereal crop had to be followed by a foliage crop so the leaves of the plants would protect the ground against weeds." My relatives always liked to joke about how Julius left Germany in 1868 to avoid a marriage his mother had arranged with the only daughter of a wealthy landlord. But it was clear from his autobiography that Julius was unhappy working as a farm manager for overbearing Prussian landlords who would berate him for the tiniest failing, including a stray potato found by the side of the road. Julius had chosen not to manage his father's four-hundred-acre farm in Rosow, north of Berlin near the North Sea, because he didn't want the responsibility of supporting his mother and nine siblings. Later, he would forever be finding ways to take care of them, but at twenty-eight, when an unreasonable boss insisted that he plow ground that was still frozen, he walked away, deciding to seek his fortune in America, where he could be his own boss.

B I O G R A P H Y
----
of Julius Eelm,

Re-written from his personal notes, by his brother Karl.

Typed by his nephew Fritz Helm, and translated into

English, at Yokohama, in the month of June, 1933.

By Fritz Hoehler friend of his eldest son Karl Julius

When Julius arrived in Minnesota, however, he could only find work as a common laborer. At one farm he slapped a fellow workman who called him a "damn Dutchman." When the man took up a boxing stance, Julius, who didn't know how to box, held him in a bear hug until the landlord came to split up the fight. At another farm, his Irish employer wanted to marry Julius to a niece. When Julius saw a farmhand lose his arm in a thresher at yet another farm, he concluded America was not the place for him. In 1869, he took the transcontinental railroad to San Francisco with plans to board a ship to China. Since the recently completed railroad was now carrying mail from the

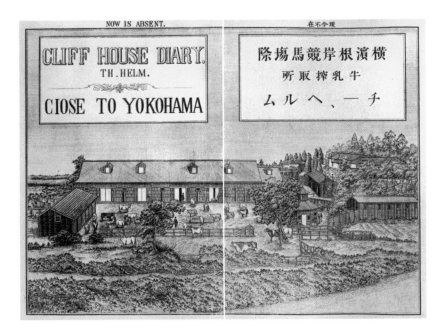

CLIFF HOUSE DIARY.
TH.HELM.

CIOSE TO YOKOHAMA

現今不在

横濱根岸競馬場際
牛乳搾取所

チ、ヘルム

East Coast, ships that had previously carried the mail had been put on new routes to Asia. Julius missed the China boat "by the length of my nose," so he booked passage on the next ship, *The Golden Age*, which happened to be headed for Yokohama.

As I read great-grandfather's story, I found myself admiring his decision to keep pushing beyond the familiar for something new. He was like no Helm I had ever known. The Helm relatives I knew were people caught between cultures. Like my father, and like me, they were quick to feel slighted, turn defensive and lash out in anger. Most had lived on three continents and spoke four languages, yet they never felt at home in any one country. The Helms I knew believed they were better than the Japanese, yet, of mixed blood and unable to read or write Japanese, they often felt insecure in the country of their birth. By contrast, Julius was as rooted in his German identity as an old oak tree, yet had no compunctions about pushing into new frontiers. Many years later, my son, Eric, with his powerful build, his sharp wit, his patience and his competitive drive, would remind me of Julius.

On weekends, I began to frequent the Yokohama Archives of History housed in the former British consulate, an historic brick building near the port. Saito Takio, a curator at the archives, helped me track down the dozens of Helms who had lived in Yokohama during the past century, each recorded in annual directories that listed foreigners living in Asia. Saito also showed me a lithograph of a dairy farm that had appeared on the cover of a history of dairy farming in Japan. "Helm Diary [sic]," it said. Julius had operated one of the first dairy farms in Japan. As Japan's key portal to trade with the West, Yokohama was the entry point for virtually every Western product first introduced to Japan, including the first bakery, telegraph and train.

Japan didn't always take well to this Western presence. Angry samurai determined to expel foreigners from Japan's sacred soil had slain some of the first residents of Yokohama. Even nature seemed intent on keeping outsiders at bay. Typhoons, which brought what the Japanese called *kamikaze* (winds of the gods), had destroyed invading Mongol fleets twice in the late 1200s.

When Julius's ship, *The Golden Age,* approached the Japanese coastline, it too was hit by a violent storm. The ship was a hybrid of sorts, sporting both sails and steam-powered paddle wheels. Toward the end of his journey, as he recounts in his memoir, Julius left his stuffy cabin for fresh air. He sat on the wood frame that covered the side wheel and felt the cool salt air whip against his face. He could feel the vibration and hear the sound of paddles churning below him. Above him, like a spear pointed at the stormy sky, the towering mast shivered and tipped as gusting winds filled the sails. Feeling cold, Julius went to his cabin to fetch a coat. When he returned to his seat, he was stunned to see a bare paddle wheel sending spray into the whirling wind. "During the short time I had been gone, a large wave had torn [the wooden frame] entirely away." Had he not left for his jacket, he surely would have died. But instead of fear, Julius felt exhilaration. All his life he had been pushed around, first by his father and later by his bosses. Now the only thing pushing him was the wild wind—and it was at his back.

The next morning, Julius awoke to discover the mast had broken and the engine room had flooded, extinguishing the boilers. The passengers helped clear the debris from the deck so the crew could re-fire the boilers. The ship limped into Yokohama's harbor passing lush narrow valleys sided by terraced hills and villages with thatched-roof houses. Yokohama harbor swarmed with sampans, some with squared sails, others powered by bronze-backed men who pushed back and forth on a single oar that reached out the back of the boat.

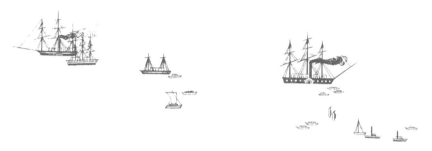

The Yokohama of 1869 was a bustling town that handled the import of cotton yarn, oils, vegetables, meats and machinery, while exporting tea and silks. Before the arrival of foreigners, Yokohama was a village of eighty households far from the main centers of commerce that stretched from Tokyo to Osaka. Now, as trade flourished, so did the population, as thousands of Japanese merchants gathered from all over Japan to engage in trade. In 1869, less than a decade after Japan opened itself to foreign trade, nearly seven hundred foreign vessels entered Yokohama harbor. Yet, as late as 1871, there were still only 1,586 Europeans and Americans living in Japan, a few hundred of whom lived in the recently opened port of Kobe, 260 miles to the southwest. Some described the foreign settlement as having a "wild west" atmosphere because of the many grog houses, gambling dens and brothels the sailors frequented. Prostitutes were often kept in street-front cages on display for customers. One British visitor described the foreign population in Yokohama as "the scum of Europe," although there were also more proper gentlemen's clubs that European merchants frequented.

Julius describes in his diary how his first task upon arriving in Yo-

横濱海岸通之圖

kohama was to find himself a new bow tie, perhaps in hopes of dif-
ferentiating himself from the common riffraff. Leaving the pier, he
walked down a street lined with shops selling lacquer pillboxes, *sumi-e*
scrolls and ivory carvings.

   To the south was the foreign settlement of two-story stone and brick
buildings. The settlement, first constructed in 1859, had burned down

The Customhouse of Yokohama, 1870. **NEXT PAGE:** Map of early Yokohama, 1893.

in 1866 and recently had been rebuilt. Two years before, the foreign settlement had also been expanded across a canal that had once served as its southern boundary. The settlement now included the two-mile stretch of hills where a community of Victorian homes had sprung up, a neighborhood called The Bluff. Along the canal, at the foot of The Bluff, was Motomachi, a shopping street where foreigners went to buy

45

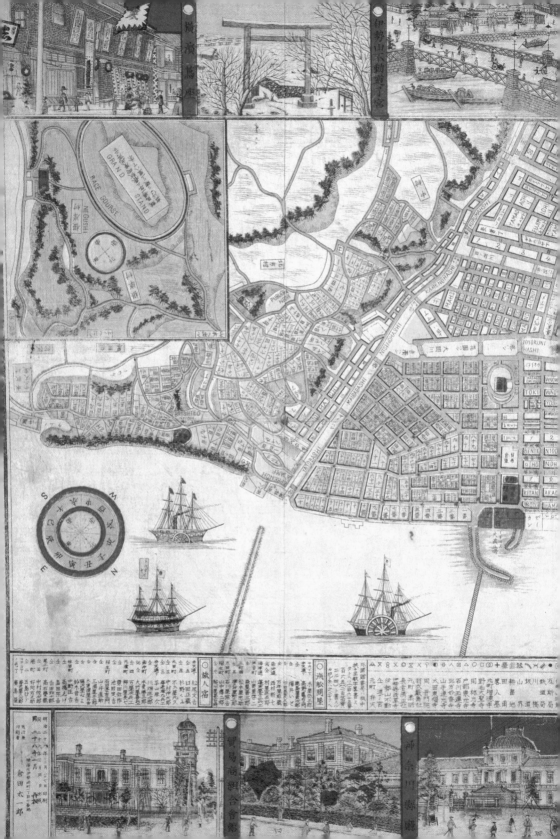

books, groceries and medicine, and where I would be born in a small clinic 86 years later.

To the north was the more densely populated Japanese town of tile-roofed compounds. There Julius would have seen peddlers balancing on their shoulders long poles with large hanging baskets filled with shellfish or vegetables. Hawkers, each with their own shrill sounds audible above the street noise, peddled their wares.

As Julius strolled through the town, he must have smelled pungent roasting teas wafting from large warehouses where the tea leaves were fired to dry before exporting. Everywhere he went, Julius would have seen colorful banners as if Yokohama had been dressed up for a special occasion. And so it was. "The town was in the state of grand festivities because of the horse races," wrote Julius.

Julius found his bow tie at a general store owned by Krause, a German. Krause introduced Julius to a German butcher who offered him room and board in exchange for work. He then apprenticed himself to a German baker. Thanks to his size—he was over six-feet tall—and his great strength, Julius finally found a well-paid job at the US Consulate in Yokohama tracking down sailors and dragging them back to their ships. He hated the work and was relieved when Carroll & Co., an American company that supplied provisions to ships, offered him a job as warehouse keeper. He was in charge of transporting goods to the ships on one of the small sampans he had admired on his arrival. Julius lived frugally in a small room in his employer's warehouse, making one dollar's worth of coal last through the winter of 1870 by using no more than a single lump per day.

Japan encouraged the introduction of Western technologies; the year Julius arrived the first telegraph was built and construction was begun on the first railway. However, Japan was also wary of its foreign guests. Its leaders knew that the West's colonization of China and consequent introduction of the opium trade had contributed to its decline. So Japan limited the movement of foreigners, requiring them to obtain a special passport to venture beyond a twenty-five-mile radius.

In early 1871, Julius received a summons from Max von Brandt, the German consul general in Yokohama. A stout, pompous man, von Brandt told Julius he had just returned from a trip to Wakayama, the domain of an important warlord several hundred miles to the west. There, von Brandt had witnessed something remarkable: A German sergeant named Carl Koppen was in the process of transforming a band of sword-bearing samurai into a modern army. "Before Koppen came, we were barbarians," von Brandt had heard one Japanese officer say. "Now we are like Europeans. We want to become Prussians." Von Brandt had heard Julius had experience in the Pioneers, Germany's engineering battalion, and said Julius would be well paid if he traveled to Wakayama to become a military adviser.

Some of Julius's experiences in Wakayama are recorded in a book I brought home from Dad's library called *Oyatoi Gaikokujin* (*Foreign Hired Hands*). It describes the activities of some of the two thousand or so Westerners the Japanese government had hired in the nineteenth century to help the nation on its path to modernization. I tracked down the author, Shigehisa Tokutaro, a history professor at the Kyoto City University of Arts. His son answered the phone. "How unfortunate," he said. "My father just died last month. He would have loved to have met you."

I was crestfallen. I had started my search too late. But the son gave me the name of another professor, Umetani Noboru, who had taken over his mentor's work. I met Umetani at a small coffee shop in Tokyo. He was a friendly man with a generous smile. He came with copies of articles about Julius's work in Wakayama that had appeared in the English language press in Japan in the 1930s.

I showed Umetani the picture of Julius with the soldiers. "If the names on the back are accurate, this is a remarkable photograph," he said. Saigo Takamori, the legendary leader of the famous samurai rebellion, Umetani explained, hated to have his picture taken and had never been photographed. If this were really Saigo, it could be the only photo in existence of one of Japan's greatest heroes.

"But the man in the picture doesn't look like Saigo," I said.

Umetani explained that the picture of Saigo used in textbooks was not a real photograph, but a composite. He showed me the line below the cheekbones where the photo of one person's broader chin and cheek had been grafted onto Saigo's younger brother's narrower upper face. Umetani suggested I visit the curator of the Wakayama City Museum to gather more information.

When I finally made the trip to Wakayama, a once-powerful castle town about 360 miles west of Tokyo, the curator of the museum showed me an exhibit he had put together about the German advisers who had worked in Wakayama, including Great-Grandfather Julius. When I showed him the names on the back of the photograph, he raised his eyebrows. We went through dozens of books in the museum, but we could find nothing to confirm the men in the picture were in fact the names written on the back of the photograph.

On a subsequent visit, however, the curator gave me something valuable: a manuscript that a German scholar, Margaret Mehl, had recently completed on Carl Koppen, the man Julius had worked for in Wakayama. The manuscript contained entries from Koppen's diary, letters he had written and scholarly analysis of the period. That summer, while vacationing on my sister's houseboat in Utah's beautiful Lake Powell where our family had gathered for a reunion, my mother, who was born German, helped me translate large chunks of the Koppen diary into English.

With that translation, Julius's memoir, anecdotes from the museum curator, newspaper articles and other research, I recreated the story of Julius's work as a military adviser. I was searching for information that would tell me something positive about my family—something that would demonstrate we had made an important contribution to Japan. What I found was something different altogether.

JULIUS AND HIS YOUNGER BROTHER, Adolf, who had recently arrived from New York on Julius's invitation, left Yokohama in the spring of 1871 on a small coastal ship. They landed at dusk the following day at Wakanoura, a half-moon bay of sandy beach. Julius and Adolf were led on horseback past temples placed around the perimeter of the city to serve as the first line of defense. Then they passed the walled residences of the city's nobles from where they could see, high above the city, Wakayama castle with its elegant sloping roof glowing in the moonlight.

In a compound at the foot of the castle, they were greeted by Koppen, a short, stocky Saxon with a receding hairline. Koppen had asked his personal cook to prepare a special French meal for Julius and Adolf. After dinner, Koppen explained the rules: They were not to fraternize with the Japanese soldiers; they were not to enter Japanese homes; with the exception of certain servants, Japanese were not to enter their home without written permission from the Wakayama government; they could leave the training grounds only if they were accompanied by guards. "The guards are there to protect you," Koppen explained, puffing on his pipe. "But they are also there to keep an eye on you."

Wakayama's position in Japan was a delicate one, Koppen explained. As a key pillar of the Tokugawa Shogunate that ruled Japan for 250 years, Wakayama had amassed great power, becoming one of the wealthiest domains. But the Western warships that had abruptly ended Japan's isolation a decade before, had also undermined the power of the Tokugawa Shogunate. In 1868, Satsuma and Choshu, two southwest domains, overthrew the shogun, moved the sixteen-year-old emperor from Kyoto to the shogun's castle in Tokyo and established a council of advisers to rule in his name. Japan remained a feudal land in which power was divided among hundreds of domains, each headed by a lord who maintained his own army. Wakayama had decided to modernize its army following the Prussian model in hopes of restoring the domain to its previous prominence.

The following morning, Koppen took Julius and his brother to the military training grounds where they watched as Koppen put the Japanese soldiers through their drills. The soldiers' uniforms consisted solely of a black wool tunic and a hat made of paper painted with black lacquer. Julius chuckled at the way many of the soldiers used sticks in place of rifles, like children playing at war. But once they began to goose-step down the field, Julius was impressed at the way their legs rose and fell in unison.

When the exercise ended, there was a single crisp *whack* as the soldiers all clapped their guns and wooden sticks to their shoulders at precisely the same moment. It was an impressive performance at a time when Western observers believed it was beyond the ability of Asians to move in a disciplined manner.

Koppen showed Julius a Prussian-made needle gun, so-called because a needle strikes a cartridge to create the explosion that releases the bullet. Unlike the traditional musket, in which bullet and gunpowder are loaded from the front of the barrel—a time-consuming process—the needle gun could be quickly loaded from the back.

Julius had seen the gun before. In the summer of 1866, when war broke out between Prussia and Austria, he had been assigned to Prussia's First Army, a force of 93,000 men commanded by Prince Friedrich Karl, the Prussian king's nephew. When the prince, eager for glory, prematurely ordered an attack on the backbone of the Austrian Army, a force twice its size, many of his colleagues in the infantry believed the rapid-firing capabilities of this needle gun had saved them from suffering far heavier losses. The Prussian soldiers could shoot as many as five bullets in the time it took the Austrian forces to load their muskets once.

Upon hearing of Julius's training as a Prussian pioneer, Koppen immediately appointed him head of a new engineering battalion. On his first day at work, Julius gathered his men at the training ground. With the help of a Japanese assistant who spoke rudimentary German, Julius quickly put the men to work. "I gathered the materials and turned an old barge into a pontoon for a pontoon bridge," wrote Julius. "Then I picked out the sixteen strongest men to carry the pontoon, but the results were pitiful."

The soldiers, Julius noticed, were mostly old men or boys. His interpreter explained that as samurai they had never engaged in manual labor. Most were unfit. Like the empty castle and the fortified temples, these soldiers were an anachronism. Samurai, the warrior class, accounted for about five percent of the population and were at the top of the social hierarchy followed by peasants, artisans and merchants. But by the 1800s, after centuries of peace, they had evolved into a class made up largely of administrators and social parasites.

When Julius told Koppen that his samurai could not perform the required work, Koppen said nothing. His answer came soon afterward when he sent Julius a hundred new recruits. They were all strong young farmers. The year before, in spite of opposition from many samurai who believed commoners would flee at the first sign of danger, Wakayama became the first domain in Japan to institute universal conscription. All twenty-year-old males, regardless of class, were required to serve in the army for three years. Koppen had taken the first recruits for his infantry. Now a new crop of men were supplied to Julius. Their first task was to learn discipline: to obey without question. For this, Julius made them goose-step up and down the training ground day after day.

When Julius announced to his soldiers that they would build pontoon bridges, the men were eager to learn. They completed their first pontoon within a few hours by lashing together old fishing boats. Unlike the samurai, these farmers were strong and could lift the pontoon with ease. They quickly assembled six more. A few days later, Julius taught them how to anchor the pontoons in place and then lash planks on top. In this way, they built a bridge across the broad castle moat.

The soldiers who gathered at the bridge were skeptical. "Sure there is a bridge," said one of the men. "But will it hold?"

At Julius's command, the whole company marched over the bridge and back. "The astonishment never ceased," Julius wrote.

Soon Julius had them working on new projects—they gathered timber to build tunnels and trenches.

Julius and his German colleagues believed that to fight like Westerners, the Japanese had to live like Westerners. Accustomed to a diet of fish and vegetables, the Japanese soldiers were forced to eat meat. Instead of eating and sleeping on the floor, the soldiers sat on chairs and slept in beds. Traditionally, the samurai shaved the crowns of their heads, allowing the rest of their hair to grow long so it could be arranged into a long queue and pulled forward in a manner to make them look fierce. This elaborate hairstyle required an assistant's help. "When Koppen explained to the Japanese that the Prussian soldier was only allowed a few fractions of a second to fix his hair," Julius wrote, "they finally agreed to sacrifice their queue."

Progress often required challenging taboos. The soldiers could not march in straw sandals, so Koppen had arranged for a German tanner and shoemaker to join their small group in Wakayama. The German advisers dined each night at Koppen's home. "So what is this word *naosu* that the men shout at me all the time?" the shoemaker asked one night over dinner.

Koppen exploded with laughter. "That is what the leather workers who fix sandals call out when they offer their services in the streets."

The Japanese were making fun of this foreigner for doing "unclean" leatherwork that only untouchables in Japan handled. The German tanner was not amused.

If the Germans were undertaking a cultural revolution inside the training camp, outside it Julius witnessed a Japan that looked much as it had for centuries. I wish I could have walked beside my great-grandfather as he explored a land where peasants still measured the passing days by phases of the moon and daylight was divided not into hours but into six equal periods, with each period expanding in the summer and shrinking in the winter.

Farmers walked on the paddles of small water wheels to lift water into their paddy fields. Most carts were pulled by hand. Captain H.C. St. John, a naturalist and hunter who traveled in Wakayama in the early 1870s, describes in *Notes and Sketches from the Wild Coasts of Japan* how badgers and deer wandered freely through the villages. Herons, cranes and mandarin ducks settled among the paddy fields, unalarmed by villagers who planted rice stalks nearby. St. John discovered, however, that when *he* approached a bird while hunting, it would immediately fly away. "The duck and geese knew at once I was not a Japanese and therefore not to be trusted," he wrote.

If Julius experienced the peace and stability that existed in much of Japan before Westerners arrived, he may not have been aware of the brutal cultural traditions that helped to maintain that social order.

When I was fourteen, I began to learn about some of those Japanese customs. I visited a workshop in the northern mountains of Japan for a school field trip. I watched an old man polish a spherical piece of wood and pass it on to an old woman who painted a sweet face on it with a few dabs of red from her paintbrush. The two were making *kokeshi*, the armless cylindrical dolls you can find in souvenir shops across Japan.

I have never looked at the dolls, or at Japanese culture, in quite the same way since the old lady told me what she believed the word meant. Years later, as I considered adopting a Japanese girl, the words would haunt me. "*Kokeshi* literally means 'to erase a child,'" the old woman explained to us. Traditionally, she said, the dolls had been used by farmers to remind them of the little girl they had drowned at birth so they would have one less mouth to feed. I later learned that many historians question the connection between infanticide and *kokeshi* dolls. Yet the historical record shows that female infanticide was so common in Japan that as late as the mid-1880s there were some villages in Japan with twenty-five percent more boys than girls. Japanese villages had found an efficient, if chilling, method of maintaining a stable population.

Regular public executions were another way Japan maintained social order at the time. Even petty thieves could be decapitated, their heads stuck on posts for public display as a warning to others. Western newspapers published pictures of such scenes to support their view that the Japanese were barbarians. Foreign advisers like Great-Grandfather Julius, of course, were busily teaching Japan European tactics for killing people far more efficiently.

In the old Japan, samurai armies were relatively small. In that fateful summer of 1871, after the Meiji emperor had been in nominal control for three years, he had only a few thousand soldiers at his command. A warlord with a modestly strong army could still take control. But to make Wakayama a power to be reckoned with, Koppen needed more

54

guns. In July, Koppen sailed for Germany to buy 4,000 more needle-nosed guns and to hire another half-dozen military instructors.

Word spread of Wakayama's efforts to modernize its military. "In a small Japanese region still closed to foreigners, German institutions are having a far-reaching influence," a reporter wrote in the July 21, 1871 issue of the German newspaper *National Zeitung*. The reporter questioned whether it was such a good idea to be teaching the Japanese the ways of modern warfare, but determined that the German advisers were helping to elevate the soldiers of Wakayama morally and socially. "Peace through war," the reporter concluded. *The New York Times* ran a similar story in the summer of 1871.

While Koppen was in Germany, Julius continued to train his men. Soon he had five hundred men under his command. But on August 29, 1871, shortly before Koppen was scheduled to return with his guns, the Meiji emperor ordered the *daimyo* (lords) of the nation's three hundred domains to disband their armies and resign their posts, passing real control to the central government.

"The [emperor's council of advisers] had planned this *coup d'etat* [against the lords] for some time, but delayed it because of some doubts about the loyalty of the warlords," wrote Julius in his reminiscences. "They took advantage of Koppen's absence as well as Wakayama's shortage of arms and war materials to eliminate the armies of the warlords."

Historians today differ over whether Wakayama ever truly posed a threat to the Meiji government as Julius believed. It is remarkable how Japan's lords succumbed so quickly to central government rule. A feudal system that had been in place for seven hundred years was dismantled peacefully in a matter of months.

Sometime later, three thousand Wakayama samurai gathered at the *daimyo's* offices for a farewell ceremony. Julius did not write about this scene, but according to historical records, all the paper doors and shoji screens were removed to create one massive room. The samurai sat in their colorful ceremonial robes as the *daimyo* thanked them for the loyal service they and their ancestors had provided over the centuries. Many samurai could not hold back tears as they were released from their service—demoted from loyal samurai with status and monthly stipends to *ronin*, leaderless men with no choice but to find new occupations. Some went to work as servants in foreign households; others pulled rickshaws. Most samurai received little more than a folding fan printed with the name of their *daimyo*. Only the most senior retainers received pensions.

Before heading back to Yokohama, Julius took a final tour of the castle grounds and recalled fond memories of how he first taught those peasants to build a pontoon bridge. Historian Shigehisa Tokutaro called Julius "the father of military engineering in Japan." Later, back in Germany, Carl Koppen would become a heavy drinker. Reading about Japan's military victories against China and Russia, he would tell anyone who cared to listen, "Those are my boys." Julius, too, would take quiet pride in what he had taught his soldiers.

I wonder if Julius ever had doubts about what he had helped to create. Julius could not have imagined that in the ensuing decades, the Prussian system of conscription Wakayama had introduced to Japan would be introduced in the national army and expand wildly as Japan pushed into Asia. By World War II, the Japanese armed forces exceeded eight million men. A quarter of them would die in battle, and they would be responsible for the deaths of as many as twenty million people in China alone.

AN UNLIKELY MATCH

WHEN JULIUS AND ADOLF RETURNED to Yokohama in 1872 with the gold they had received in payment for their work in Wakayama, the town was in the midst of a cultural revolution. Barber shops had popped up and were doing a thriving business cutting off the top knots of samurai and trimming their hair in the Western fashion. A railroad to connect Yokohama with Tokyo was near completion. And gas lanterns, which the Japanese called magic lights, had been installed along the main boulevards.

Adolf found work teaching German. Julius tried his hand at trade and failed before going back to work for his former employer, Carroll and Co. Sometime during those next two years, Julius met Hiro, my great-grandmother, and fell in love. Today it is hard to understand how unusual that special relationship was for its time. I cannot imagine it was love at first sight. Hiro must have been initially repelled by Julius, a man whose shoes would have seemed like buckets, whose nose would have appeared grotesquely oversized and whose hairy face and arms would have seemed beastly. Over time, she must have become accustomed to these Western features. Perhaps she was attracted by Julius's self-confidence, his strength and his kindness.

Julius, too, would have initially given little thought to Hiro, this small, but tough-minded woman. But he would have come to enjoy

the special meals she fixed. He would come to appreciate her slender figure and find alluring the slope at the nape of her neck as she bent down to serve tea or sweep the floor. One day, perhaps, he discovered that he was obsessed with Hiro. Prudish Lutheran that he was, Julius would resist the temptation to make her his mistress. At a time when Prussian Protestants had little tolerance even for Catholics, Julius must have assumed that his mother would disapprove of him having any kind of relationship with a Japanese woman.

Over time, Julius started to look at the world in a new way. Yokohama was part of a different world. Few in Japan believed there was any shame in having a mistress. Indeed, it was a sign of status. Wealthy men were expected to have mistresses. And if Julius's mother might have disapproved of Hiro, she was two oceans away. What his mother would have wholeheartedly approved of was Hiro's frugality. I imagine Hiro substituted delicious local vegetables and fish for the expensive imported meat and potatoes Julius had been eating. One day in early 1875, Julius asked Hiro to share his room and hired another maid to clean his house. That was the beginning of their long life together.

YOKOHAMA, TOO, CONTINUED TO UNDERGO great change. In 1873, a delegation of Japanese diplomats returned from a two-year tour of Europe and the United States with shocking news for Japan's leaders: The country was behind the West not just in military might but also in virtually every other area from transportation to communications. The good news was that most of the West's advances had been made in the previous fifty years, as a consequence of the Industrial Revolution. By aggressively importing Western technology, the delegation declared, Japan could quickly catch up.

The Japanese government began employing hundreds of Europeans and Americans to help establish key institutions such as schools and government agencies, and to build lighthouses, telegraph lines and shipyards. Julius's brother, Adolf, was appointed professor of German at the newly created Tokyo School of Foreign Languages.

An uncle once told me that Adolf had received a samurai sword from the emperor for teaching German to members of the Imperial family. I was skeptical at the time, but while reading the diary of Kido Takayoshi, the Meiji emperor's powerful counselor and the man responsible for his education, I came across a simple entry on December 12, 1875: "I met with the German Helm," Kido had written about Adolf in his diary.

Yokohama in those days still had a rough, frontier atmosphere, and Western women were rare. Liaisons between Western men and Japanese women consequently became common. British diplomats, even as they complained of Yokohama's loose morals, often sneaked out to apartments where they kept courtesans.

These relationships were almost always illicit and when the men returned to their homelands, as they usually did after a few years, their mistresses were invariably left behind. If there were children involved, perhaps there would be an extra stipend. Was this the nature of the relationship between Julius and Hiro? Did he sometimes stroll the Bund, letting her walk three steps behind, as a Japanese wife should? Or did he keep her closeted at home, out of view of the gossiping Western community?

I like to think Julius stood up for Hiro from the beginning, but I doubt it. I remember the day in 1999, when my dad's cousin Lillian guided me to a neglected section of the Foreigners' Cemetery in Yokohama to help me find a grave. She was seventy-eight, so I held her elbow as we walked down uneven stone steps toward a dark corner of the cemetery. Lillian was the youngest daughter of Julius's eldest son, Karl. Her dark hair and eyes made her look vaguely Spanish, and even at her advanced age, she was still beautiful.

"It's somewhere around here," Lillian said in a voice high and thin, waving her arm across a terraced area of overgrown weeds and shrubs. I moved from gravestone to gravestone pushing aside bushes and wiping away, with my bare hands, the moss that had collected on the gravestones. Finally, I found it: the name "LINA" was engraved in large letters across a grave marker the size and shape of a milestone. The date, written in small Japanese letters, and the inscription, engraved vertically on the lower right, read: "December 31, Meiji 8." The eighth year of the Meiji emperor would have been 1875. Hiro and Julius's first child, Lina, had probably died at birth. Carved into the stone above the name was a wisteria blossom.

I felt a pang of sadness that Lina's grave had been neglected for so long. The grave site was far from the other Helm graves, most of which were at the top of the hill. *Why was there no last name on the headstone?* I wondered. *Was Lina born out of wedlock?* Julius had written in his memoir that

he had married Hiro in 1875, but was that possible? At that time, Japanese law required Japanese citizens to get government approval before marrying a foreigner. When Kido, the emperor's adviser, helped a Japanese diplomat marry a German woman in 1876, he wrote in his diary that it was the first officially sanctioned marriage between a Japanese citizen and a Westerner.

If Julius named his daughter Lina, honoring his mother, Caroline, he must have intended to raise her as his own. Hiro was no mere mistress. Yet, I wondered if Lina didn't bring shame to Julius and Hiro. Did Lina's early death feel to Julius like a divine rebuke? His Lutheran mother would have been horrified to learn that Julius had a child by a Japanese Buddhist. Hiro, who had been cut off from her own family, as I would later discover, would have borne her suffering alone. To make matters worse, Julius lost his job with Carroll and Co. not long after his daughter died.

Julius was an enterprising man, and before long, he found new work. In Yokohama in 1876, there were only two draying companies to transport cargo between the customs house and the warehouses of the various trading houses. What kept more companies from launching their own businesses was the high cost of the horse-drawn trucks used to move the cargo. The trucks, imported from America, were so heavy they each required a large American dray horse to pull them. At the time, there were only twelve such dray horses in Yokohama, each imported at a great cost.

Julius came up with a simple solution. He designed and built a wagon that was lighter and rigged it so it could be pulled by two of the smaller Japanese ponies that were readily available. When he found the new wagon worked to his satisfaction, he paid a Japanese carpenter to build three more. With these wagons, he set up an office at No. 124, just a block away from his home, and put his first advertisement in the English-language newspaper, the *Japan Gazette*: *Julius Helm: Landing & Shipping Agents*. He called on his friends at the stevedoring companies to drum up business.

By 1879, he was so successful that for $6,500, Julius acquired one of his main competitors. He borrowed the money from a friend at two percent interest a month and soon made enough profits to pay off the debt. He acquired new warehouses and stables in an ambitious expansion drive. "I rebuilt the houses and stables according to my requirements, and as soon as everything was ready, I saw that my ten years in

Yokohama had not been wasted," Julius wrote in his memoir. "I was proud of myself as the owner of a profitable business."

The things Julius sought—the challenges, the thrill of competition, the recognition from his peers—he now found in his life as an entrepreneur. He had left Germany because he wanted to be free. And now, although he was always working, he had never felt freer. Business was the purest expression of who he was. The very manner in which he structured his business reflected his character: He insisted on absolute order, a tireless pursuit of efficiency and an unflinching loyalty and honesty with every customer. As Julius hired new employees, he trained them to his way of thinking. The new warehouses and barges, like his wagons, were built to his own specifications, and Julius found it fulfilling to see those efforts boost revenues.

J. HELM.

Landing & Shipping Agents.

Yokohama Drayage Company.
Office : No. 124.
Yokohama, Feb. 3rd, 1880.   6m.

"I worked as hard as three men all week, and on Sundays you would find me with my accounts," Julius wrote. "The more people called me a slave to my business, the happier I felt. I was working for myself and I could see the results of my efforts."

In 1878, Julius acquired the Cliff Dairy, one of Yokohama's first dairy farms. He put in charge his thirty-one-year-old brother, Theodore, who had come to Yokohama a decade before and had worked in a general store. Because the dairy farm was located outside the boundaries within which foreigners were permitted to reside, Julius had to register the farm in the name of a Japanese friend. Since the Japanese did not like the smell of dairy products—they disparagingly referred to anything Western as *batakusai* (stinks like butter)—all the milk was sold to Westerners.

Julius's own household would become a big consumer of that milk. His home was soon filled with the cries of children. His eldest daughter, Marie, was born in February 1877, and his first son, Karl, followed in 1879. I wondered what Julius thought of his children who looked so unlike him. How did Hiro regard her life with Julius?

For many years I had no idea. Hiro remained a mystery. Once, not long after I began working as a reporter in Japan, Dad took me to his favorite sushi shop on a quiet side street in Yokohama where he shared a curious story about Hiro. Dad had been loudly berating the sushi chef for the slow service, and I was embarrassed, as I so often was when he drank too much. I went into my reporter mode, my standard response to any awkward social situation, and asked Dad a question I had been curious about for some time.

"What did you know about Hiro, your grandmother?" I asked.

Dad turned to me with tired eyes and sighed. He wrinkled his nose and slowly shook his balding head. It was that look of resignation he had shown me so often since I had returned as a correspondent, no longer beholden to him and his money. Looking back now, as a father, I think I understand how he felt. He wanted my respect, but he didn't know how to gain it. It was easier for him to pretend to be the uncaring, deadbeat father.

"I never knew her. My father never talked about her," Dad said, shrugging his shoulders. "But I have a cup with her family crest, two crossed eagle feathers. Did I ever show it to you?" I nodded. I had heard that story before.

Then suddenly, Dad's eyes lit up, and he put his little finger in the air. "Did I tell you she was missing half of her little finger?" He called for another flask of *sake* and leaned on the counter to tell the tale.

"They say Hiro was one tough woman," Dad began. "Well, this Japanese warlord's retinue was passing in front of Julius's house. The warlord was being carried in one of those *kago*, you know, those sedan chairs enclosed in bamboo shades. Samurai guards walked at his side. Julius's gardener was clipping the camellia bush that hung over the

compound wall when one of the branches fell at the foot of a samurai guard. The samurai, furious at the insult to his lord, pulled out his sword, kicked down the gate and ran into the compound to chase down the gardener." Dad's story had me on the edge of my stool. I couldn't believe he had never mentioned this before.

"The gardener clambered down the tree and fell to his knees. Touching his forehead to the ground, he begged forgiveness. The samurai raised his sword and was about to cut off the poor bastard's head when Hiro jumped in front of the gardener and put out her hand." Dad put his right hand up, palm out, to demonstrate. "The samurai was bringing his sword down on the gardener when suddenly he saw this little woman standing in front of him."

"'Stop!' she shouted. Well, the samurai stopped his sword just as it sliced through Hiro's little finger."

At that, Dad beamed a smile that was so warm, so captivating, it caught me by surprise. I had often seen that smile as a child. But it had always been directed at someone else, usually a beautiful woman he was trying to charm. Now, as it came my way, I felt a surge of pleasure. It was as if Dad had opened himself up to me so I could enter his thoughts, and, with his playful eyes, had unfolded the hard fist of my resistance so he could enter mine.

We both knew the story was probably untrue. That was why Dad had never bothered to tell it to me. By the time Hiro was living with Julius, the days of sword-swinging samurai were over. Even so, Dad had painted in my mind a vivid picture of a samurai with a fierce grimace staring down at this unyielding woman. And somehow, I knew that Dad had the exact same picture in his mind because he suddenly wrinkled his nose.

I laughed. Soon, Dad, too, was laughing. Much later, I would come to treasure this story and that special connection I would never again experience. Dad would die before I had children. They would never know the indescribable pleasure of having that bewitching smile directed at them.

Sometime later, I was going through old Yokohama newspapers when I came across a story that brought back the memory of that evening with my father. The article, which appeared on the front page of *The Japan Gazette* on July 2, 1879, never mentioned Hiro or a samurai. Yet it was hauntingly familiar. It began:

66

We have to record the story of a crime happily without precedent in Yokohama for many years past. In the compound of Mr. Helm, carrier, lived a coolie with his wife; both were in his employ. The woman bore the reputation of being very loose in her morals. At about one o'clock this morning Mr. Helm was aroused by the [maid] rushing into his room and thence into the room in which another Japanese woman slept.

Julius followed the maid into "the other woman's" room, the article went on to say. The maid, sobbing hysterically, said her husband was going to kill her. Seconds later, the maid's husband, the coolie, pounded on the door downstairs. Julius tried to persuade the husband to go home quietly. When he refused, Julius went out into the street to summon a policeman. Julius had walked barely half a block when he heard the screams. He ran home to find the husband, knife in hand, fighting with the gardener. Julius pushed the men aside, and ran up the stairs to the room where he had left Hiro with his maid.

[Julius] was horrified to find the whole place literally covered with blood and both the women in an unconscious state, bleeding profusely from wounds about the head and body, one having had her left hand almost severed by some sharp instrument. He lost no time in procuring medical assistance.

In the meantime, a small crowd had gathered in front of Julius's house, where the gardener lay dead, evidently slain by the maid's husband, the coolie. Since the crime occurred in a German compound, under the rules of the so-called "unequal treaties" Europeans forced Japan to sign, a German constable was in charge of the investigation. The constable concluded that the coolie had come home to find his wife, the maid, in bed with the gardener, and had gone mad. After chasing his wife into "the other woman's room," next to Julius's room, the coolie had stabbed his wife, the maid, and ran into the compound next door to hide.

There (the coolie) committed suicide, first by stabbing himself with the sword right through the neck, and then by a deep gash in the abdomen—this latter wound almost completely disemboweled him. Mr. Helm says the husband was always a quiet man and he can only account

for his conduct by supposing that he was exasperated beyond control by the conduct of his wife.

It was a gruesome story. As I reread it, however, I realized that the coolie must have been a former samurai, for only a samurai would commit suicide through *seppuku*, the excruciatingly painful ritual of disemboweling oneself, which was supposed to restore honor. This was the first hint of a parallel with Dad's story of Hiro. But it was the next passage that left absolutely no doubt:

> It must have been while attempting to protect (the maid) that the other woman received her wounds, for the cut on her left hand appears to have been inflicted through that hand having caught hold of the blade.

The article concluded by noting that while the coolie's cheating wife died, "the other woman," who I now understood was clearly Hiro, had a better chance of surviving her severe wounds. What kind of courage does it take to grab the razor-sharp blade of a madman's sword? Hiro must have been a woman of unusual spunk. And what of the children? Hiro and Julius's daughter, Marie, two years old at the time, must have been in the corner trembling, and six-month-old Karl must have been wailing as his mother fought. The reporter probably referred to Hiro as "the other Japanese woman" because she and Julius were not married. And it must have been to save Julius embarrassment that the newspaper made no mention of the children.

I imagine Julius scooped up his two frightened children and held them to calm their cries as he watched Hiro, on the edge of death, taken away on a stretcher. I like to think that at that moment, Julius knew how close he had come to losing his family.

Julius had built a successful business and was raising a fine family. The carnage that ended the lives of his three employees and resulted in Hiro's near death had shaken him. If there were records kept of the marriages that occurred in Yokohama during those years, I imagine they might show that Julius and Hiro quietly recorded their commitment to each other sometime soon after those horrible murders. Did the strong bonds that then developed between Julius and Hiro help them build a fortune and begin a family dynasty against great odds? Or were the murders an inauspicious start to the family's troubled history in Japan?

KOREAN KINGS
& VIRGINIA
GENTRY

06

IN 1992, I VISITED TRUDY WEBSTER, Karl's daughter, then living in Los Angeles. She was proud of her middle name, Hiro, and had collected a trunk full of family photos. Among them, I found one of Hiro taken in 1883 when she was twenty-nine. She seemed like an entirely different person from the woman I had seen in my father's picture of her. Hiro had a pretty, oval face. Her mouth had a touch of insolence; her upper lips formed a pout. Her hands were slender and delicate. Hiro wore a kimono of rough grey flannel tied at the waist by a narrow *obi*. The small bead on the thin, braided cord tied across the middle of her sash was placed slightly off center.

In my father's picture taken in 1898, fifteen years later, by contrast, Hiro wore the formal kimono of a wealthy woman with sleeves displaying her family crest: two crossed eagle feathers. Seated in an arm chair, stiff and austere, Hiro looked drained of life. Her feet, encased in white *tabi*, the split-toe socks, rested on a low, cushioned stool. Her cheeks were gaunt with her mouth almost in a frown. Hiro's hands were thick and swollen at the knuckles, worn from years of hard

OPPOSITE:
Julius Helm and Hiro Komiya with children, (L to R) Marie, Jim and Karl, ca. 1883.

Julius and Hiro, ca. 1898.

work. What happened in those intervening years to diminish Hiro, even as her fifty-eight-year-old husband, standing behind her, still looked as strong as an ox?

Julius's sense of obligation to his siblings must have been an enormous burden on Hiro. Most Sundays, Hiro had to cook for the whole extended Helm family that included his brothers Adolf and Theodore. Then in 1880, Julius's younger sister Anna, recently divorced, came with her two sons and stayed with Julius and Hiro for nine months. They paid little attention to Hiro, and their long hours of conversation in German must have grated on her ears.

Hiro, like many of Yokohama's Japanese residents, must have felt odd to be living in a foreign settlement ruled by white men. Under the humiliating treaties of "extraterritoriality" the West imposed on Japan, Japanese authorities had no jurisdiction over foreigners living in Japan's foreign settlements. This was why the murder in Hiro and Julius's house had been handled by a German constable. Julius benefited from the system, according to newspaper reports of the time. Once a German judge ordered a Japanese merchant to return $350 Julius had loaned him, and another time, Julius was not found liable when he delivered a barrel of palm oil to a Japanese customer that was undamaged, yet proved to be empty.

When a cholera epidemic struck in 1879, a German ship ignored the quarantine imposed by Japanese authorities and sailed into Yokohama escorted by a German man-of-war ship. If the captain had done the same in a European port, the action would have been regarded as an act of war. But Japan was powerless to respond.

In spite of such arrogance, the Japanese began to treat the Germans more favorably. The Meiji government had chosen to pattern many of its institutions on German models because they reflected similar values on the important role of the state. A German noble was hired to become chamberlain and reorganize protocol at Japan's Imperial Palace. The German constitution provided the basic model for the Japanese constitution. And in the wake of Wakayama's success, German officers replaced the French as advisers to the Japanese army. Jealous Englishmen complained that Japan had acquired "a bad case of the German measles."

German merchants like Julius were also successful in Yokohama because they made an effort to learn Japanese and worked hard, eschewing the leisurely lifestyle of the British colonialists who took long lunches and retired early to their country clubs. While Julius's business prospered, he remained unsatisfied with his life. One March day in 1885, he sold his dray company to a group of Japanese businessmen and told Hiro he wanted to move the family to America. "I had always missed a particular line of business, and that was the farm business," Julius wrote.

Just as he waited for word from friends and relatives about the availability of land for sale in the United States, he met Paul Georg von Mollendorf, a German diplomat-turned-adviser to the Korean king who was visiting Yokohama. Mollendorf sported a long wispy beard, hair that flowed past his shoulders and round horn-rimmed glasses. Yokohama's German Club was scandalized by Mollendorf's appearance and refused him entry because he wore "native" clothes, the heavily embroidered, padded robes of a Korean noble. Mollendorf told Julius that his task was to help the Korean king modernize his country. He had already established a customs office and was now in Yokohama to find talent to help him set up a medical college, build railroads and develop new industries. When he learned of Julius's training in agriculture, Mollendorf invited him to come to Korea to establish a model farm.

Enticed by the offer, Julius put his plans for farming in America on hold. He handed over the Cliff Dairy to his brother Theodore, placed a few plows in a wagon and set out for Korea, leaving his wife and children in Yokohama. At the port of Chemulpo, Korea, now called Inchon, Julius learned that to get to Seoul, 26 miles away, he was expected to take a sedan chair carried by eight Korean coolies. The coolies, he was told, had to be paid in advance so they could eat ahead of the arduous journey. Repelled by the idea of sitting on the shoulders of eight men, Julius chose to walk, pulling the wagon he had brought with him along the muddy road to the capital.

In Seoul, Julius met Mollendorf and the cadre of German experts who had signed up for the mission to modernize Korea. One German had imported and planted 100,000 mulberry trees and was trying to raise silk worms. Another had been asked to build a glass factory. When the man discovered the sand in the vicinity of Seoul was useless for making glass, Mollendorf tried to persuade him to build a match factory.

Julius was excited to be part of this important enterprise. It reminded him of his early days in Wakayama. He purchased a horse and rode out to explore the open plains outside Seoul that Mollendorf wanted him to cultivate. When Julius reported that the soil was too poor to farm, Mollendorf told him to take fertile land occupied by Korean tenant farmers. Julius didn't like the idea, and when, not long afterwards, a mud stable collapsed in a rainstorm killing his horse, Julius headed back to Japan. Mollendorf would later become infamous for trying to sell French Catholic missionaries the exclusive right to proselytize in Korea. Under pressure from the British and Chinese, the Korean king would later be forced to fire Mollendorf for secretly negotiating a treaty that would have expanded Russian influence in Korea.

Julius was lucky to have left Korea when he did. In 1886, a year later, successive smallpox and cholera epidemics killed an estimated ten thousand people in Seoul. Travelers described ugly scenes of roving dogs feasting on smallpox-scarred children left outside the city to ward off demons.

Back in Japan, Julius took Hiro and his three children to Ashinoyu, a hot-spring resort near Mt. Fuji. Julius walked the thirty-five miles, while Hiro and the children rode a horse. It would be the last time Julius lavished so much time on his family. Soon afterward, having heard about property available in Virginia, he ventured there by steamship and train. Two months later, Julius was on a real estate agent's buggy turning down a long, cedar-lined driveway in Yorktown to inspect Lansdowne, an old tobacco plantation. When he stopped in front of the mansion, Julius decided he had found the home of his dreams. The massive house, built in the 1690s of brick brought from Britain as ballast in sailing ships, sat on 1,100 acres of farmland, forest and swamp. From the house, there was a stunning view across a terraced garden to the wide expanse of the York River. The man who built the mansion had been one of the original founders of Yorktown, and the adjacent plantation had housed two Virginia governors. On December 14, 1885, Julius signed the deed and paid $2,700 to purchase what he concluded was "one of the finest pieces of property in the world." The sum was equal to about fifteen years of wages for a US farm worker, who typically made about $15.50 a month.

Julius immediately wrote to Hiro asking her to join him. He spent the winter repairing the house and building the barns and stables. In the spring, he bought two horses, a few cows and several pigs. Hiro, who probably spoke little or no English, set sail from Yokohama in the spring of 1886 with her nine-year-old daughter, Marie, and her two sons, seven-year-old Karl and three-year-old James. There is no record of that long journey, but my Uncle Ray, my father's younger brother, heard a family story of how Hiro, while on that train journey, had looked through the window from her train seat to find herself staring into the face of a Native American. She didn't know what to make of this man with the Asian-looking face dressed in shabby garb. The Native American seemed equally surprised to find this woman, who looked so much like one of his people, wearing kimono and sitting among the wealthy white passengers.

No doubt Hiro tried to see the glory of Lansdowne through Julius's eyes. It was late spring when she arrived, so the peach trees would have been in full bloom and she would have smelled the sweet fragrance of the honeysuckle. Hiro had been raised as a farm girl and was not afraid to work in the fields, care for the animals and clean house.

But Hiro must have missed Yokohama's energy, its boisterous open-air markets crowded with shoppers and noisy with hawkers. Williamsburg, the former capital of colonial Virginia, about twenty minutes away by carriage, would have seemed to her like a ghost town. The very vastness of Lansdowne would have heightened Hiro's sense of isolation. Her entire village could have fit on this estate. Indeed, there was a little village of small huts in which slaves on the plantation had once lived and where a few sharecroppers were still resident.

I wonder if Hiro sensed the shadows that haunted the land. In 1622, Native Americans had massacred 347 English settlers in the area. In the years that followed, thousands of Native Americans died of smallpox, which, according to some accounts, was deliberately spread by settlers. The wife of the former owner of Lansdowne, a captain who had been a member of Robert E. Lee's personal staff, had been murdered by renegade soldiers at the end of the Civil War in the very house in which Hiro now lived.

If Hiro sometimes felt like an outsider in her old home in Yokohama because she was married to a white man, in Virginia, where colored people were treated as barely human, she must have felt like an outcast. Her children Marie and Karl would not have been permitted to attend the local school because of Jim Crow laws banning "colored" people from attending the same school as whites. When Hiro learned she was pregnant with her fourth child, she pressed Julius to return to Yokohama.

Julius stubbornly clung to his dream estate, but there was one thing Hiro could rely on—Julius's restlessness. Sure enough, in January 1887, midway through his second winter on the farm, Julius told Hiro to pack up. He had figured out that the plantation would never generate even a small fraction of the profits he had made with his Yokohama business. Rather than part with Lansdowne, he persuaded his brother Gustav, a tailor in New York, to take over the plantation. He would ultimately hand the deed to his brother whose family would live there through the early 1930s.

Julius moved to New York and lived briefly in a Brooklyn tenement while he worked as a longshoreman, declaring himself "lucky" that jobs had opened up thanks to a major strike, one of the nation's first general strikes. He was a scab, though I'm sure he did not see himself that way. It was during this short stay in Brooklyn that my grandfather, Julius Felix Heinrich Helm, was born on March 30, 1887. The boy was named after his father, but Hiro called him "Julie-chan," and the name Julie stuck. It was because of my grandfather's chance birth in New York that he, my father and I were all born American citizens.

As soon as Julius had earned the fare, he took his family on the long journey back to Yokohama, arriving in the hot summer of 1888 where a bittersweet surprise awaited him. Julius's youngest brother, thirty-three-year-old Paul, who had moved to Yokohama soon after Julius's departure for Virginia, had exploited the familiarity in Yokohama with the Helm name to launch his own dray company, offering trucking services between the piers and the warehouses.

Paul generously invited Julius's family to stay with him. Julius was proud of Paul's success, but embarrassed that he, the older brother, had to start over at the age of forty-seven. Had he stayed in Yokohama instead of yielding to his desire to farm, he would have been master of a thriving business. It would have been Julius who arranged a job for Paul just as he had done for Adolf in Wakayama and Theodore with the dairy. Instead, with four children to support, Julius had to depend on his youngest brother for work and shelter.

"There is nothing to be ashamed of," Hiro told her husband, as Julius would later recall. "You had the right to sell your business; you never hurt anyone; you only fooled yourself. Don't worry about what people think. Do your best, and better days will come."

Hiro was right. Within weeks Julius had found a job, and within months he had been promoted to manager. When Julius's Japanese

(L to R) Elsie, Marie, Jim, Julius, Willie, Julie, Karl, Louisa, Hiro, ca. 1895.

bosses learned that he had managed a farm, they asked him to raise sheep.

Japanese entrepreneurs in the late 1800s in Yokohama had a tendency to latch onto the latest fad. For a while, every Japanese company wanted to own its own steamer. Whenever a ship came into port, a Japanese company would acquire it as soon as its cargo was unloaded. *The Golden Age,* on which Great-Grandfather Julius first came to Japan, was purchased by Mitsubishi Mail Steamship Co. and became the Hiroshima-maru, the first steamship ever boarded by the Meiji emperor. Later there was great interest among Japanese entrepreneurs in rabbits because of their astounding ability to breed, and the animals were imported from California, Australia and China. Sheep were the latest fad. Unfortunately, after fattening the sheep, Julius discovered that the butchers in Yokohama preferred the larger sheep now being imported from China, and he had to sell the sheep at a loss. When his Japanese boss sold the business in 1891, Julius bought the assets and merged the company with his brother Paul's company to create Helm Brothers.

Julius wanted to be his own boss, so he moved his family to Kobe, a port 260 miles down the coast, to open a branch office for Helm Brothers. Ever restless, he then closed the branch and borrowed 15,000 yen to buy a half share of his largest competitor, Nickel & Co. Meanwhile, Hiro was even busier. With the birth of Elsie, Willie and Louisa, she and Julius now had seven children.

Julius's business benefited from a rapidly expanding Japanese economy. Japanese steamships now plied every port in the Pacific, and Japanese merchant houses quickly wrested much of the tea and silk trade from China. With economic power came a desire for a broader political presence in Asia. In 1894, when China sent troops to Korea to help the Korean king suppress a rebellion, Japan countered with its own expeditionary force, which replaced the existing government with a pro-Japanese government, leading to war with China. Even liberal Japanese intellectuals supported the war against China, calling it a great conflict between the forces of progress, represented by Japan, and the backward forces, represented by China.

Julius's main competitor in Kobe was a company run by a Chinese man named Jack Yong. When Japan declared war on China, Yong asked Julius to take over his business to protect it from Japan's anti-China frenzy. Julius sold his share of Nickel's business and took over Yong's.

Japan's decisive victory over China in 1895, thanks in part to its German-trained army and advanced German weaponry, established Japan as a new power in Asia. However, Western doubts about Japan remained. In the final invasion of Port Arthur, when the Japanese entered a Chinese village to find tortured Japanese prisoners nailed to stakes, the army was said to have retaliated by massacring every man, woman and child in the village. Western observers would point to the massacre as evidence the Japanese were uncivilized, although the action was reminiscent of similar acts by the US cavalry against Native Americans not long before.

There was a surge of patriotism in Japan at its victory over China and the territory it wrested from China, including the strategic Port Arthur and territory in Manchuria and Taiwan (then called Formosa).

In less than a generation, a country that had once been threatened by colonization had itself become a colonial power.

Despite its rise as an international power to be reckoned with, Japan had not yet been accepted by the exclusive club of white colonial nations. Germany, Russia and France banded together to pressure Japan to return much of the Chinese territory. Japan felt it had been treated unjustly by the Western powers, particularly since Germany then proceeded, a few years later, to establish its own colony in Tsingtao, halfway between Shanghai and Beijing, while Russia took over Port Arthur. It would take two wars for Japan to win those territories back.

In early 1897, Julius received word that his brother Paul was ill and planned to leave Yokohama for Germany. Julius sold the Kobe business back to Yong and bought Helm Brothers from Paul. This time he planned to remain in Yokohama for good.

The port of Yokohama, which had few facilities when Julius first arrived in 1869, now had a large harbor and two long piers built to accommodate the big passenger liners of the seven steamship companies that now made scheduled calls to Yokohama. Julius expanded Helm Brothers' business to represent many of the major European shipping companies. He also added stevedoring, landing and forwarding services to his dray business. Hiro was now recognized in the community as Julius's wife and business partner. "Helm and his wife [Hiro] rolled barrels and pushed their shoulders to the wheel unloading ships," wrote the daughter of Robert Meikeljohn, who owned the *Japan Daily Advertiser*, in her unpublished autobiography.

But nationalist sentiment was rising in Japan. Newspapers warned that foreign employees of the Japanese government were leaking Japanese national secrets and demanded they be replaced by Japanese. In 1899, the Japanese government terminated the widespread use of foreigners in its modernization.

Foreign businesses also faced tougher times. Japanese trading companies, which handled a growing share of Japanese trade, used Japanese shipping companies with which they were affiliated to transport their cargo and Japanese stevedoring firms to unload it. Consequently, many foreign stevedoring firms went out of business, and Julius saw an opportunity to consolidate the industry. On March 8, 1899, Julius took Helm Brothers public, registering the company in Hong Kong and valuing it at 250,000 yen. According to the public offering docu-

No. 12 Bluff our home in 1904, later Carl's family lived in there till 1923 big earthquake, when it burned.

ment, the money would be used to acquire all of Julius's assets, including "launches, boats, drays, carts, horses, plants, live and dead stock." The new company would also acquire land, wharves, warehouses and carriages as well as "horses, mules and other draught animals" needed to carry out its business. Julius had to guarantee a ten percent dividend in the first year to attract shareholders.

Now, at the age of sixty, for the first time in his life, Julius had both time and money in abundance. He purchased a large piece of land on The Bluff overlooking Yokohama Harbor and built a Victorian-style mansion. It was not as imposing as Lansdowne but was far more elegant: It had five bedrooms, a library, a parlor, a living room and a dining room. Each room had a fireplace. The new dining room table, when extended to its full length, could seat twenty people. The kitchen and pantry were in a separate building that was connected to the house by a covered walkway. There were four maids' rooms above the kitchen for the cook, the upstairs maid, the downstairs maid and the chauf-

81

feur. Julius's gardener landscaped the large garden, planting a hillside of azaleas that bloomed white and blazing red in the spring. There was a circular driveway so that horse carriages could bring their passengers right up to the front door.

Then Julius did something which, as a parent, I find it hard to understand. Perhaps he was determined to give his children the solid education they could not get in Japan. Or perhaps he worried Hiro was spoiling the children. Whatever the reason, in 1900, Julius put another executive in charge of Helm Brothers and took his eldest daughter, Marie, and the four youngest children on the long journey to San Francisco. Hiro and their two oldest sons remained in Yokohama. In San Francisco, Julius rented a house where Marie, then twenty-three, would take care of three of the children—Elsie, eleven; Willie, nine; and Louisa, six—while simultaneously attending St. Mary's School of Nursing. Then Julius took thirteen-year-old Julie, my grandfather, across the country by train to Virginia and left him at Lansdowne to help his Uncle Gustav with his accounts. Finally, Julius sailed to Germany to visit his mother for the first time in thirty years. "I was proud of my great success in business and enjoyed the well-earned rest long denied the ever advancing American farmer and forwarding and shipping man in Japan," Julius wrote.

Julius spent several weeks in a sanatorium in Germany for relaxation. He attended the 1900 Paris International Exposition, looking with pride on exhibits displaying Germany's advances in electrical, chemical and optical industries. He later took a separate trip to Berlin to inspect the elaborate new irrigation systems put in place to expand the range of arable land.

On his return to Yokohama in 1901, Julius took back the reins at Helm Brothers and proceeded to boost its performance. He liked to pick up the *Japan Chronicle* each day to find Helm Brothers listed on the front page with its stock price alongside the twenty or so other publicly listed Yokohama companies. Now, with money to spare, he began investing his personal fortune in mines. Perhaps it was in connection with these investments that Tanaka Shozo, the renowned Japanese environmentalist, visited Julius on July 1, 1903, as Tanaka recorded in his diary. Tanaka had been spearheading efforts to help villagers whose paddy fields and forests were being poisoned by sulfuric acid from a nearby copper mine. The Japanese military, in dire need of copper, was pressuring the government to allow the mines to continue operat-

Helm Hill (Hachioji-yama) in Honmoku.

ing. There is no record of whether Julius was sympathetic to Tanaka's concerns.

About the same time, Julius bought a hill in Honmoku, just outside of Yokohama, that locals would later come to call Herumu Yama (Helm Hill). There he built a large summer villa overlooking the ocean. Only when it was completed did he finally call his children home. Hiro must have been happy to have her children back. The family gathered at the new villa on holidays and spent most of their summers there.

The following year, Julius's youngest sister asked for money to start a school in Germany. Julius sent her a generous sum as well as new students—his four youngest children now ranging in age from ten to seventeen. This time, the two older boys, Karl, twenty-five, and Jim, twenty-one, accompanied their younger siblings on the trip. Jim would fulfill his military service requirement in Germany, while Karl would stay at a sanatorium in Switzerland to attend to his poor health.

When Karl completed his respite in Switzerland, he traveled across the Atlantic to visit Uncle Gustav and his family at Lansdowne. When Karl returned to Yokohama, he told his father he was in a fix. He had fallen in love with Gustav's daughter, his first cousin Louise.

Hiro (Komiya) Helm, ca. 1898.

"Don't let that bother you," Julius told his son. "Kings and queens marry their cousins. If it is good enough for royalty, it is good enough for you." On January 6, 1904, Karl married his cousin in a lavish wedding in Yokohama. Not long after Hiro's fiftieth birthday, Karl and his new bride left for Lansdowne to visit his new in-laws.

Soon after Karl left, Hiro began to lose weight. She had cancer, but I wonder if perhaps her spirits weren't sapped by being cut off from her children for so long. Julius sent telegrams calling the children home, but the trip from Germany took eight weeks. Hiro died on July 18, 1904, at age fifty. By the time the children returned, their mother had been dead for two weeks.

Julius buried Hiro in a plot in the foreign cemetery overlooking the harbor marked by a white marble gravestone. He had a portion of Psalm 90:10 inscribed in copper letters and nailed to her gravestone. It reads: "We have seventy years to live, or if blessed, as many as eighty, but it is all but toil and sorrow."

Hiro's courage and pluck, her "toil and sorrow," drew me closer to her, and I began stopping by her grave site on every subsequent trip to Yokohama. I would weed the area around her grave and prune back the bushes, often wondering what her family was like and if I might ever meet some of their descendants.

Hiro had served Julius faithfully, but Julius wanted to give his children a future as Europeans. That meant separating them from Hiro and from Japan. I wondered, *Was the family crest on Hiro's kimono showing two crossed eagle feathers her effort to reconnect with her Japanese family?* This strong woman had never demanded anything for herself, and in the end she had nothing left to give.

Hommoku, Yokohama

横濱本牧十二天

Yokohama Pier.

橫濱棧橋

Bund of Yokohama.

横濱海岸通り

(Y411) *View of Fuji Mt. from Ishikawa, Yokoh-*

横浜石川玉泉寺前ヨリ富士ヲ望山

Mayeta Bridg, Yokohama

横濱前田橋

Motomachi dori, Yokohama.

横濱元町通り

Canal near Yokohama Station

横濱柳橋川岸

R. YAMA[...]-YA.
WINE SPIRIT & PRO[...] IMPORTER
No. 131 MOTOMACHI SAN[...] YOKOH[...]

Sengenyama, Yokohama.　　　　　山間淺町元（所名名濱横）

IN THE SUMMER OF 1910, Julius celebrated his seventieth birthday with a grand party at his summer villa. Paper lanterns hung across the large garden and down at the beach below. The servants had spent days preparing the feast that included roast beef, several large hams and lots of potatoes. Julius's brother Paul was there with his wife. His sister Anna was there with her husband, two children and a grandchild. His three daughters—Marie, Elsie and Louise—were there, although Julius was disappointed that none had married. His two eldest sons Karl and Jim were there with their German-American wives. Karl and his wife had already given Julius two grandchildren. Julius's youngest son, Willie, now eighteen, was also there. He was popular among the women with his charming smile. The only child missing was Julie, my grandfather, who was in New York studying accounting.

Julius sat on a chair in his garden surveying the scene. Periodically, a Helm Brothers employee would come by to pay his respects. Julius now employed hundreds of Japanese, and he had invited all of the managers to the party. He was immensely proud of his success.

Standing at the edge of the garden clutching something in her hand was his granddaughter Margaret, Karl's dark-haired six-year-old. Eighty-five years later, the moment was still vivid in Margaret's memory as she described her conversation with Julius: "Grandpa picked me up and put me on his lap. He asked me what I had in my hand. When I opened my hand to show him my coins, he asked me if I had saved that money. When I said, 'Yes,' he took another coin from his pocket and put it in my hand. Then he asked me, 'So what is it you want more than anything else in the world?' I told him: 'I want a cousin with golden hair like Goldilocks.'"

I wonder if Julius didn't then reflect again on the challenges his half-Japanese descendants faced. He had tried his best to help them overcome the stigma of their mixed-race heritage. He had sent his children overseas to be educated. When Hiro died, Julius married Alma, a distant cousin from Germany, so that his youngest children would have the benefit of being raised by a German mother.

He was proud of his children, and he had provided well for them. If the foreign community sometimes looked down on them as half-caste, his family was large enough and wealthy enough to have created a community of its own with large family dinners on Sundays and lavish costume parties. What Julius hadn't foreseen were the two forces that would pull the family apart: One force, as old as history, was Alma, the new stepmother. The other was something completely new to mankind: a world war.

Julius thought he was doing his children a favor when he brought Alma to Yokohama from Germany to manage the household as his new wife. Alma, who had been active promoting voting rights for women in Germany, brought her girlfriend with her to keep her company. She was everything Hiro was not. She was tall, heavy and wore round, steel-rimmed spectacles over her icy blue eyes. She was a stern disciplinarian who held the Japanese in contempt and made her stepchildren ashamed of their Japanese heritage.

Julius's eldest daughter, Marie, showed her loyalty to her dead mother Hiro by moving out. Later, Marie would abandon her Christian Science faith in favor of Buddhism and purchase a large piece of property by the sea in Zushi, not far from Yokohama, with plans to open a sanatorium for victims of tuberculosis.

Marie's two younger sisters, Elsie and Louisa, had no such escape. Alma was intent on training them to be upper-class Germans, so she pressured them to study piano and art. When other mixed-race suitors came to call, Alma would turn them away, insisting the girls deserved better. My Aunt Louisa once warned me seventy years later never to go out with a Japanese girl because she would "only be after your money."

Julius at 70th birthday party with son Karl and granddaughter.

None of Julius's three daughters would ever marry. Louisa would be the only one of her generation I would come to know, and what I remember best about her was the extremes to which she took thrift. Although Louisa was wealthy in her later years, she would hand the bus driver a ten-thousand-yen note, knowing he had no change and would have to let the old woman on for free. She once took my mother out to lunch for her birthday at the German Bakery in Motomachi. When it came time for Louisa to order, she pulled a slice of bread from her purse and asked the waitress to toast it. "My stomach is not feeling well," she explained.

Alma's greatest impact would be on Willie, Julius's youngest son, with tragic consequences. Willie was a handsome boy with the same intense eyes and restless soul as his father, but with the delicate mouth and rounded chin of his mother, Hiro. At age seven, he had been sent to L'Ecole de L'Etoile du Matin, a French Catholic boarding school in Tokyo. At nine, he lived in San Francisco with his three sisters while attending the Moulder School for Boys. At eleven, Willie returned to Yokohama to attend a boys' Catholic school. Then Alma insisted Willie travel to Germany to attend prep school, business school and to do his military service.

When Willie returned to Japan from Germany, he hopped from job to job, never quite satisfied with his work. In 1914, when Willie was twenty-two, he worked for a British trading company. Perhaps because of his good looks, his money and his cosmopolitan ways, Willie developed a reputation as a playboy. It was bad luck that he came of age when, for the only time in its history, Germany would become Japan's enemy.

At the beginning of the twentieth century, Japan was intent on reversing the injustices it suffered following its victory over China. It created an alliance in 1902 with Britain, the world's greatest naval power, and quadrupled the size of its standing army. In the summer of 1904, when Russia tried to expand its presence in Korea, Japan attacked. In a series of bloody battles that cost it more than eighty thousand lives, Japan defeated Russia and retook Port Arthur, becoming the first Asian country to defeat a modern European power. Japan now controlled Korea and had established its long-desired presence in Manchuria, a new frontier rich in all the raw materials Japan lacked. When World War I broke out in Europe in the summer of 1914, Japan invaded Tsingtao, China, considered Germany's "Pearl of the East."

Willie Helm is the center of the party, ca. 1928.

Germany called on all its citizens in Asia to come to the defense of Tsingtao. Most Germans in Japan at the time did not respond to what seemed to them a hopeless cause. Willie, whose mother had been Japanese, seemed compelled to prove he was a German patriot, and volunteered.

Willie was assigned as sergeant in the artillery division and sent to Tsingtao, but the small German force defending the German colony never had a chance. By November 1914, a few months after Willie reached Tsingtao, German forces surrendered, and the captured soldiers were sent to Japan as prisoners of war.

I wanted to learn more about Willie's experiences as a prisoner of war, so in 2003 I traveled to the home of one of Japan's largest prison camps. It was pouring rain when I got off the train at Kurume, a sleepy town of 300,000 on the southwestern island of Kyushu. Tsutsumi

Yukichi, an official from the town's cultural affairs department, was waiting at the platform with an umbrella to usher me to his car. Tsutsumi wore the dark suit and tie of a bureaucrat, but he had the relaxed mannerisms of a college professor.

Over lunch, Tsutsumi told me that he first learned about the POW camp when the curator of a German museum called Kurume City Hall to say they were holding an exhibit of memorabilia from the Kurume prison camp and wanted the city's cooperation.

"'What prison camp?' we said. We didn't know what he was talking about." Tsutsumi began asking elderly residents if they knew anything about the camp. One old man remembered a German prisoner who paid him five sen (about a penny) for each frog he collected. The man fed the frogs to his pet snake. Another man had earned money chasing after tennis balls that had gone over the prison camp fence.

Tennis? Pet snakes? It was hard to believe.

"At first the mayor was reluctant to let us dredge up old stories about the war," said Tsutsumi. But Tsutsumi soon learned that Bridgestone Tire, the town's largest employer and one of the world's largest tire manufacturers, had once been a maker of footwear and had acquired technology for building tires from a German prisoner at the camp. The town decided the camp was an important piece of the town's history.

After lunch, Tsutsumi showed me the collection of camp documents and memorabilia he had gathered for an exhibit. There was a model sailing ship in a bottle, a table of inlaid wood and other items that prisoners had built while at Kurume. There were calendars with drawings of the camp. There were printed concert programs that listed pieces by Beethoven and Wagner performed by the prison orchestra. There were photos of a dozen musicians practicing, of men drinking beer and of a man dressed as a woman walking a tightrope. *What kind of prison camp was this?* I wondered. I was impressed by the enterprise of the prisoners but also by the freedom the Japanese had given them.

"Willie was quite popular among the reporters," said Tsutsumi, handing me a folder filled with newspaper clips. "Girlfriend of the Mixed-blood Helm Causes Problems" declared one headline. "Prison authorities complained that they were staying up until late at night translating and censoring letters from Willie's Japanese girlfriend who wrote in English." Tsutsumi laughed.

It was a funny story, but what struck me were the headlines that identified Willie as "mixed-blood Helm" as if "mixed blood" were his occupation. Worse, the tiny letters placed about the kanji characters to signify how they should be pronounced read *ainoko*," which means mixed-race child, but is also a word used to describe mongrel dogs.

What was it like, I wondered, *to be compared to a mongrel dog?* Was I also an *ainoko?* Since I could pass as white, I had never thought of myself as mixed blood. I wondered if this explained the strange attitude of Japanese to whom I revealed my Japanese heritage.

According to the news accounts, Willie had initially been housed in a large temple in Kumamoto. Willie contacted a representative of Helm Brothers in the nearby town of Moji and arranged to have a telegram sent to his father. When Julius received the telegram, he made the two-day journey from Yokohama to visit Willie. Satisfied that his son was being treated well, he donated money to the temple to help provide for the prisoners. According to prison camp records, the money was used to purchase five butcher's knives, three vegetable knives, three whisks, five roast pans, one square wooden bucket, three forks, eight pots, three steak forks, ten cooking spoons, three scales, eight meat hangers and one rice cooker.

When reporters asked Willie about his living conditions, he told them, in a statement that was splashed across the top of the local newspaper, that the temple would be "a great place to have a geisha party." Six months later, Willie was moved to Kurume, which, with 1,370 prisoners, was Japan's largest prison camp: seven rows of barracks surrounded by a tall wood fence.

Although Kurume had a reputation as Japan's strictest prison camp, Japan was eager to show it was civilized so prisoners were treated according to the strictest interpretation of the Geneva Convention. For example, the prisoners received the same wages they had received as part of the German military, even though the average salary was about six times that of a Japanese policeman. The prisoners used their salaries to buy beer, hire cooks and purchase a printing press they used to publish a weekly prison newspaper in German called *The Barracks.*

Willie was more comfortable than most of the other prisoners. His family sent care packages of canned milk, coffee and sausages, but after nearly two years, he was desperate to leave. So when the camp's barber offered to help him escape, Willie could not resist.

According to a newspaper account, on the night of July 19, 1916, the barber distracted the sentries while Willie and a friend, wearing *yukata*, a light cotton kimono, sneaked out the gate and made their way toward the train station. Before they had gone very far, however, they were surrounded by guards.

Willie and his friend were put in solitary confinement where they received half a bowl of rice and some weak miso soup three times a day. Willie later told his children how he saved his rice from breakfast and lunch and pressed it into a ball to eat with dinner so he could feel full at least once a day. He berated himself for being so stupid as to wear his army boots under his cotton *yukata*. He would later tell his children that was the reason the soldiers had caught him.

The truth, I discovered, was far more interesting. One day, Jan Baerwald, a friend whose family had lived for several generations in Japan, was showing me an old family guestbook that contained the signatures of prominent visitors to Japan like Albert Einstein. We were turning the pages when a yellowed newspaper clipping fluttered to the floor. Jan's grandparents had not known the Helms, so I was surprised when I picked up the clipping and discovered it was about Willie.

"Curious End to a Strange Adventure," read the headline on the article dated August 31, 1916. "It will be remembered that on July 19 two German prisoners—W. Helm (well known in Kobe and Yokohama) and Hugo Tandain—escaped from the camp at Kurume but were arrested before they had proceeded far." Evidently the article had been clipped from an English-language newspaper in Japan.

Willie and his friend were brought before a Japanese court and charged with attempted escape, the article reported. If convicted, they could have lost their privileges as prisoners of war and been placed in a regular prison as common criminals. However, in the course of the proceedings, the Japanese judge discovered that camp commander Mazaki Jinzaburo—who would later play an important role in the rise of militarism in Japan—had ordered the barber to help Willie escape, according to the newspaper account, "for the mere pleasure of having them arrested." I wondered then if Mazaki had chosen Willie for the scheme because he was of mixed blood and had a reputation for being a playboy, something he might have associated with the decadence of the West. Willie was released from solitary confinement and moved to another prison camp.

Tsutsumi introduced me to the mayor before taking me to a nearby cemetery to visit a stone memorial for the half-dozen German prisoners who died, mostly of disease, while living in the camp. Tsutsumi handed me a bouquet of flowers to place on the grave while members of the press photographed the occasion.

"How do you feel about this?" one of several reporters called out to me. "Willie must have felt a little confused fighting for Germany knowing that his own mother was Japanese," I said, feeling at a loss for words.

It didn't seem appropriate to mention that having grown up reading comic books and watching movies in which the enemy was always German, I felt odd putting flowers on a memorial to German soldiers. I remembered how some of my American relatives would disdainfully refer to "the German Helms." World War I, I realized, had driven in the first wedge dividing the Helm family.

At the beginning of the war, Japanese authorities took no action against German residents living in Japan who had not chosen, like Willie, to fight against Japan. But as the war dragged on, Britain pressured its ally Japan, to crack down on its enemy. Julius and his second son, Jim, also a German national, were forced to resign from Helm Brothers. Julius left Yokohama on April 26, 1915 for San Francisco where he boarded the Danish steamer, *The United States,* to Copenhagen because it flew a neutral flag. Then he sailed to Germany where he met up with his wife, Alma, and his two daughters.

Back in Yokohama, Helm Brothers was able to continue to operate because it was registered in Hong Kong and was managed by Julie, who was American because he happened to be born in New York, and Karl, who had taken Japanese citizenship so he could register Helm Brothers' ships in his name, bypassing Japanese laws that prohibited foreign-owned boats from plying internal waterways. Taking Japanese citizenship was not easy, even then. To become a Japanese citizen, Japanese law required you to be included in the birth registry of a Japanese family. I wondered how Karl had managed to pull this off. But Karl, his children said, had always considered himself Japanese by passport only, sending his children to the German school.

Now that Germany was an enemy to Japan, Karl began to distance himself from his German heritage as well. He began to use the name Charles instead of Karl, and moved his children from the German school in Yokohama to Sacred Heart, a French convent school in Tokyo, seventeen miles away.

The Charles Helm family now lived in the large house Julius had built for himself on The Bluff. They had a cook, a downstairs maid to clean and serve the table, an upstairs maid to clean the bedrooms and bathrooms and to build fires in the fireplaces in each room. There was also a governess to take care of the children, and a seamstress for the family.

On Sunday afternoons, the girls would look at magazines to select their favorite fashions. When the seamstress could not handle something, a tailor was brought in. The shoemaker came to the house to measure the children's feet for shoes. On Mondays, the kids would be bundled into a buggy that would take them to Sakuragicho Station. From there, they took the train to Tokyo. When the girls reached Tokyo, there would be a dozen rickshaws lined up and men wearing large straw hats waiting to take them, each on a separate rickshaw, on the forty-five-minute ride to the convent school. In 1913, their father Charles was among the first in Japan to purchase a Model T Ford, but he was so uncomfortable riding in the contraption that he often walked to work, having his driver meet him with the car at the office.

When Armistice Day was announced in November 1918, marking the end of World War I, there was a big parade in downtown Yokohama. Fifteen months later, on a cold January night, a thin, sickly looking man with a bad cough showed up at the Helm house. Charles looked at him quizzically and then gave him a hearty handshake.

"Willie! By Jove, it really is you," he cried, Charles's daughter Trudy would later recall. Willie had been imprisoned for more than five years.

Not long after Willie's return, Julius, now eighty, came home to Yokohama with Alma and his daughters, Louisa and Elsie. They settled into Julius's large summer home in Honmoku. Julius was not the same man. His exile in Germany during the war had taken a toll on his health and crushed his spirit. He spent his days sitting in the garden of his villa on Helm Hill from where he could see the sun play across the sparkling sea.

When Willie asked his father for an advance on his inheritance to start a business in Manchuria, the next frontier, Julius thought of his own pioneering days and readily agreed. Soon after Willie's departure, Julius died in his sleep on May 16, 1922. Willie, struggling to make his way in Manchuria, never made it back for his father's funeral, which took place at the Foreigners' Cemetery where Hiro had been buried. Perhaps because Julius's second wife, Alma, could not stand to see Julius buried beside his Japanese wife, she took his ashes back to Germany where they were buried next to his mother. Ironically, Alma, who hated Japan, was buried in Kobe, while Julius, who loved Yokohama, was buried in distant Germany. Hiro, who had left her community to marry Julius, was left all alone in the Foreigners' Cemetery far from her kin.

Before dying, Julius put his estate into a partnership that was equally owned by each of his children and which was virtually impossible to dissolve. He hoped to preserve his legacy by keeping his family united and in control of Helm Brothers. As it turned out, that was too much to ask of a family whose members were citizens of three powerful countries, each increasingly at odds with the other two.

Passport 1

旅券
PASSPORT

🌸 日 本 国 🌸 JAPAN

型/Type　発行国/Issuing country　旅券番号/Passport No.

P　　JPN　　MN0941311

姓/Surname
KUROKAWA

名/Given name
MARI

国 籍/Nationality　　　　　生年月日/Date of birth
JAPAN　　　　　　　　　　　19 JUN 1989

性別/Sex　本 籍/Registered Domicile
F　　TOKYO

発行年月日/Date of issue
20 JAN 1993

有効期間満了日/Date of expiry
20 JAN 1998

発行官庁/Authority
MINISTRY OF
FOREIGN AFFAIRS

所持人自署/Signature of bearer
Mari Kurokawa by mother

P<JPNKUROKAWA<<MARI<<<<<<<<<<<<<<<<<<<<<<<<
MN0941311 4JPN8906197F9801200<<<<<<<<<<<<<<<8

Passport 2

旅券
PASSPORT

🌸 日 本 国 🌸 JAPAN

型/Type　発行国/Issuing country　旅券番号/Passport No.

P　　JPN　　MN0941312

姓/Surname
KASHIWABARA

名/Given name
YUKI

国 籍/Nationality　　　　　生年月日/Date of birth
JAPAN　　　　　　　　　　　26 JUL 1992

性別/Sex　本 籍/Registered Domicile
M　　FUKUSHIMA

発行年月日/Date of issue
20 JAN 1993

有効期間満了日/Date of expiry
20 JAN 1998

発行官庁/Authority
MINISTRY OF
FOREIGN AFFAIRS

所持人自署/Signature of bearer
Yuki Kashiwabara by mother

P<JPNKASHIWABARA<<YUKI<<<<<<<<<<<<<<<<<<<<<
MN0941312 5JPN9207260M9801200<<<<<<<<<<<<<<<4

TWO MONTHS,
TWO CHILDREN,
ONE FAMILY

ABOUT FIVE MONTHS AFTER OUR adoption orientation at Tokyo City Hall, I flew to Seattle to spend a month with Marie, who was teaching at the University of Washington. The *Los Angeles Times* had agreed to let me work in Seattle during Marie's three-month teaching stint. One evening near the end of my stay, we received a telephone call from Maruoka-*san*, our social worker in Tokyo. A girl almost three was available for adoption. Were we interested?

Three? The child was far older than we had hoped, but we knew we might never get another chance, and so we quickly said yes. Maruoka-*san* mailed a photo not much larger than a postage stamp. The girl looked like a Japanese doll with big rosy cheeks and short black hair. Marie was thrilled; I was uneasy. Since Marie wouldn't be able to return to Tokyo for a few weeks, we agreed I would go to the orphanage alone to meet the child.

On the flight back to Tokyo, I read a small paperback book called *Your Three-Year Old* that Marie had bought. A child's character is fully developed by the age of three, the book explained. This was unsettling. *What was the joy of parenting a child whose character was fully formed?* I thought. Besides she looked nothing like me. Adoption books were filled with nightmarish stories of adopted children who never bonded to their parents.

Yet, multiracial adoptions had become relatively common in the

United States by 1992. So why the anxiety? As a child, my mother took me on her annual trip to the orphanage a few minutes from our home to drop off old clothes. I didn't like to visit that place, which always seemed to me filled with sad-eyed, sickly looking children, often the offspring of American soldiers and Japanese prostitutes. My mother and great-aunt did various "good works" for the orphanage, but I had never heard of anyone actually adopting a child. Adoption was part of a shadowy realm that I could not easily equate with my idealized notion of what a family should be.

Was it this dark view of adoption that troubled me or was it really about race? I couldn't sort it out. I thought of the deep insecurities my father and his Uncle Willie seemed to feel, in part, from being half Japanese. Didn't a mixed-race family present many of the same challenges? Nobody would ever mistake this girl for my biological child. The issue hadn't come up when Marie and I had visited the orphanage in Tokyo and I had held the young boy. Yet now that a child was available, I couldn't help but feel a strange foreboding.

A few days later, I was sitting on a couch covered with doilies in the waiting room of an orphanage on the outskirts of Tokyo. It was not just jet lag that made my mind fuzzy as the director of the orphanage, a small, elderly woman, walked into the room and introduced herself. I felt something cold and hard at the pit of my stomach.

As she led me down the dark hallway, I trembled. A door opened at the end of the hallway. At about knee height, a little round face peered through the crack. My heart lurched.

Mariko's black bangs were cut short across her forehead. She had big, dark eyes that seemed filled with life, yet were also a little sad. She was beautiful. And yet, I felt myself hesitate. Could I learn to love this child who looked so different from me?

Mariko stretched out her arms asking to be picked up. She guided me to a basket of toys and picked out her favorite doll. Then she told me to walk to the window.

I looked out the window at the small dirt playground with a jungle gym. Mariko nudged me and pointed to a colony of ants milling about on the window sill. I knelt down so we could both get a better look. Our heads touched as we watched the ants going about their busy lives. I was totally unprepared for it when Mariko looked up and suddenly burst into song in Japanese: *Mr. Ant meets Mr. Ant walking down the way. They face THIS way and nod. They face THAT way and nod.* Mariko's voice, so filled

Mariko, two, celebrates children's day at orphanage.

with intensity and the sheer joy of being, seized my heart and tugged at it until I thought it was going to tear.

When she had finished singing, I gave Mariko a hug, and she looked at me and smiled. I felt lightheaded. Then a surge of warmth spread through my chest. It was as if something was beginning to heal. Looking back now to that summer day in 1992, I wonder if I wasn't choosing, at that moment, to affirm life and embrace Japan in a way that my father never would.

Mariko now pointed to the railing that separated the toddlers from the older kids. "Be careful," I said as I lifted her onto the railing. I held her left hand in my right hand as she walked slowly, perfectly balanced, along the narrow wood rail.

From where she stood, balanced on that railing, she was not much shorter than me. And as we walked side by side, our arms outstretched, we might have been dancing.

WHEN MARIE RETURNED TO TOKYO from Seattle a couple of weeks

later, we visited Mariko together. The orphanage director showed us Mariko's photo album. It contained a dozen or so pictures that recorded Mariko's two years at the orphanage: blowing out the candles of a birthday cake; hanging upside down on the jungle gym. One picture showed Mariko at two, wading in the water on her first visit to the seashore. "She ran fearlessly into the water and began to sing a song about the sea," read the caption underneath.

Then we were taken to the nursery where we got a chance to watch as the children played, ate and then all took their turns on the little potties. When it was playtime, the director encouraged us to take Mariko on a walk, which we did on our daily visits. Each time, we learned something new and wonderful about Mariko. Once she stopped to stare intently at a spider spinning its web. Without hesitation, she reached out and picked the hairy spider off its web with her bare hands so she could look at it more closely. Marie had taken to Mariko immediately and wanted to bring her home as soon as possible, but we sensed reluctance on Mariko's part. Usually, after twenty or thirty minutes, Mariko would want to return to the orphanage. We were told we had six months to let Mariko get accustomed to us, but we couldn't imagine waiting that long. Every day apart seemed to us another precious day lost.

We soon learned that Maruoka-*san* had persuaded the authorities that Mariko should be placed with us rather than a Japanese family. Mariko craved physical affection like a morning glory craves the sun. Yet most Japanese mothers avoid hugging their children once they pass their toddler years. Mariko was stubborn and independent, traits many Japanese parents considered to be tragic flaws in a girl. Maruoka-*san* told us she thought Mariko's strong spirit would have a better chance of surviving with a foreign family.

June 18, 1992. I do not remember how that fateful day began, but I will never forget how it ended. I do recall that we believed we were fully prepared. The spare bedroom in our Tokyo apartment was furnished with the large white baby crib we had purchased when we had expected an infant, its mattress encased in pink-flowered sheets. A mobile of tropical fish hung over it, pinned to the ceiling. The closet was filled with dresses of every color and pattern: orange polka dots, blue stripes and red roses. All were for size one hundred centimeters. Mariko was three foot three.

The living room was scattered with stuffed animals, the most prominent of which was a shaggy brown teddy bear, about Mariko's height, with shiny black eyes and a black felt nose that a Japanese friend had sent us. A rubber ball the color of the ocean sat on our cream-colored couch. On the far side of the living room was a shiny new red plastic desk so low we had to be careful not to trip on it. There was a high chair in the dining room and a birthday cake in the fridge. It was the day before Mariko's third birthday.

Only a few weeks had passed since we had first met Mariko, and she still seemed hesitant about coming home with us. Although the adoption process was supposed to take as long as a year, since Mariko was already turning three, the orphanage director decided it was time for Mariko to leave. It was a cool, overcast day when we arrived at the orphanage to pick up Mariko. The glass door rattled loudly as we slid it open. We entered and announced ourselves. *"Gomenkudasai!"*

Inside, the wooden floors seemed cold and the hallways dark. I shivered. There were whispers and the sounds of shuffling slippers. The orphanage director invited us into her waiting room. She was polite but all business.

"Tell Okuyama-*san* to bring Mariko," the director told the lady who was serving us green tea. Okuyama-*san*, an attractive young woman with a warm smile, came into the room. She had always been Mariko's favorite nanny at the orphanage. Mariko, wearing a straw hat with an aqua blue band around it, was hiding behind Okuyama-*san*'s skirt.

"Why don't you take Mariko on a short walk and talk to her," the director said to us. We crossed the small street to the park. Mariko squatted beside a drain in the gravel path. She picked up little pieces of gravel and dropped them through the slots of the wrought iron grate, one by one. *Plop. Plop. Plop.*

"You are going to leave the orphanage today. You are coming home with us," I explained to her.

Plop. Plop.

"We will be your mother and father. Would you like that?"

Plop. Plop.

"We have a special room for you with lots of toys."

Plop. Plop.

She would not look at us. "You shouldn't throw stones down the drain," I finally told Mariko.

I had grown impatient. I didn't understand why she had been so warm a week ago and now was so cool. I wondered if the orphanage had already told her we would be bringing her home and she had been unhappy about the news.

Mariko stopped dropping stones for a second and looked at me briefly. Her eyes darkened. Then she ran into the nearby cemetery, her tiny body immediately hidden by the black gravestones. Marie and I separated and went after her. We ran all around the cemetery but couldn't find her. We were in a panic. Should we go to the orphanage and tell the director we had already lost her? What would they think? What kind of incompetent parents were we? We decided to look a little more. Finally, we spotted her next to a huge urn filled with ash just outside a temple. Mariko was squatting, scraping the packed dirt on the ground with a little stick.

"Let's go back," I said softly. She shook her head. I squatted down beside her. Marie stood patiently by. After a while, Mariko stood and headed back to the orphanage. We followed. She would not hold our hands.

Mariko slipped off her shoes in the *genkan* and ran down the hallway. She had spotted Okuyama-san and hid behind her skirt. The orphanage director came out of her office. "You must pick her up and take her. Delay will do no good," she said firmly.

I hesitated, confused. I felt like a child ordered to do something he knew was wrong. I knew the delay would make it more difficult for Mariko to bond with us. She was about to turn three. Every day she remained at the orphanage was a precious day of her childhood lost to us. Also I knew that Mariko would soon have to leave the orphanage in any case. The orphanage only kept children up to the age of three. But in my gut I also knew that it was not right to force Mariko to leave the orphanage against her will. That was no way to start a relationship with a child.

"Do it *now!*" said the orphanage director, a little louder.

Was it because I had been the first one to meet Mariko and spoke better Japanese, or was it simply a question of physical strength? I don't know, but Marie and I instantly agreed that Marie would get the car, while I carried Mariko out of the orphanage. I walked down the hallway toward Okuyama-san. There was fear in Mariko's eyes.

"You must go with them," Okuyama-san said to Mariko. "Everything will be okay."

"No. No! I don't want to go!" Mariko said. There was steel in her voice.

Okuyama-*san* looked pained. She knelt down and, holding Mariko's shoulders, firmly pushed her out from behind her skirt. Mariko's body was stiff.

"Quickly!" commanded the director.

I scooped up Mariko and held her in my arms as I did that first day when we saw the ants, but this time her body was unyielding. She turned her head and called out in a plaintive voice, "Okuyama-*san!* Okuyama-*san!*"

Okuyama-*san* handed Mariko a little doll with a straw hat identical to Mariko's. Mariko took the doll and pressed it to her breast. It was the only toy she had ever owned. Okuyama-*san* turned and left. Tears welled in Mariko's eyes as her nanny disappeared down the dark hallway. I headed for the front door. As I walked out the open door, Mariko cried out, "I don't want to go! I don't want to go!"

I felt like a kidnapper as I slid into the back seat of the car trying to ignore her screams. I took off her straw hat and put it on the seat beside me. Marie drove us through Tokyo traffic while I held Mariko against my chest. I could feel her heart beat fast like a bird's, tapping out a Morse code of fear.

"Okuyama-*san!* Okuyama-*san!* Okuyama-*san!*" Mariko started to cry again. Her small body was wracked with sobs, and soon, I was crying too. I gave Mariko a hug, but even though my tears fell on her shoulders and her tears wet my shirt, we might as well have been on opposite shores of a great ocean. There was nothing I could do or say to console her on that first ride home.

When we finally reached our apartment complex, Marie parked the car and walked ahead of me to open the door. I carried Mariko into the apartment and put her down.

"This is your new home," Marie said, kneeling down next to her. Mariko was quiet for a moment. Her eyes were still glistening with tears, but she was curious. Her eyes widened as she walked farther into the living room and saw all the toys.

"What is this?" she said, pointing to the large teddy bear.

"It's a present for you." She grabbed Teddy's arm and dragged it behind her.

"How about this?" she asked, pointing at a blue ball.

"Yours," I said. She picked it up and clumsily cradled it in her left arm.

She nodded to the red desk. "What about that?"

"It's Mariko's."

Mariko leaned the teddy bear carefully against the desk and placed her doll from the orphanage and the rubber ball next to the teddy. Then she went about the room pointing at other toys. "And this. Is this mine too? And that?"

Each time, Marie and I nodded, then Mariko picked up the toy and took it to her desk. Soon all the toys were in small piles next to her desk.

"Are these all mine?" she asked.

We nodded.

Mariko pulled out the little red seat tucked under the desk and sat down. She leaned over, put her arm on the table and rested her cheek on it. Soon her body was trembling. At the orphanage, all toys were communal. I wondered if it suddenly struck her as terribly lonely to have so many toys and no other children to share them with. But no, it was something far more disturbing, for soon she was moaning. It was a wretched, mournful sound. Tears poured from her eyes like a mountain spring, and I wondered, *How can a girl of three possibly hold within her so much pain?*

It was unbearable to watch Mariko's grief. Marie and I each started crying too. We hugged, wondering what we had done to this poor girl. Then Marie went to the kitchen. I picked up Mariko and put her in her high chair. Looking for a way to distract her, I took a silver one-hundred-yen coin and flicked it so it started spinning across the dining room table. Mariko looked up. She was enchanted by the flashing, spinning coin. Her tears stopped. Soon I had emptied my pockets of change and I was sending dozens of coins spinning across the table. I tried to show Mariko how to do it, but it was difficult with her little fingers. Soon she was crying again.

It was late, and the windows were now sheets of black obsidian. I was holding Mariko in my arms and pacing the apartment. She had finally quieted. Marie and I were exhausted. I told Marie to go to bed, and I would put Mariko to bed. As soon as I tried to put Mariko in her crib, she started to cry. If I sat on the couch, she wailed. At two o'clock in the morning, Mariko finally fell asleep, her head lying on my shoulders. I inched down slowly on the couch, but as soon as my butt touched the couch, Mariko lifted her head and started to bawl. She was fighting me with every ounce of her power. At four o'clock, I surrendered. I climbed into the crib and sat there with Mariko asleep in my arms. As the light of dawn started to filter through the windows, Mariko was finally asleep. I could feel her heartbeat slow. I could feel the hard wood slats of the crib digging into my back as I too finally drifted to sleep.

When I awoke, Mariko was in the dining room having breakfast with Marie. When I bent over to give her a kiss, she turned her head away from me. My chest tightened. My new daughter had been barely home for a day and already, like my father before me and, perhaps, like his father before him, I was proving to be a terrible father.

In those first months, I tried to woo Mariko every way I could. I reached deep into the well of my memory as a child growing up in Japan. *Clap your hands, then just close them, open them up again, and raise them high.* Mariko knew many of the same games and songs I had learned as a child; for the first time, I felt truly blessed to have been raised in Japan. Marie had taken a sabbatical from work and since she could spend the whole day with Mariko, the two were growing closer by the day. But I had something else I shared with Mariko—a childhood in Japan. At bedtime, I pulled out my guitar and a Japanese songbook and sang until my voice went hoarse. Mariko loved to hear me sing. I found myself singing haunting melodies I had loved as a child, but whose lyrics I had never completely understood.

When was it?
Picking wild mulberries in the fields
With my nanny who was sent off to be a bride at fifteen.
Her family could not support her.
We saw the red dragonfly alight on a reed,
Set afire by the setting sun.

Mariko would often join me. Her voice was bright and loud and always on key. Soon she knew all the verses of even the longest and most complex songs. At first when I sang those sad songs, I thought of the pain Mariko had suffered in the first three years of her life—then I thought of my own bittersweet childhood in Japan. I remembered dancing in my *yukata* at the festival of the spirits, feeling awkward as the only foreigner in a ring of dancers; I remembered the elaborate gardens of a famous restaurant where, after dinner, they released thousands of fireflies. I would run through the garden chasing after that cloud of stardust that always seemed just beyond my reach.

It had been nearly a month since Mariko had come home with us. I was up early, making Sunday breakfast in our tiny kitchen. The morning sun lit up the apartment and warmed the kitchen floor. I turned to find Mariko standing by the refrigerator looking at me with her dark, sleepy eyes, her hair sticking out every which way. She was in her blue pajamas—the ones with tiny rocking horses that I had picked out for her. In her left hand, she held her teddy bear. I picked up an egg and held it out to her between my thumb and forefinger.

"Do you want to help Papa crack it?"

She looked at the egg, intrigued, but eyed me suspiciously. She did not move. My left hand stayed on the stainless steel bowl where I had already measured out the flour. My extended right hand, still holding the egg, grew heavy, but I did not move. We were two gunslingers facing off at high noon. Who would blink first?

Mariko furrowed her brows. She dropped her teddy bear and walked over to me. She took the egg from my hand. I lifted her up on the kitchen counter, then I leaned over her shoulder and put my right hand over her right hand to help her crack the egg on the edge of the bowl. Then I put my left hand over her left hand and guided her tiny fingers to pull the two sides of the broken egg shell gently apart. The glistening yellow sun of the yolk slid out and came to rest in a small depression in the flour.

"Again!" Mariko demanded. I took another egg out of the carton, though the recipe didn't call for it. "I will mix," she announced grandly, after successfully cracking the second egg.

I gave her the whisk and showed her how to mix. Her warm back leaned against my chest as she began to stir the batter. I gently kissed Mariko on the cheek. She turned her head briefly, as if I were distracting her, but she was okay with it. From that day forward, we often cooked together. Even today as a young adult, she likes to show off the scar on her wrist from when I let her get a little too close to a frying pan. She shows it as if it were a badge of our shared adventures.

Most mornings Mariko awoke before us and crawled into our bed. I would pick her up and place her between Marie and me. While Mariko lay on her back, Marie would smother her with kisses from the right side. I would attack her with kisses from the left. Mariko would giggle, showing us deep dimples on her big round cheeks. She was ticklish, but she always wanted more. It was Mariko's favorite treat—the kiss sandwich.

WHEN THE HEAT AND HUMIDITY descended on Tokyo that first summer together, we rented a cabin at Lake Nojiri, a mountain retreat for Christian missionaries. The cabin was drafty and the bathroom dank and smelly from the open-pit toilet. Mariko was an early riser and, afraid to go by herself, she would shout, "toilet!" I would walk her to the bathroom and wait while she squatted over the hole and told me her plans for the day in her rapid-speak Japanese: "I'm gonna go on the swing, jump in the water from the tree, and draw a nice picture for Mama."

One evening, I parked the car behind a restaurant in the little village nearby and let Mariko down from her car seat. Suddenly she ran out into the street laughing joyously. I heard the sound of a revving engine. I raced after her and swept her up in my arms. At that instant, a dozen motorcycles roared by. Mariko looked at me wide-eyed. Motorcycle exhaust lingered in the air. My heart pounded. It had been just six weeks since Mariko had come to us, but already I could not imagine life without her.

One Sunday, Marie and I took a walk with Mariko between us. Every few steps we would go "wheeee!" and lift her up into the air. "Again," she would demand. As we were walking by the boathouse, we noticed a new sign posted. "Newborn baby looking for Christian family," it said. I wasn't religious, but it was easy to believe, here in this Christian retreat, that God had a hand in putting that sign there, as Marie and I had our hearts set on having a second child.

That afternoon Marie was on the telephone. A Japanese pastor in the northern city of Fukushima was looking for a family to adopt a boy born to a teenage girl in a local hospital two weeks before. Japanese authorities didn't like to put babies up for adoption until they were at least a year old so they could assure parents there were no birth defects. This Christian pastor thought the boy should be adopted right away and had asked a minister in Nojiri to find a family. Within a week of making the phone call, Marie, Mariko and I were on a bullet train bound for Fukushima. We borrowed a small bassinet and purchased a pack of paper diapers, a box of powdered milk and two milk bottles. The pastor met us at the station. He was surprisingly young and clearly nervous. We were also anxious. Mariko just skipped along the station platform singing her made-up songs.

Leslie Helm and wife Marie with Eric and Mariko.

"Mariko seems to be a happy child," said the pastor, as if reassuring himself that we would be good parents.

"Mariko is excited about getting a younger brother," I replied.

We had chosen a Western name, Eric, for the baby boy. His biological mother had named him Yuki, but we worried that name might subject him to teasing in America. We decided Yuki should be Eric's middle name. The pastor took us to a bland meeting room in a hotel with a large conference table. Eric's paternal grandmother and grandfather greeted us first. They were formal and polite. His maternal grandmother was warm and smiled broadly. The young mother entered the room with Eric. She was a shy, quiet girl. She gave little sign of how she felt about giving up her newborn. Perhaps on the advice of the pastor, the birth mother had not seen Eric since the day he was born. I thought I saw a tear glisten as she handed the baby to Marie. Marie took a bottle of milk she had prepared and gave it to Eric. He drank hungrily.

While Marie was with the birth mother and the two grandmothers fussing over Eric, I looked on from a distance as I tried to make small talk with the pastor and the grandfather, an elegant man in his early forties who worked for the government's forestry department. The formalities had been dispensed with quickly. The pastor had made sure all the papers were in order. Since the city of Tokyo had already approved us as adoptive parents, the authorities agreed to process Eric's adoption application together with Mariko's application.

As we visited with the birth family, we were having trouble finding something to say. The things we wanted most to know we did not feel comfortable asking. Why had the mother decided to have the child? How did she feel about giving up this baby to strangers who would very likely leave Japan? What was the birth father like? At a loss for words, we focused on Mariko, who bubbled with excitement about the baby. Then it was time to leave.

The pastor, the grandparents and the mother came to the train station to see us off. We all bowed. There was no hugging, but as we boarded the train, suddenly there were tears. We cried. They cried. How odd it was, this emotional farewell. They had been strangers a few hours before. Now they were family. Soon they would be strangers again. They waved to us as the train pulled away. We waved back. I thought about how Eric's two grandmothers, his grandfather and the pastor had come together for us and would now return to their lives without the baby. Now we were a family of four. My two children were as Japanese as Hiro; I was something in between; and Marie was Caucasian. Each of us came from a different world, yet here we were bound together, ready to create something new for ourselves and be a family. When the train pulled out of the station, Mariko looked down into the little basket. She petted Eric's downy hair. "*Nen-ne*, Erikku," she said. "Go to sleep now."

As the bullet train hurtled through the darkness, we sat in our seats peaceful and content. Little did we know of the challenges we would face as we forged a new identity for our family.

Lake Nojiri, ca. 1940.

THAT SUMMER OF 1992, MARIE and the two kids stayed at the cabin we rented at Lake Nojiri. I joined them most weekends, always looking forward to spending time with the family in the cool mountain air. During the week, when I was alone, I thought often of Charles, who took Japanese citizenship for business reasons and slipped out of his German identity, chameleon-like, when Germany became Japan's enemy. I thought of Willie, who took the opposite tack, bravely—some might say foolishly—volunteering to fight for Germany's interests in China to prove he was a loyal German. How did it feel then to be identified at the prison camp, above all, as a child of mixed blood? I have avoided that stigma because I look white. Yet that experience of being an outsider, of being part of Japan, yet separate, was always an irritant. It was like a persistent itch I longed to scratch but could never quite reach. What does it do to our sense of self when there is no group to which we belong, except, perhaps, to that ill-defined group of those who don't quite belong anywhere? I found myself revisiting past events and viewing them from a new perspective—one that was both eye-opening and alarming.

I thought back to the sunny afternoon in August 1991, just a month before my father's death, when I had taken the subway to a Tokyo suburb for an assignment. I was standing on the street corner when a white Mercedes Benz with tinted windows pulled up in front of me. The driver, a young Japanese albino wearing a brightly colored Hawaiian shirt and his white hair in a crew cut, opened the door for me. He was my ride. I was on my way to meet with a *yakuza* boss to do a story on Japan's mafia-like gangsters.

As the driver navigated his big car through the narrow streets, I noticed something odd about his right hand as it rested on the steering wheel—his pinky was a short stub. It reminded me of a scene from a Japanese movie about *yakuza* in which a gangster chopped off his own pinky with a butcher's knife as a way of making amends to his boss for botching an important job. I shuddered. Gangsters could turn violent if they believed someone was impugning their honor. Yet I had to ask. Screwing up my courage, I leaned forward. "So what happened to your finger?"

When the driver turned his head, his pale face flushed a bright red. "I wrecked the Boss's car," he said, embarrassed.

I sank back into the plush leather seats, feeling a mixture of amusement and relief. Perhaps he was a gangster, but he seemed like a sweet kid.

He parked in a quiet neighborhood and led me to a small, second-floor apartment, leaving me in a small living room. At the far end of the room, a five-foot-high wood carving of a cobra stood ready to strike, a gold sake cup in the snake's mouth. A samurai sword hung on the right wall at chest height.

A middle-aged man with a pockmarked face strode into the room, followed my eyes to the sword and smiled. "We need that to defend ourselves," he said. "The police won't let us have guns."

It was hard to know if it was just bravado. I knew the Boss's parent organization was expanding into new areas in Tokyo and faced threats from rival Tokyo gangs, but did they really fight with samurai swords?

The Boss went to the galley kitchen and poured himself a glass of milk. "Bad liver," he explained as he sat down on a sofa and beckoned me to sit on the easy chair beside him. He was a short, stocky man with a blunt nose and thick eyebrows. He wore a batik shirt, a heavy gold bracelet, a gilded John F. Kennedy silver-dollar belt buckle and a diamond-studded Rolex. He had an ugly scar under his jaw that moved when he spoke.

Apologizing in advance for being rude, I asked him about his driver's lost pinky.

"I never asked him to do that, you know, but it was a nice gesture," he said with a smile. "It made me feel like a father toward him."

For the first time I was afraid. When I was growing up in Japan, the only time we heard about gangsters was when warfare broke out between gangs or when the papers would run photos of gang members all dressed up in their dark suits waiting for a prominent member's imminent release from prison.

The conventional view in Japan was that *yakuza* were a necessary evil. In a society without a developed consumer loan business, *yakuza* were a source of credit. In a society where the courts were inaccessible, the *yakuza* helped resolve disputes. In popular movies, the *yakuza* were often portrayed as heroes of the downtrodden. Police tolerated them because they absorbed fringe elements of society—misfits, members of the untouchable tribe and half-castes. They took these people who were excluded from mainstream Japanese society and employed them in organized criminal activities like gambling and prostitution, preventing them from getting involved in more serious crimes.

However, in the bubble era of the 1980s, *yakuza* had emerged as a serious social problem. Developers, frustrated by strong tenant laws, used gangsters to drive renters out of buildings they wanted to demolish so they could build large, new buildings. In addition, the *yakuza* were getting involved in the stock market and expanding overseas.

I had gotten this Boss's name from a long list of gang members that a Japanese investigative journalist friend had gotten from a police contact. This Boss had been the only one on the list willing to talk. I asked him about the décor in his room. The snake, he explained, was a symbol of virility. The shrine in the kitchen was a reminder of the traditional Japanese values that *yakuza* honored.

When I asked him about the police crackdown on the *yakuza*, however, the Boss gave me a wry smile. His right eye twitched as he pulled out a stack of business cards from his pocket and spread them on the table like a pack of playing cards. I could see at a glance that many of the cards were from police detectives. "We have our contacts," he said. "They won't bother us."

There was something about the Boss's arrogant tone of voice and the smirk that passed for a smile that made me feel uneasy. Perhaps it was the violence that I knew lurked beneath his calm demeanor.

Now as I look back, I realize there was something else. The Boss reminded me of my father. It was his spirit of defiance, the "me against the world" attitude. Like Dad, he pretended not to care what anybody thought of him, and yet I knew it was all that mattered. Perhaps it all came down to this: Although their lives moved in vastly different orbits, this gangster and my father shared something important—they were outsiders who hungered for respect.

As I thought about it, I realized that the world of the gangsters and the world of the mixed-blood foreigner were not as far apart as I would have liked to think. Half-castes, as they were referred to then, often lived in a murky world in Japan. Many of my mixed-blood childhood friends adopted the foot-dragging saunter and tough dialect of the *chimpira*—punk gangs from which *yakuza* recruited. One of the few avenues open to half-castes in those days was the entertainment world, a world filled with gangsters.

Perhaps because of our family's outsider status, my father sometimes found himself dealing with *yakuza*. One of the last big deals Dad handled in Japan was the sale of his Uncle Jim's summer house on the seashore in a small neighborhood called Maiko on the western edge of Kobe. Dad told Jim's family that the buyer was a gangster. Only a gangster can pay such an exorbitant sum for a house in cash.

Dad knew that only a gangster would buy a house in which a tenant was still living, since Japanese laws made it so difficult to get the tenant to leave. Only a gangster would be willing to live in a showy house with such a stink of wealth: only a *yakuza*, that is, or a half-caste foreigner.

The Maiko house, as the Helms called it, was legendary for the beauty of its large garden. One day in the fall of 1992, I happened to be in Kobe on assignment, so I took the train to Maiko, about half an hour away, to look at the house. It was easy to find because Jim's daughter had explained that it was by a wooded park across the street from the octagonal house, now a museum, where Chinese Nationalist leader Sun Yat-Sen lived in exile in the early 1900s. The Maiko house was surrounded by an eight-foot-high wall of white plaster topped with blue tiles. I rang the doorbell. When nobody answered, I climbed a tree to get a better view. I was nervous. As far as I knew, the house, one of the few pre-war buildings left in the area, was still owned by a *yakuza*. Recently I had written a story about a gambler who had been killed by

Julie Helm, ca. 1907.

yakuza for failing to pay his debts. The assassin had scaled a wall much like this one and slain the gambler with a samurai sword. *What would the yakuza owner of the Maiko house think if he saw me sitting in a tree spying on him?*

From my vantage point in the tree, I could see over the wall onto a stunning garden that included a dry brook of smooth river stones lined with large craggy rocks and a thirty-foot-high stone pagoda. The house was built on one side of dark wood siding, while the other side was built of exposed half-timbers and white plaster.

Eighty years earlier, Jim had hosted a party here for his younger brother Julie and his bride Betty. It felt strange and thrilling to think that somehow, through earthquakes and fires, this building had survived. I had seen a picture of Grandmother Betty as a young woman looking exotic with her hair cut short and wearing a tight-fitting dress from the flapper era. She didn't look the least bit Japanese, although she was mixed race, Japanese and Caucasian. There are also many pictures of her holding me, although I was too young to remember her. I wondered what she would have thought if she could look over the wall, eighty years into the future, and see me sitting in a tree trying to imagine her life with Grandfather Julie.

I never knew Grandfather Julie. He died before I was born. My father kept a photo of Julie on his dresser. He had a big nose that was out of sync with his narrow face. His ears stuck out and his thin lips

were curled down at the edge. Somehow Julie's face and his features didn't mesh.

Would my grandparents provide the key to understanding my father and his awkward relationship with Japan, and ultimately, with me? I tried to imagine what it must have been like for Julie and Betty living in the early 1900s in both Japan and the United States as half-castes.

ALTHOUGH JULIE WAS A COMPETENT man who did a good job managing the family business, he never received much respect from the Helm family. "Well, you know, Uncle Julie was the bookkeeper," one great-aunt told me a little contemptuously. "He would give us pocket money and then tell us not to buy candy. It was silly. The only reason we wanted money was to buy candy."

As I thought about it, I realized I knew little about Julie as a young man. In a family photo taken when he was about eight years old, there is an intensity in his big eyes that drew my attention to him. At fourteen, when he completed eighth grade at St. Joseph's College on The Bluff, Julie went to work for Helm Brothers. Later he would help his Uncle Gustav in Virginia with his accounts, study at his aunt's school in Germany and complete an accounting program in New York. "I believe Dad had a very difficult upbringing with little or no adolescence," explained my Uncle Larry. "From the age of fourteen, he was working in an adult world that told him emotions were a sign of weakness."

When Julie graduated from accounting school in 1912 at age twenty-five, he was appointed secretary and treasurer of Helm Brothers, working under his older brother Charles. The job proved to be a perfect fit for Julie. He had a mind for numbers and a sharp eye for cutting costs. He recorded every penny the company spent and established strict rules to eliminate waste. A pencil had to be worn down until it was less than an inch long before it could be replaced. Bits of string any longer than the distance between an outstretched thumb and forefinger were added to a ball of string always kept on hand. Julie began to collect old clocks, admiring their intricate, predictable mechanisms and their white faces painted with elegant numbers. These seemed to be the very embodiment of his well-ordered life.

Though he was wealthy and his English perfect, being of mixed blood, Julie was barred from the Union Club, the exclusive lunch club on Yokohama's Bund where the expats hung out. Many of the foreigners in Yokohama were envious of Julie's ability to speak Japanese and to be at ease in any Japanese setting. Once, after a few drinks, my father told me how, as a child, he had walked into his father's office to find a large man with a bald head bowing deeply before his father, a little too deeply. It was only much later that Dad would understand the man was a *yakuza* and he was either in Julie's employ or deeply in-

Lovingly always
Betty

Julie's wife, Betty (Stucken) Helm, ca. 1928.

debted to him. I would later discover that Helm Brothers had little choice but to work with the gangsters who represented the day laborers the company employed to load and unload ships for a new transport company Charles had established called Toyo Unso. A man who always appears in pictures of Helm Brothers employees wearing sunglasses was the man charged with dealing with the labor groups. A retired Helm Brothers employee told me the man in sunglasses once returned from an encounter with a *yakuza* with knife cuts all over his face. He had refused to be intimidated. In the early 1920s, when laborers were becoming increasingly militant and frequently threatened the company with strikes, these men of the underworld played a key role in cowing the workers to assure labor peace.

In 1922, when his father died, Julie was suddenly wealthy. He began to have fun, frequenting the racetrack and having a relationship with a Japanese courtesan. He frequently went drinking with his two friends, Mike Apcar, an Armenian who exported Japanese antiques and imported Ariel motorcycles from Britain (he once took an Ariel halfway up Mt. Fuji as a marketing gimmick), and an Australian who ran the Japanese subsidiary of an American record company.

In November 1922, Julie took a trip to New York that changed his life. The trip was ostensibly to establish contacts with a shipping company in the city. But in truth, Julie had been intrigued by a letter from his older brother Jim, who was then staying with his mother-in-law in Brooklyn. There was somebody there Jim wanted his brother Julie to meet.

Julie had always been a little envious of his older brother Jim, who seemed to be everything Julie was not. Jim was tall and athletic, and his performance in crew races and other athletic feats would often appear in the local Kobe English newspaper. By contrast, Julie was short and somewhat awkward. While Jim sported a great bushy moustache, Julie could hardly grow stubble on his face. Jim had light skin and could easily pass as Caucasian, while Julie was dark and might pass perhaps as someone from Latin America. While Jim was at ease in society gatherings, Julie avoided them.

Jim had a cosmopolitan air about him. He had worked at a bank in St. Petersburg, Russia, and as an executive at a large New York corporation before taking over Helm Brothers' Kobe operation. What was most impressive of all was that Jim had wooed and married a musically accomplished Caucasian-American girl. True, his eldest brother, Charles, formerly Karl, and his younger brother, Willie, had also married white women, but Charles's wife was a first cousin, and Willie's wife was a widow with two children.

In Kobe, where Jim ran Helm Brothers' local branch, he and his charming wife moved in high circles. Jim raced in regattas, joined a water polo team and contributed large sums of Helm Brothers' money to various charitable causes. His wife, Elizabeth, a brunette with a commanding presence and a beautiful voice, served two terms as president of the Kobe Women's Club and often sang at special occasions. Still it was hard to escape the issue of race. Jim would never forget overhearing his friends talk about him in the locker room at his sports clubs. "Jim's a good sort," one man said. "Yes," said the other. "He knows his place."

Among the many ladies in the foreign community who Jim's wife Elizabeth had befriended in Kobe was Betty Stucken, a charming, well-brought-up Eurasian girl whose father came from a good German family. When Betty moved to New York in 1920, Elizabeth had suggested Betty room with her mother in Brooklyn. It was Elizabeth's idea to match up Julie with Betty.

Julie must have been filled with both excitement and foreboding as he disembarked from his ship in New York. Ever since attending accounting school in New York as a young man, he had developed a special affection for the city. He liked the crowds of people brimming with energy and purpose, the sense of freedom and the anonymity amid the polyglot of races and languages. What he may not have been aware of was the extent to which racism had infected every element of American society.

Earlier that year, the US Supreme Court had affirmed legislation denying Japanese immigrants the right to American citizenship. American politicians and citizens were becoming increasingly bold in their racist pronouncements. "If you were to go abroad and someone was to meet you and say, 'I met a typical American,' what would flash into your mind as a typical American, the typical representative of that new Nation?" Senator Ellison Du Rant Smith of South Carolina would later ask the US Senate in support of a new measure to prevent all people of color from migrating to the United States. "Would it be ... the son of any of the breeds from the Orient, the son of the denizens of Africa? ... It is the breed of the dog in which I am interested."

Eugenics, which sought to prove the superiority of whites over other races, was all the rage among "scholars" in the United States. Edward Byron Reuter, who would later serve as president of the American Sociological Society, asked rhetorically in his 1918 book, *The Mulatto in the United States*, whether the United States would continue to be welcomed among the club of civilized nations if the proportion of non-whites in its population kept increasing. Eurasians, he said, "stand between two civilizations, but are a part of neither. They are miserable, helpless, despised and neglected." Why? "In infancy [the half-caste] is nursed, and in youth pampered by his native servants upon whom he is dependent. As a consequence, all the strong traits of manhood are feebly developed in him ... In manhood he is wily, untrustworthy and untruthful. He is lacking in independence and is forever begging for special favors ... Socially the Eurasians are outcasts. They are despised by the ruling whites and hated by the natives."

I wonder if Julie didn't sense this new attitude in the glances of the man at the bank who cashed his check or the taxi driver who took him to Jim's mother-in-law's brick townhouse in Brooklyn. I wonder if it didn't give him pause when Jim and Elizabeth introduced him to the pretty Eurasian girl who was living with Elizabeth's mother.

Long afterward, Betty and Julie might have smiled at what Julie would later admit had been a carefully arranged meeting. But at the time, I wonder if Julie didn't feel vaguely insulted that Jim, who had been so proud of his white wife, would feel that a Eurasian girl was good enough for his younger brother. Julie was acutely aware of the relationship between skin color and class. When he saw Joyce, Jim's ten-year-old daughter, and David, his two-year-old son, Julie might well have intuited that David, with no hint of the Japanese blood in him, would live a comfortable life. He would marry a white woman and his children would not be identifiable as Asian in any way. By contrast, Joyce, who had black hair and lovely Asian features, would find her way littered with obstacles.

It was a self-fulfilling prophecy. Decades later, when Joyce married a Portuguese man from Macao, Jim and Elizabeth would refuse to attend their own daughter's wedding to this dark-skinned man. In his will, Jim granted his darker-skinned daughter just half of what he gave to his two other lighter-skinned children.

In the eyes of Betty, then twenty-three years old, Julie must have seemed far less the prize than her friend Elizabeth had promised. Julie looked like an odd old man. At thirty-five, he was already bald and

Jim Helm's children: Joyce, Ruth and David, ca. 1926.

had a huge purple birthmark on his head. His large ears stuck out awkwardly. He was short, quiet, and though he played the mandolin, a little boring. It would not have occurred to Betty that she and Julie had much in common even though both their fathers traveled to Japan from Germany a half century before and married Japanese women. Although the Helms were rich, Betty's father, Edmund, came from old wealth.

By the end of Julie's two weeks in New York, as I imagine the meeting, he had fallen for Betty as if he had fallen from a horse carriage, hit his head on the pavement and stood up to find the world a different place. He had never known anyone as beautiful, talented and vivacious as Betty. He loved to watch her paint in Central Park, her lips pursed, her eyes focused. He loved to hear the soft Japanese words and lyrical French she threw in her conversations that spiced up her English. It intrigued Julie that Betty seemed to be proud of her Japanese blood. She had studied Japanese *sumi-e* painting and *bonseki*, miniature landscapes. She had learned to read and write Japanese, something none of the Helms had ever attempted.

At the same time, Betty was very much the modern Western woman.

Her slim body looked stunning in the body-hugging flapper fashions of the time, and Betty delighted in taking the staid Julie to the dance halls then popular in New York. Watching Betty dance, twirl and laugh gave Julie a sense of joy that was foreign to him. When he talked to her, her eyes sparkled. He wanted to buy her furs and jewels. It was as if all the money he had been saving all his life finally had a purpose.

It took much longer for Betty to fall for Julie. He was not the tall, handsome man she had envisioned for herself. Still, she found with Julie a sense of security she craved, for Betty was hardly the carefree woman she appeared to be.

Betty's father, Edmund Stucken, came from a wealthy merchant family in the large German port of Bremen. His mother, born in Cuba to a family of German diplomats, died while giving birth to Edmund, and so the boy was raised by a bevy of nannies and tutors. He moved to Kobe in 1870, at age twenty, just a year after Julie's father, Julius, had arrived in Yokohama. Stucken, who may have been trying to avoid being sent to the front in the Franco-Prussian War, received a stipend from his wealthy father and had established his own trading company that represented the Tsingtao Brewery, a German beer company in China.

In a publication of the Club Concordia, a German club, old timers recalled Edmund as a debonair man with a handlebar moustache who would put his brandy snifter on the club's grand piano and sit down to play a stormy rendition of Beethoven's "Tempest." Edmund married a Japanese woman who died, like his mother, in childbirth. His daughter Betty, at age four, was sent to live at a French convent in Tokyo with her two sisters.

Toward the end of World War I, Edmund, as a German, had to shutter his business. To save money, he pulled his children from the convent school and let his servants go. Betty was disturbed when her father started coming home drunk and collapsing on the living room couch. When Edmund died in 1920 at age seventy, his obituary in the *Japan Chronicle* noted how he had fallen "on evil ways" toward the end of his life.

Soon afterward, at age twenty-one, Betty traveled to New York. She worked as a secretary at the New York branch of a large Japanese trading company. She quickly learned that Americans saw Japanese women as exotic playthings. In 1917, "My Yokohama Girl" was a popular tune whose refrain was "My Yokohama pearl. Run away, run away, run away in your silk pajama." Then there was the song "Yokohama Lullaby" about a "Yama mama" who sings a Yokohama lullaby to her "Happy little Jappy."

Betty began dating a well-educated Japanese man at her office. He took her to see the Charlie Chaplin comedies and Valentino romances that she loved. One evening he mentioned that his mother had arranged a bride for him and he would soon be returning to Japan to be married. It hurt Betty deeply that this man she had opened her heart to had never seriously considered her. Betty would always wonder if it was because she was only half Japanese.

Julie, by contrast, clearly loved her. When it came time for Julie to return to Japan, he asked Betty if he could see her again. She told him that she would like nothing better.

But life was not to be so simple. The US Congress would soon pass the Exclusion Act, which barred East Asians from immigrating. If Betty traveled to Japan, she might never be able to return to the United States. Julie, a US citizen, had planned to return to New York the following fall to woo Betty. Instead, he found himself caught up in an event that the insurance companies would call an "act of God," but that even God might have disavowed.

THE YEARS BEGINNING WITH World War I, sometimes called the
Taisho era after the imperial reign that followed Meiji, were Yokohama's golden era. Japan had expended little money in the war effort, yet, as a victor nation, it was permitted by its allies to occupy
German interests in China and the Pacific islands. Japan also did a
booming business supplying its allies with war materials. Trade soared,
boosting the fortunes of both Yokohama and Helm Brothers. I imagine it was a little like the early Meiji period when Great-Grandfather
Julius first arrived, and after World War II when I was growing up in
Yokohama. Foreigners and Japanese alike flocked to a city that seemed
to combine the best of Japan and the West—a place that seemed open to
new things. But that era of prosperity would be short-lived.

September 1, 1923, eleven fifty-eight in the morning. Summer was
winding down, but it was still hot and humid in Yokohama. The sun
was heating up the corrugated steel roof of the Helm Brothers building at #43 Yamashita-cho. Julie and his older brother Karl, who now
called himself Charles, were on the second floor drenched in sweat
as they stuffed yen bills into long slender envelopes for their employees' payday that afternoon. They were almost finished, and Julie was
beginning to place the envelopes back in the safe when the floor rose
abruptly and then lurched to the side as if the building were on the

back of some giant creature that had suddenly awoken from its slumber. Julie was thrown to the ground. He heard a distant roar like the sound of the surf. When he came to his senses, a yellow cloud of dust hung over him. And outside of what had been a second-story window, he saw a bicycle lying on its side.

"The entire first floor had collapsed under them," explained Trudy, Charles's daughter, as she recounted what happened that day. They were lucky the roof had been made of light corrugated iron instead of tile, which would have crashed down on them. Julie looked over to see Charles dust off his three-piece suit and pull a pocket watch from his vest. From the watch chain, which was attached to a button on his vest, hung a two-inch tiger's tooth given him by a ship's captain as a good luck charm. Charles opened the watch cover and put the watch to his ear. "It's still ticking," he said.

"I'll see to things here," Julie told his brother. "You'd better get back to your family."

Charles's family was spending the summer at their vacation home on Helm Hill in Honmoku, a seaside village three miles away. Charles and his wife Louise were respected members of the Yokohama community. They frequently invited for dinner the ship captains who were important customers of the Helm Brothers' stevedoring and forwarding services. Julie had always been the quiet one, and I suspect he envied the confidence and social ease of Charles and his wife Louise, who arranged flowers at the Union Church. She had become the matriarch of the extended Helm family, and everyone referred to her as Auntie Mama-Lou.

At two minutes before noon, Auntie Mama-Lou was making jam on a big stove using figs from her orchard. Her two daughters, Trudy, thirteen, and Lillian, nine, and her son Walter, fourteen, were sitting together on the couch in the veranda. They were reading comics from two weeks' worth of the *Los Angeles Times* that had arrived on a recent freighter when the house began to sway violently. Japanese houses, with their wood beams notched together, were meant to flex during an earthquake and thereby dissipate its force. But this temblor was too powerful. Trudy would later recall how the house swayed so sharply the sliding glass doors along the veranda popped off their rails and crashed down into the house, sending shards of glass across the room. A big beam supporting the roof overhang groaned horribly and then fell. In the kitchen, the stove toppled on its side and coals spilled across the floor. Trudy screamed. Later she recalled, "I was sure it was the end of the world."

Auntie Mama-Lou grabbed the big jar of coarse salt she kept on the shelf for making pickles and dumped it on the hot coals. Then she rushed the children out of the house and through the garden gate. Just as she thought she had gotten her children to safety, she put her hand to her mouth in horror. "David! Where's David?" She had agreed to take care of her nephew, David, and his two sisters for a few weeks. How could she have forgotten? The maids must have put two-year-old David down for his noontime nap. Auntie Mama-Lou rushed back into the house. She gasped when she saw that the heavy wardrobe had fallen forward, crushing the crib where David had been sleeping.

On The Bluff, the cook who was taking care of Louise and Charles's main home in their absence was pleased to see how well the grand old Victorian had withstood the earthquake. The cook doused the stove and returned everything that had been thrown to the ground back to its proper place. Then she locked the doors and set off on foot on the walk to the Honmoku summer house. She would have good news to report to the mistress: the house was safe.

Julie, still standing inside the fragile shell of the Helm Brothers' headquarters, was in shock, as he would later tell my father. He had been through many earthquakes. He often laughed when newcomers to Yokohama would turn white just because a lampshade had begun to waver, but he had never experienced anything like the one that had brought this building to its knees. He quickly made his way to the safe. He spent the next five minutes picking up the pay envelopes and cash strewn about. He put the notes in neat piles, secured them with rubber bands and returned them to the safe. There was an aftershock and the roof swayed. Julie knew it could collapse at any moment. He quickly locked the safe and made his way out onto the street headed for home.

For the first time, Julie noticed the full extent of the devastation. Virtually all of the buildings in the area, most of which were built of brick, had collapsed. A thick cloud of dust and a strange silence hung in the air. People seemed to be moving in slow motion, as if in a trance. As Julie walked down the street, the whole city seemed to gradually awaken. Soon he could hear cries and moans from every direction. The mid-day sun was blazing. Here and there he saw wisps of smoke rising from the ruins. Later Julie would learn that many of the hibachis restaurants used to prepare lunch had tipped over, spilling hot coals and starting fires. In the distance, he heard the clanging bell of a fire engine. Then he heard a sharper cry.

"Over there!" a man shouted. Soon half a dozen men appeared. When my relatives retold the story, they would laugh about how a mob of Japanese carried sharpened bamboo sticks and chased Julie through the city. But it couldn't have been funny to Julie. Later, he heard that the mobs were hunting down Koreans. They apparently mistook Julie for a Korean. Julie darted through back streets, clambering over fallen telephone poles and tangled wires. When he stopped to catch his breath, he felt trapped. Ahead of him was a raging fire; behind him were the vigilantes.

Charles had barely made it to the Motomachi tunnel, which led to Honmoku and his summer house, when he faced townspeople running in the opposite direction. "Fire!" he heard someone yell. He drifted to the side of the road and looked up to see the entire area around the tunnel a wall of flames. Charles turned and joined the crowds headed back toward the canal. At the canal, firemen were pumping water in a valiant but vain effort to slow the fire. The water mains, busted during the earthquake, had rendered the fire engines useless. Hundreds of people were now jumping into the canal to escape the heat, but Charles knew how polluted those waters were. *The pond in the park*, Charles thought, as he later told the story to his daughters. When he reached the park, six blocks away, he discovered the pond was already filled with hundreds of people up to their knees in water. Water mains beneath the park had burst and flooded the area. The park had once been the location of Yokohama's entertainment quarters. During the fire of 1866, hundreds of prostitutes locked into their brothels had burned to death. The foreign community had designed the park in part to act as a fire break.

Charles climbed into the pond, not bothering to remove his shoes and pants. There he waited, occasionally pulling out his watch to check the time. A man offered him a cigarette. Charles had never smoked before, but he found the smell of the tobacco familiar and comforting—it camouflaged the greasy odor he began to detect amid the smoke, the scent of burning flesh. Charles had always assumed his wife and children were safe in the summer house. Now as he watched the firestorm, he wasn't so sure.

Auntie Mama-Lou tried to move the large wardrobe from on top of the crushed crib, but it was too heavy. She looked pathetically at the

146

corner of the pink wool blanket sticking out from under the wardrobe. My great-aunts said Auntie Mama-Lou berated herself, telling herself that she should have known better than to place the crib next to such a heavy piece of furniture! She should have grabbed the child on her way out of the house! But where was the child's nanny? And where were the two girls? Suddenly it dawned on Auntie—David and his two sisters had left with their nanny the day before. By now they would be safe in their parents' arms in Kobe.

With a sigh of relief, Auntie Mama-Lou ran out into the street to join her children. A chasm about five feet wide and ten feet deep had opened up in the mud road, and somebody had thrown a wooden shutter over the crack to act as a bridge. When they got to the orchard, it was hot. Louise pulled some leaves off a fig tree and gave them to the children to shade their heads. The servants had placed *shoji* doors on the ground and put futons on them for makeshift beds. With nothing more for the servants to do, Louise released them to join their families. She worried about Charles. Why hadn't he come home? By late afternoon, the cook had joined them to report the good news that their main house was safe and locked up.

Motomachi, the little village at the foot of The Bluff, was ablaze. Hundreds of people who had jumped into the canal to escape the fire had drowned. The fire, fed by heavy winds, was now rapidly consuming houses along Jizozaka, the steep road up to Charles's house. The road had been named after the temple halfway up the hill that honored the guardian deity of children. Charles's main house was soon in flames. Now hundreds of foreign residents and their servants were running away from the fire toward the sea cliffs carrying their valuables. Several priests heard sounds from the St. Maur International School farther up The Bluff and stopped to pull survivors from the wreckage. A few of the sisters had been saved, but most of the nuns and all of the children were trapped inside.

"I have a great big stone on my chest. Take it off. Oh, take it off please!" a priest heard one of the girls inside call out, as a family friend would later recall in a lengthy account of the earthquake.

"Be calm. Help is coming!" the priest shouted encouragingly. It was a lie. Already the fire was descending on the school. The priest called to the girls to join him in prayer, but as he did, he heard blood-curdling screams. Twenty-six children and ten nuns died in the school that day.

Farther down the road, another man called for help. It was Mr. Meyer, an employee of Helm Brothers. His leg was caught under a heavy beam that fell when his house collapsed. A few good Samaritans had stopped to help him, but the beam was too large to dislodge, and they could already feel the heat from the advancing fire. Mr. Meyer begged them to cut off his leg so he could escape, but nobody was willing to undertake the gruesome task. They left him screaming as he was engulfed in flames.

A large crowd had now gathered on The Bluff along the edge of a fifty-foot precipice. A few residents knew a path down and led the way. When one old lady refused to move, a man grabbed her bag of valuables and threw it over the cliff. The woman quickly scrambled down. Soon the smoke hid the way and the crowds were overcome by the smoke and heat. Some desperate mothers jumped to their deaths, hugging their young children in their arms.

In downtown Yokohama, Julie felt trapped, blocked by a wall of flames. When he looked back, the men who had been chasing him were gone, evidently scared away by the approaching fire. Julie made for the sea wall. He climbed down some steps and stood in the water as he watched Yokohama burn. It was a dazzling sight. Telephone poles lit up like giant candles and then came crashing down. As the wind picked up and the flames grew higher, pieces of wood, paper and all manner of litter filled the air, carried by the heat and the wind. As Julie watched, he calculated the damage: the warehouses, the residences and the offices. How many employees survived? And what of the horses? Helm Brothers, he quickly concluded, was ruined.

In Honmoku, Auntie Mama-Lou and her children huddled together on futons in the fig orchard as they watched gangs of men carrying lanterns run up and down the street. They were searching for Koreans, a neighbor told them. "The Koreans have poisoned the wells," he said. In the ensuing days, thousands of Koreans were captured and beaten or stabbed to death.

The fire was still burning in the distance when Louise and her children woke up in the orchard and made their way several miles along the water to the foot of The Bluff where a large congregation of foreigners had gathered. They were waiting to board a tugboat that would ferry them to the *Empress of Australia,* which was anchored offshore. Auntie Mama-Lou tried to keep the children from staring at the dozens of blackened bodies that washed up against the sea wall. After several hours, it was finally their turn. A nice man helped Auntie Mama-Lou lift the children into the tugboat. On board the *Empress of Australia* she found Charles there looking for her. Charles told her the shipping companies were offering free passage to Kobe and on to America. It appeared that the United States had offered citizenship to foreign residents who were victims of the earthquake. Charles told his wife to take the ship to Kobe with the children and stay with Jim's family. There was little food or shelter in Yokohama now. He promised to join her when matters were in hand, then got a lift on a tugboat back to shore.

A day later, the ship *Empress of Canada* arrived to help in the evacuation. The passengers were transferred to the ship from the *Empress of Australia*. Now, with 1,400 refugees aboard, the *Empress of Canada* steamed off to Kobe. That night rich and poor slept side by side like sardines on the deck of the ship. There were few Japanese on board—they had been left to fend for themselves.

In the morning, as Julie surveyed the damage, he realized there was no point in counting up Helm Brothers' losses. Yokohama was now nothing more than a vast wasteland of blackened rubble. It was as if Yokohama had shed its foreign skin in the intense heat. The only sign that this land had ever been a great international port was the occasional brick chimney, steel safe or the ridiculous sight of a bath tub floating twenty feet above the ground, held up in the sky by its iron plumbing while the house had collapsed around it.

One hundred and forty thousand people died in Yokohama and Tokyo that day in 1923. In Yokohama alone, at least 31,000 of the city's population of 441,000 died. In Tokyo, the death figure was more than double that. A vacant lot where city residents had gone to escape the fire had become a giant crematorium when the warehouses around it burst into flames and 44,000 people burned. Some two-thirds of the buildings in Yokohama were destroyed, most of them by fire. Forty-five percent of Yokohama's workers were instantly unemployed. Most of Yokohama's foreign residents were quick to abandon the city.

Anybody who had felt the world tremble that day, anybody who had run from the firestorm, would find it difficult to ever feel completely safe in Yokohama again. Newspapers reported that insane asylums were filled with people who could not take the strain. Many foreign residents returned to their homelands in Europe or the United States. Some emigrated to Australia or New Zealand. Most of the rest moved to either Kobe or Shanghai.

大正十二年九月一日横浜市大震災惨状
港町の亀裂

THE YOKOHAMA SPCAIE BANK 狀慘の近附行銀金正濱橫 （濱橫）

THE DAY AFTER THE QUAKE, Julie made his way amid blackened timbers and rows of corpses, across cracks in the earth and piles of rubble, to the office where he had been when the earthquake hit. As he had expected, Helm Brothers' warehouses had all collapsed. In 1866, following a devastating fire in the foreign settlement, foreigners had chosen to build in brick. But if buildings of brick could resist fire, it was now apparent that they were useless against a major earthquake. The city offices, banks and churches made of stone were now crypts burying the dead. The livery, where the horses and wagons were kept, was made of wood and had survived the temblor, but it had burned down in the aftermath like the rest of Yokohama. Nobody had thought to let the horses out.

Searching through the crumbled remains of the old office, Julie found the safe. It looked to be in good condition. At least they would be able to pay the employees their wages. Julie turned the dials on the combination lock, opened the heavy fireproof door of the safe and reached in, but everything had turned to ash. Now there wouldn't even be enough money to pay the workers. The company had fire insurance, but he suspected—and he would be proved right— that the insurance companies would find a reason not to pay out. The Helm Brothers operations in Kobe and other ports around Japan had tended to operate at a loss. Without the operation in Yokohama to support them, they would quickly go bankrupt.

The only money the brothers had left was a few thousand dollars deposited in a New York bank account. They questioned if they should take that money and make a new life elsewhere. Julie could move to New York to be with Betty. But what would he do for work? And would Betty still want him without his wealth? Julie wondered if he even wanted to live in an unfriendly city like New York without money, the one security he had always relied upon.

Julie and Charles spent the next two days with a small group of Westerners helping the police line up and identify the bodies of the foreigners who had died. The police didn't want to touch them for fear they would be accused of stealing from the corpses. The Japanese government was expected to send troops to help, but with communications systems down, the government was relying on carrier pigeons.

Immediately, Julie and Charles put their employees to work. They used the barges that had survived the fire to help unload and deliver emergency materials. They built a shack to serve as the company's temporary headquarters. Later they traveled to nearby forests to collect wood to build new barges and tugboats.

As foreigners left Yokohama, Charles and Julie used the money they had deposited in New York to acquire property in downtown Yokohama and on The Bluff. Julie also loaned money to friends who wanted to rebuild their homes in Yokohama.

So often did Japan experience fires and so often did it bounce back afterward that there was a saying in Japan: "After fire, prosperity." And so it was with the Helms. Their commitment to Yokohama in its darkest days set the Helms apart. Yes, they were outsiders. Yes, they were foreigners. But Yokohama was their home. And their fates were tied to this land in a way true to few other foreigners, most of whom fled the ravaged city. Some have suggested that the Helms profited from the hardship of others. Perhaps, but they also fought to rebuild Yokohama. Although I have never found concrete evidence of it, one old-timer in Yokohama whose grandfather had worked for Helm Brothers told me that he had heard Helm Brothers was given special favors by the city of Yokohama in its business dealings because of its contribution to the city after the earthquake.

Auntie Mama-Lou and the children arrived in Kobe on the *Em-*

曠野と化したし横濱
The devastated Yokohama.

Barrack, temporary quarter of Helm Bros Ltd

press of Canada where they were greeted by Jim and Elizabeth, and taken to their family's expansive home in Maiko with its beautiful gardens. While the Helms in Yokohama had escaped disaster, there was trouble closer to home. A week after the earthquake, Jim's daughter, Dora, who was thirteen and had just returned from Yokohama with her siblings, grew hysterical when she heard of the Yokohama earthquake. "The anxiety seems to have started some kind of brain disturbance," reported the *Japan Weekly Chronicle,* which covered the foreign community. "She complained of headaches and when her relatives arrived from Yokohama on the fifth, the disease had made such progress that she could take but little interest in them."

Dora died on September 10, 1923, just nine days after the great earthquake. Doctors today will say a girl cannot die of anxiety, but hospitals in Kobe were so busy taking care of the injured that she did not get the care she required. She was the only earthquake-related death in the whole Helm family.

Dora's death was a great blow to Jim and Elizabeth. They withdrew from their social engagements and in 1924 journeyed to New York to stay with Elizabeth's mother. Betty was still renting a room from Elizabeth's mother, so Betty comforted Elizabeth, and once again they became close friends.

Did Elizabeth, trying to forget the pain of her lost daughter, be-

Julie and Betty are married in Yokohama surrounded by Julie's brothers, Karl and Jim with their families, and his sisters Marie, Elsie and Louise, 1925.

come once again engrossed in Betty's suspended relationship with Julie? I do not doubt it, for when she returned to Japan in the spring of 1925, Betty was with her.

Betty and Julie were married in Yokohama on September 5, 1925, just two years after the great earthquake. Betty, twenty-six, wore a garland of flowers in her hair. She looked like a child bride next to her thirty-eight-year-old, balding groom. Elizabeth's four-year-old son, David, the child who might have been crushed during the earthquake had he stayed in Yokohama a day longer, was the ring bearer. Charles's youngest daughter, Lillian, dark-haired and with olive skin, was the flower girl.

via Amerika!

CARTE POSTALE
UNIVERSELLE
HELM BROS.
YOKOHAMA

Herrn
Arthur Hofmann
Zwickau i/Sa.
Germany
Köhlerstraße N° 8

TELEPHONE
YOKOHAMA NO. 524 & 3159
TOKYO, NANIWA, NO. 2581
KOBE, NO. 3489

Forwarding Agency

14 NANIWA MACHI
KOBE.
P. O. BOX 147

W./No. 1633 **HELM BROS., LIMITED.**

43 Yamashita-cho, Yokohama, P. O. Box 116
Nihon-Bashiku Koamicho 3 chome, Kubanchi, Tokio.

Yokohama, 6ᵗʰ May 1912

Messrs Röbling & Co
Bremen

Dear Sir,

We have the pleasure to acknowledge the receipt of your Waybill
dated 16/4 for £ S 7084/6 3₰ per S. S. Goeben which will
receive our most careful and prompt attention.

Hoping to be favoured with your further esteemed consignments.

We are, Dear Sir,
Yours faithfully,
HELM BROS., LTD.

10ᵗʰ regard to your draft of
MK 4114⁵⁵ we will let you know
in a few days.

ON THE EVE OF
A NEW WAR

THE SAME EARTHQUAKE THAT DESTROYED Yokohama created a
giant tsunami off the coast of Hayama, a seaside resort thirteen
miles from Yokohama. A young woman they called Tsuru ("crane")
because of her long white neck was taking her lunch break from her
work as a maid at the Hayama Imperial Villa when she heard cries.
Tsuru-*san* ran outside to see the ocean receding, leaving a vast expanse
of beach. "Run," people were screaming. She ran for higher ground,
turning around just in time to watch as the ocean rushed in like a
moving wall then crashed down on the Villa, reducing it to splintered
timbers.

Afterward, when she walked back to the beach she saw thieves going through the pockets of corpses. "It was a horrible sight," the now
elderly Tsuru-*san* told me when I visited her at her home in Yokohama
about a year after my father's memorial. At the memorial, she had
looked elegant in her formal kimono, but now, wearing a plain flannel
kimono and peering at me through eyes like black marbles, she looked
decades older.

Tsuru-*san* recalled fond memories at the Villa. She remembered
one night in particular, when Hirohito, the crown prince, spent the
night. The next morning, before cleaning the crown prince's bath,
she had taken off her clothes and slipped into the lukewarm water. "I
bathed in the same water as the crown prince," she said. Her eyes spar-

kled as she leaned her head back and chuckled, covering her mouth to hide her teeth. And when she folded his highness's futon, she told me, putting her face close to mine conspiratorially, she laid down on the warm tatami mat where the futon had been, feeling the warmth that still remained under the futon where the crown prince had been sleeping. I was a little shocked when Tsuru-*san* told me this story. I had always heard how the emperor was revered as a god, so this seemed sacrilegious.

But most of the time, she continued, the Imperial Villa job had been boring. Her supervisors had always complained about her and often used to say, "You are so lazy; you should go work for a foreigner." So after the earthquake, she made her way to Yokohama where, after three years she met with Betty, who was looking for a nanny for her first son, Don, my father.

It was good work. Tsuru-*san* was paid a salary that was more than that of a policeman. She lived in one of three small rooms behind the kitchen that also housed the cook. The chauffeur and his family lived in a small room above the garage. There was a chicken coop where the maids fetched fresh eggs for breakfast. In the fall, there was always a turkey being fattened for the holidays.

"We were always curious about blue-eyed people," said Tsuru-*san*, using a description that referred to all foreigners. "I remember there was a popular song about blue-eyed dolls."

The blue-eyed doll from America.
At the pier her eyes are full of tears.
"I don't speak Japanese. I will get lost," she cries.
"Gentle girls of Japan, play with me! Be my friend."

In 1927, I learned later, some twelve thousand American dolls were sent to Japanese schools as a gesture of goodwill. Japan reciprocated by sending fifty-eight dolls made by the best dollmakers to America. When World War II began, the Japanese burned most of the American dolls as evil symbols of the West, but the song remained popular.

"The mistress [Betty] was kind to me. She always liked me," said Tsuru-*san*. "She even included me in her will."

While Julie would fine Tsuru-*san* every time she let the screen door slam, Betty always paid her back afterward. Tsuru-*san* knew Betty trusted her when Betty shared her system for testing maids. She would throw a few coins under the couch and then ask the maid to do a thorough cleaning: If the money was left untouched, she knew the maid hadn't cleaned properly; if the money was gone, she knew the maid was dishonest.

Tsuru-san told me she felt sorry for Betty on the many nights that Julie would come home late, long after the children had been put to bed. On those nights, Betty would turn to the cook and say, "The master is working late. Please put away the dinner." It became clear to Tsuru-san that Julie had a mistress. Then one day a beautiful woman in a kimono came to the door. She had the good manners and bearing of a geisha. Julie led her to the living room. Betty held her son Don in her arms while she paced back and forth in the dining room. Tsuru-san was so curious she piled up two boxes in the hallway and climbed onto them so she could peer through the small glass window at the top of the living room door. "I was standing on the boxes when they tumbled down. I fell right on my bottom." Tsuru-san laughed. "The Master didn't hear me. He was busy negotiating."

Tsuru-san concluded that the lady had been Grandfather Julie's concubine before he had married Betty. Finally Betty had put her foot down and Julie had arranged a settlement. "I think she came to the house because she felt she didn't get enough separation money," said Tsuru-san. "He always was such a stingy man. Served him right!"

Julie's stinginess was partly from his father Julius. It may also have had something to do with the tough economic times in Yokohama in the aftermath of the earthquake. The silk trade, on which Helm Brothers had depended for the bulk of its stevedoring business, had largely moved to Kobe after its warehouses had burned down in the earthquake.

Slowly business began to recover. The Japanese had been impressed by the trucks and cars brought in from America to help in Yokohama's reconstruction following the earthquake. Soon demand for those vehicles soared. Ford opened a factory near Yokohama in 1925 and General Motors soon followed. Cars replaced horse carriages as the preferred means of transportation among the rich. The occasional car or bus could now be heard honking its horn as it jostled for space with the streetcars, bicycles, rickshaws and handcarts that crowded the roads.

As Yokohama industrialized, it became a major destination for foreign travelers. In 1927, the Hotel New Grand was built. It was a three-story luxury hotel of stone overlooking the harbor that would host

Hosei University baseball team travels to Hawaii.

such luminaries as Charlie Chaplin, Babe Ruth and Prince Henry, the Duke of Gloucester. Helm Brothers also served many of the new world travelers. In June 1928, when the pilots John Mears and Charles Collyer arrived in Yokohama by ship, only Helm Brothers had a floating crane, a fifty-eight-ton, German-built machine capable of lifting their single propeller plane off of the ship and onto shore so they could carry on their "Round the World" voyage. The two pilots would circle the planet in a record-breaking twenty-three days and fifteen hours. The year before, Charles Lindbergh had piloted the *Spirit of St. Louis* on its famous flight across the Atlantic.

Culturally, too, the world seemed to be converging in those final years of the 1920s. Dance halls, jazz and automobiles—those crowning glories of the West—had already become an integral part of Yokohama. There was even a Japanese word for the flapper. Taking the first syllables of the English words "modern" and "girl," the Japanese called these party-loving, cigarette-smoking Japanese girls *moga*. Cultural exchange blossomed.

Julie and Betty were swept up in the new mood. In May 1929, Julie loaned a Hawaiian friend $1,500 in gold to pay the cost of sending the sixteen-member Hosei University baseball team to Hawaii. The team arrived in Honolulu on the *S.S. Shinyo Maru* on May 18, 1929. Julie must have felt good when he received newspaper clippings in the mail with such headlines as "Hosei Japanese Collegians Smother Fils." The team stayed in Hawaii for five weeks and played more than twenty games.

In October 1929, just when Julie thought everything was back on track, the New York stock market crashed. Overnight, the substantial investments Julie had made in the United States were worthless. His Hawaiian friend never repaid the loan for the fares of the baseball team. The US economy plunged into an economic downturn that led the US Congress in 1930 to raise tariffs on imports by more than fifty percent. After championing free trade for half a century—it was America that had forced Japan in 1859 to open its doors to trade—the United States was slamming the door in Japan's face. The volume of trade passing through the port of Yokohama fell by half from 1929 to 1931. Unemployment in Japan soared. The few Yokohama banks that survived the earthquake were now knocked out by the plunge in trade. Virtually every bank in Yokohama was forced into bankruptcy by 1930.

CHARLES J. HELM DIES AT YOKOHAMA

———

Well Known Businessman There Succumbs After Long Struggle Against Blood Poisoning

———

FAMILY PRESENT AT END

———

Was Managing Director of Stevedoring and Landing Agents Firm for Many Years

———

Helm Brothers was still struggling to recover from the Great Depression when Charles died unexpectedly of pneumonia in 1933, at age fifty-three. Julie took over as boss. Life steadily improved for Betty and their three children: Don, seven; Ray, three; and Larry, one. They moved to a large, two-story Western house high on a hill. In the living room was a large glass chandelier. A big pantry off the kitchen was packed with Betty's large collection of antique Japanese ceramics.

Julie also built a summer home for the family in Honmoku, near his father's summer house on Helm Hill. Today, the hill looks over a vast plain of highways and oil refineries, but at the time it was an idyllic place. There was a long wooden staircase with more than a hundred steps that took the kids from their summer house on the cliff down to "Society Beach," where other foreigners rented temporary bamboo shacks. At the beginning of every summer, the foreigners paid for the construction of a wooden pier for swimming and boating that was dismantled every September before typhoons could destroy it. Up at the house, a fisherman would come by the kitchen door with a large basket filled with seafood caught that morning. The cook would select a nice fish for dinner and buy a bag of baby clams to put in the miso soup. At dinner time, the cook would ring a gong to call the children to dinner. After dinner the kids would play hide-and-seek or use a can and string to talk between houses. Too soon, summer would be over and it would be back to school and a stricter regimen.

Dad remembered dinner with his father, Julie, as an unhappy time. "He would flip my ear with his finger whenever I used my hands to eat and it would sting like hell. I was very scared of him always."

Tsuru-*san* later recalled that sometimes Julie would come home to find Dad playing cards with a friend while yapping away in Japanese. Julie would grab him by the ear and drag him across the room to his office, take off his slipper and hit Dad on the bottom until he was howling. Julie didn't want his son to end up speaking "Japlish," a tangled mixture of Japanese and English spoken by so many children of mixed parents. How well you spoke English was a critical determinant of class, and Julie was intent on making sure his kids could pass in the best society.

One day Dad came home crying after being taunted by Japanese kids who shouted, "*Gaijin mame kutte papiya, papiya.* (Foreigners eat beans and fart.)" He had bruises all over his body.

A few days later, recalled Tsuru-*san*, Julie pushed the coffee table to the side of the room, laid tatami mats in the middle of the living room and began teaching Dad judo.

Tsuru-*san* remembered another disturbing incident. On February 2, 1936, Tsuru-*san* and the cook were warming themselves by the stove when my Dad, then nine, came rushing through the door. "A terrible

Betty and Julie with sons (L to R) Larry, Ray and Don.

thing has happened,' he said. "Takahashi-*san* has been murdered!"

Tsuru-*san* and the cook looked at each other skeptically.

"It's true!" Dad insisted. "The gardener is dead. I heard it at the store."

Then they both burst out laughing. How typical of a *gaijin* child to assume that the Takahashi-*san* he heard mentioned at the store must be the one that worked for him. Dad didn't know that Takahashi was about as common a name as you could find in Japan.

Takahashi had indeed been murdered. And just as the servants suspected, it was not the gardener. But it was no laughing matter. The victim had been Takahashi Korekiyo, Japan's finance minister. Early that morning, 1,483 soldiers had marched into Tokyo, occupied government buildings and murdered politicians they considered corrupt. They were stopped before they reached the Imperial Palace where they had planned to "free" the emperor.

Tokyo was thrown into chaos for three days before the leaders of the insurrection were captured. The man who had been the inspiration for many of the rebels was General Mazaki Jinzaburo. He was the xenophobic commander of the World War I POW camp who had tried to frame my Great-Uncle Willie.

The leaders of the insurrection were put to death, but the murders intimidated the politicians and made it difficult for them to stand up to the military. Without strong opposition from the central government, the Kwantung Army, Japan's army in Manchuria, pushed farther and farther into North China, setting Japan on a collision path with the United States.

In spite of these incidents, Julie was optimistic about the future. In 1935, Yokohama felt good enough to celebrate its economic recovery in the Grand Yokohama Exposition. The city held the expo at Yamashita park, which had been built along the waterfront with rubble from the earthquake. A year later, the International Olympic Committee announced that the 1940 Olympic Games would be held in Tokyo. Japan saw the games as an appropriate way to help celebrate what it claimed was the 2,600th anniversary of the founding of Japan by its mythic first emperor.

In 1936, Julie decided it was time to build a headquarters building for Helm Brothers—one that would survive any fire or earthquake, anchoring the family in Yokohama far into the future. The new headquarters would be completed just as the Olympics was being held and

Japan was center stage on the global scene. The timing could not have been more auspicious.

TWO YEARS LATER, GRANDFATHER JULIE was dressed in a tailcoat as he stood for a photograph to celebrate the grand opening of Helm House, a five-story, reinforced concrete building that would serve as the new headquarters of Helm Brothers. The firm my Great-Grandfather Julius had founded now had several hundred employees, close to a hundred barges, a dozen tugboats, two of Japan's largest floating cranes and stevedoring operations in all six of Japan's largest ports. So confident was Julie of the company's survival far into the future that he had arranged for a time capsule to be placed under one corner of the building. It contained paintings by his wife Betty, who had done the interior decorating of the building. It also contained other valuables and mementos which, when the capsule was unearthed in some distant future, would offer a record of that moment in history.

Great-Grandfather Julius was present in the form of a poster-sized portrait placed at the center of the room beside an elaborate flower arrangement. Julie, perhaps aware of his father looking on, straightened his tie and pulled back his shoulders as the photographer began to shoot. In the picture Julie looks diminutive, flanked by his two tall, mustachioed German brothers, Jim and Willie.

Julie was proud of the building. It was just two blocks away from the South Pier, where passenger ships unloaded travelers from around the globe, and was visible from the harbor. In the fifteen years since the earthquake, Yokohama had quadrupled in size as it incorporated more and more of the towns and villages around it. With its jazz bars, dance halls and many movie theaters, Yokohama had come to epitomize Japan's embrace of the West. Helm House represented another important step.

Julie took his family and guests on a tour of the building. The first floor of the Helm House included an elegant dining room with art deco lighting, a bar and the Japan headquarters of the Banque de l'Indochine, as well as the headquarter offices of Helm Brothers. From the second floor up, the building contained thirty-one fully furnished apartments designed to attract wealthy international guests with the latest in Western comfort and convenience.

It was one of the first buildings in Japan to have a telephone exchange and central air conditioning. Each kitchen had a gas range, a refrigerator, a coffee maker and a toaster, all imported from the United States. The living rooms boasted American couches and Chinese carpets. The dining-room table and chairs were custom-made in Japan as was the china, each piece stamped with the Helm Brothers HB logo.

The Czech architect, Jan Josef Svagr, who had come to Japan on the invitation of an assistant to Frank Lloyd Wright, designed Helm House's blocky, modern look, full of angles and corners, to assure each apartment had good views and plenty of privacy, an amenity still rare in Japan.

"You could slam the front door shut in one apartment and you wouldn't even hear it in the apartment next door," a Helm Brothers employee would recall decades later.

British, Japanese, German and American flags flew on a row of flagpoles alongside the symbol of Helm Brothers. Visitors could see over the roof of the nearby Hotel New Grand and watch sunsets through the prism of Yokohama's industrial smog. For those who stayed at the hotel, that smog was just another sign of Yokohama's emergence as a major industrial center, an economic power whose growth would drive Helm Brothers' prosperity far into the future.

Every morning, dozens of new employees poured into the building in freshly pressed uniforms. There were maids to clean the rooms daily, cooks to provide meals in the fancy dining room and *boysans* to respond to the customers' every whim. They were all a part of the Helm Brothers family. "Every maid hired was the daughter, sister or mother of a Helm Brothers employee," recalled Ozawa Matsuko, a former maid at Helm House. Her father was a carpenter who had built barges and tugboats for Helm Brothers. The Ozawa family lived in a row of houses Helm Brothers had built for its employees near the dock where the company built and repaired the boats.

Helm House's success in attracting diplomats and wealthy business executives as residents made it the envy of Yokohama real-estate devel-

opers. In his novel *Alien Rice,* writer Kawasaki Ichiro, who served as a Japanese diplomat between the two world wars, quotes a "Mrs. Hertz" (a lightly veiled reference to Grandmother Betty Helm) commenting on the success of Helm House. "After my husband built Hertz House, many Japanese real-estate people came to get the building plan and other information. When we declined, they sent a spy to steal the plan from us."

With the Tokyo Olympics scheduled for 1940 when Japan would be center stage, Julie believed that Helm House had been completed at the perfect time. He could not have known that another world war would soon shatter the peace and that Helm family members would

NEXT PAGE: Helm Brothers employees behind Helm House, ca. 1939.

once again be scattered across four continents. Instead of being a beacon for a new era of internationalism, Helm House would be a flickering light in that waning era. Its apartments' Western conveniences would come to symbolize not the comforts of modernity, but the decadence of Western materialism.

Once Helm House's operations were in place and the company running smoothly, Julie decided to take his family, including my father, Don, then eleven, on their first vacation to the United States and Canada. In San Francisco, he bought a brand-new 1938 Ford and drove the family across the recently completed Golden Gate Bridge. Dad was impressed by the wide roads and the tall buildings of San Francisco. The family went to Yosemite where they saw the firefall launched over those immense granite cliffs. Dad stared in wonder at the endless miles of wild forests, mountains and deserts where there was not a soul in sight. His parents were dazzled by the news of great progress. One day it was the Mallard, a steam locomotive reaching a high speed of 126 miles an hour. A few weeks later, it was millionaire Howard Hughes flying around the world in ninety-one hours.

When Julie and Betty returned to Yokohama in the fall of 1938, the mood was somber. The Japanese government, now dominated by militarists, had decided in July to relinquish hosting the Olympics, in part because the government needed the money to pay for its war in China. Instead of an international celebration, the government decided to have an even more elaborate celebration than planned for the 2,600th anniversary of the year when the first emperor, Emperor Jimmu, descendant of the Sun Goddess, began his reign.

Julie learned that his brother Jim, who had been running the Kobe branch of Helm Brothers, had become uncomfortable with the growing anti-Western sentiment in Japan and had decided to move to the United States. Although Helm House proved to be a great success, Julie must have understood that the factories going up north of Yokohama were busy producing steel and ships and armaments to support the fighting in Manchuria. I wonder if he heard the stories of how Japanese soldiers had butchered hundreds of thousands of civilians in Nanjing and whether he believed them. Did he begin to see an ugly side to Japanese nationalism?

Did Betty, too, begin to look at Yokohama through new eyes? She had often seen school kids at the train station waving their flags to give the soldiers a warm sendoff. She had seen women in front of the train

stations and department stores asking passersby to add a red stitch to the red sun on a Japanese flag. Such a flag with a thousand stitches sewn by a thousand different women was supposed to protect their men from bullets. The practice had always seemed quaint to Betty, but in the months that followed her return from America, she began to see another increasingly common sight: mothers receiving small wooden boxes wrapped in white cloth, the ashes of the sons they had sent off to China.

Parents stoically accepted the sacrifice for the good of the nation. "Great Japan, Great Japan. Its emperor is a descendant of God," went a poem Japanese children were required to learn in school. "We have never lost to our enemies. Day by day our country shines greater with glory." Japan believed it was invincible.

And what did Betty and Julie think of the alliance between Japan and Germany, their parents' homelands? Initially, Betty must have felt some pride. I have first-day-of-issue stamped envelopes Betty collected that commemorate Japan's 1937 Anti-Comintern Pact with the future axis powers, Germany and Italy. One shows portraits of Adolf Hitler, Benito Mussolini and Konoe Fumimaro, the Japanese prime minister. Another stamp shows an eagle marked with the swastika and the rays of a rising sun, together fighting back the scourge of communism, represented by a river of blood.

Julie preferred not to think about Germany. And since it was so far away, he didn't have to. Not, that is, until his younger brother, Willie, decided to take his children to Germany for their education.

On May 28, 1940, Julie arrived at Sakuragicho Station to see Willie off. The family was already there, all dressed up and waiting for the train to take them on the first step of their long journey across Siberia to Germany.

A Japanese reporter asked questions of the family and then stood by while a photographer took their portrait. No doubt the newspaper editors felt Japanese mothers sending their children to die in Manchuria would find comfort in a story about a Western mother who was sending her children to a war zone in Europe.

But Julie was saddened and confounded by the sight of his forty-nine-year-old little brother embarking on this dangerous journey. Julie may have wondered, *What had compelled Willie to take four of his children to be educated in Germany just eighteen days after the Nazi army had poured into Belgium and France?* Julie's older brother Charles had died and Jim had moved to California. Julie did not want to lose Willie too.

There was so much about Willie that Julie did not understand. Why, at age seventeen, had he volunteered to fight to protect Germany's colony of Tsingtao from the Japanese army—an army that represented his mother's country and which his father had helped to train? Why, after five years in a prisoner-of-war camp, had Willie given up his safe job at Helm Brothers and rushed off to Manchuria? He had returned penniless from Manchuria with his white Russian wife, Agnes, and six children, including two from Agnes's previous marriage to Bobrovnikov, the former Russian consul general in Manchuria. Even so, Charles had welcomed him back, given him a job at Helm Brothers and even taken in Alex, Agnes's son from her previous marriage whom Willie had refused to adopt. And when their sister, Marie, was dying of cancer, she had felt sorry for Willie and left him her entire fortune. With his money, his big family and the rising status of Germans in Japan, Willie should have been happy in Yokohama.

Perhaps Willie had inherited Julius's restlessness, his drive to explore. But perhaps Willie's need to keep moving had less to do with Julius's impatience than with the absence of a place he could call home. After all, his father had him change schools nine times in six cities on three continents over twenty years.

An article that appeared in the Japanese newspaper the day after

Willie left Yokohama shows a picture of him with the four children he was taking to Germany: Myra, Willie Jr., Dorothy and Rudi. They are standing on a crowded train platform as curious bystanders peer over their shoulders to see what is going on. The two boys are wearing suits with Hitler Youth pins on their lapels and carrying packages wrapped in brown paper tied up in string.

"Rudi seems to be happy about leaving," the article says. "When her young daughter begins to cry, mother Agnes scolds her," it continues, praising the strong will of the "German" mother.

In Berlin, Willie left his three children with cousins who would see to their education. Then he visited a minister in charge of trade with Japan in an effort to win business for his Yokohama company. As he later described the meeting in a letter to the US Occupation authorities in an effort to persuade them he should not be labeled an "enemy alien," he was turned away by the German minister because he had an American brother and because he had Japanese blood. The Nazi regime, he wrote, "treated Eurasians in the same manner as Jewish people." The war in Europe continued to escalate as Willie headed home to Yokohama in July 1941.

Richard, who stayed behind in Yokohama with his mother and sister, recalled being pleased by the news of war, because it meant his strict father, Willie, might not come home to Yokohama. "It's not a nice thing to say, but he was that strict." Once when his father found the water running from the garden hose, Richard recalled, his father had forced two of his brothers to whip each other until one of them finally confessed to the crime.

At the end of July 1940, not long after Willie left for Germany, President Roosevelt put an embargo on scrap metal exports to Japan, hoping to force the country to pull out of China. A year later, he stepped up the pressure by imposing an oil embargo. Japan had already sacrificed so many of its youth to conquer China and had no intention of retreating. The stage was now set for war in the Pacific.

DAD, THEN THIRTEEN, HAD FOND memories of the summer of 1940 at their villa on Helm Hill. "I spent more time sitting on that pier enjoying the cool breezes, watching the Korean women dig for clams," he once wrote me in a letter responding to questions I had asked about his youth. "My friends and I would play twenty-one for shells all day long." Among Dad's friends were Germans, Armenians, Australians, British, Russians, Americans and Portuguese, but everybody spoke English and nobody cared what nationality their friends were. The foreign community in Yokohama was a place in which a family like the Helms could have brothers of German, Japanese and American nationality and nobody found it any more remarkable, say, than two brothers in New York dividing their loyalties between the Mets and the Yankees.

On September 27, 1940, when Japan signed its tripartite alliance with Hitler and Mussolini, which acknowledged Japan's primacy in Asia, things began to change. The Japanese government began its crackdown. Teahouses and dance halls in Yokohama that offered "Western" forms of entertainment were shut down as decadent. Authorities banned commonly used English words and insisted everyone employ Japanese words to describe objects of foreign origin. Instead of *beruto,* the Japanese pronunciation of the English word "belt," for example, Japanese were now required to use a Japanese term meaning "waist rope."

In October 1940, the American Embassy sent out the first of a series of letters advising Americans to leave Japan. Charles's widow moved to California. Her daughter Lillian, who had married a British man who was also half-Japanese, was turned away in San Francisco because the Exclusion Act prohibited people of certain Asian nationalities from entering the country. The family was forced to live out the war years in Argentina. Her father-in-law, Charles Bernard, the British tea merchant and artist who had lived in Japan most of his life, chose to stay with his Japanese wife, fully aware of the risks he faced.

In Yokohama, a few Germans began to fly swastika flags in front of their residences. Foreigners, who had largely escaped the hand of Japan's increasingly totalitarian state, now felt its bite.

Julie had laughed some years before when his older brother Jim had told him of a visit the family had gotten from the secret police. A neighbor had seen Jim's daughter, Joyce, roll up a newspaper and pretend to use it as a telescope. The police suspected the girl was making fun of the Taisho emperor, a mildly retarded youth, who was said to have peered through rolled up papers during an official ceremony. The police were satisfied when Jim assured them that his daughter would not have dared mock the emperor. Now the military police

visited foreign residences and interviewed maids, recruiting some as spies. Even though Tsuru-*san* had by then left the Helms' employ, the police visited her at her new home where she lived with her husband to ask about Julie.

In spite of the repeated warnings from the American Embassy and the departure of most of his American and British friends by the end of 1940, Julie would not leave Japan. Now the US Embassy warned that it could not take responsibility for American citizens who remained. Friends pointed out that if he tarried, authorities might bar him from leaving because his knowledge of Yokohama harbor could be useful to the enemy in time of war. In the summer of 1941, Julie finally booked passage on the Kamakura-maru, a ship bound for San Francisco. He planned to return to Yokohama six months later after depositing his family in California. He would not return for nine years.

Yokohama's South Pier, ca. 1915.

There is a photo of the family sitting on thick tatami mats laid out along the deck. Julie, Betty and the three boys had their shoes off and sat around a low round table covered with rice bowls, sake flasks and dozens of dishes. Betty is holding a pair of chopsticks and tending to a skillet filled with beef and vegetables cooking over a hibachi. Dad, now

178

fourteen, is wearing a vest and tie, and looks anxiously at the camera. Julius had warned his children that this easy life would come to an end. They would face a different life. They would have to do their own chores, carry their own weight. Dad's youthful face, alone among those at the table, seems uneasy—sensing perhaps that nothing would ever again be quite the same.

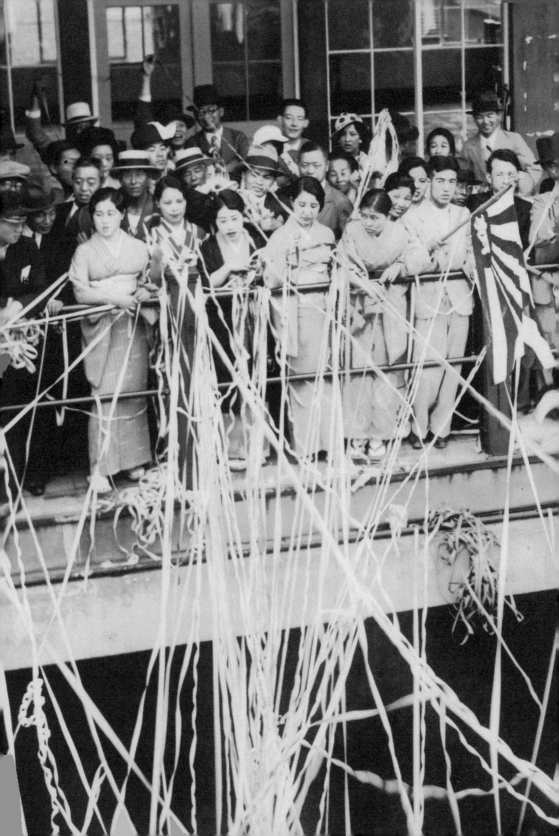

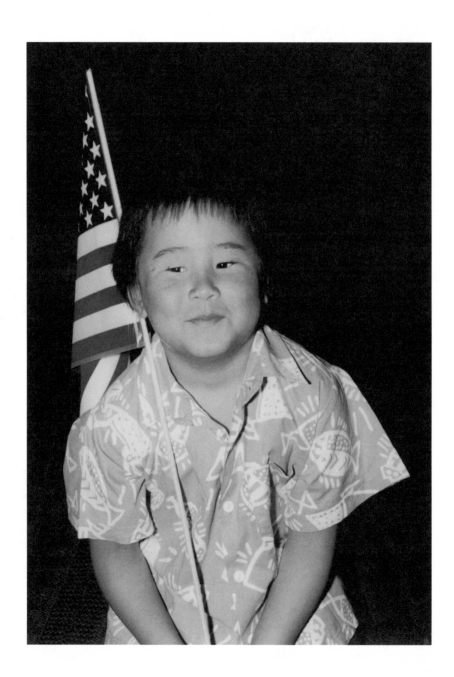

RETURN TO
AMERICA

LIFE WAS FULL IN TOKYO in that first year following our adoption of Mariko and Eric. I still worked long hours, but now would come home to a house buzzing with activity. Marie, who had once worried that children would get in the way of her career, was now on maternity leave and happily absorbed in her new role as mother. When I got home from work, she would be playing on the carpeted floor of our Tokyo apartment with Mariko and Eric while a tape recorder blasted out cheerful Japanese children's songs with bright marching rhythms. Mariko would run to the door to greet me. If I looked tired, she would tilt her head slightly and say, "Are you okay Papa?" When I picked her up, she would hug me so hard her face turned red. Then I would pick up Eric and toss him in the air until he laughed with joy.

Once the children were in bed, I would put my laptop on the dining room table and get back to work. Often, I was still working at two in the morning when it was time to feed Eric. I would lay him on my chest, put the nipple of the milk bottle in his mouth, support the bottle with the crook of my elbow and type my article while he finished drinking. I could feel his chest move as he sucked on the bottle. Often, when I put him back into his crib, I would stroke his fine black hair, moist with sleep. He had long eyelashes that curled up like a girl's, like mine. I thought of his joyous belly laughs and wondered with a pang if he would one day stop laughing, as I had when my father had become a fearful presence in the house. Then, as if to reassure myself, I thought of my father's favorite Sinatra song about the "very strange enchanted boy" who brought to the world a message of love.

In the morning, I kissed Eric on his forehead and then set out for work. I put Mariko on the child seat at the back of my bicycle, buckled her in, put on her helmet and took her to her bilingual nursery school. As I pedaled down the street, I pointed to a car and said, "Red car," and she repeated, "Red car." Then I said, "Big red car," and she would repeat after me, exaggerating the *big* by opening her eyes wide. Mariko was quickly picking up English words, although it wasn't always clear whether she understood what they meant. She liked to sing, "There was a farmer had a dog and Bingo was his name, Oh! B-I-N-G-O." The "Oh!" came out of her as an explosion, as if this was one word she could comfortably pronounce in English. Her favorite song, which she learned from Marie's mother during a visit, was "America the Beautiful," which she would end grandly with "from she to shining she."

Almost every day we had to stop at the train crossing as the red lights flashed and the traffic bar came down. We didn't mind. We liked to stay right next to the bar on our bicycle so that when the train blew past us we could feel the rush of wind on our faces. Mariko would give a belly laugh that grew louder and more joyous with every passing week. The sadness that we saw so often in her eyes in the first weeks after her adoption was now rarely apparent.

It quickly became clear that Mariko had a flair for the dramatic. If you told her something remotely silly, she would open her eyes wide, raise her eyebrows and open her mouth in an expression of total surprise, as if this were the most incredible thing she had ever heard. Then her cheeks would blow up like a chipmunk and she would explode into loud giggles. She loved to wear dresses, and she often stuck out her stomach as if proud of her rounded belly.

I tried to come home early now so I could spend time with the kids. Eric was almost one and walked confidently around our little apartment kicking a small ball. I would pick him up and throw him in the air and feel a thrill as he gave a full-throated squeal of delight. Often I built towers out of blocks just so Eric could knock them down.

The children brought me more joy than I ever dared to hope for. Work, too, was fulfilling. My stories were still often critical of Japan, but my perspective had been subtly changed, grounded not just in logic, but also in empathy.

In May 1993, I learned that Japanese children were getting encephalitis, a serious brain disease, from a vaccine for measles, mumps and rubella, commonly known as MMR. A perfectly safe MMR vaccine was available from a US company, but Japan's Ministry of Health and Welfare wanted to nurture its domestic pharmaceuticals industry and so had decided to distribute a vaccine developed in Japan even though it caused disease, often fatal, in one out of five thousand cases compared to one out of a million for the American vaccine. The story made me heartsick.

One weekend I was invited to a small town in the mountains to give a talk about "internationalism and international relations" to a group of volunteers preparing for the 1998 Winter Olympics. Often I was invited to give such talks. Japanese loved having foreigners present an "outsider's" view of Japan. I knew they expected a speech about how Japanese should do a better job of learning foreign languages and cultures to prepare for the new global age. Instead, I addressed the other side of the same coin: Japanese insularity. If Japanese families found it so difficult to adopt Japanese children just because they were biologically unrelated to them, I asked, how could they ever hope to accept people from different cultures? That evening over drinks, a city official confessed that when he was seven years old, his father told him one day that he would soon move in with his uncle and aunt because they weren't able to have children. The man said he cried so hard that his father decided to send his five-year-old brother instead. This man never got over the guilt he felt after he learned that his younger brother cried through the night for months.

I was disturbed to hear the story and to discover, sometime later, how common such adoptions are among families. At a time when there were still many children in Japan who needed parents, it seemed senseless to tear a small child away from his parents to send to a childless relative.

It would not be long before I would feel the brunt of that insularity—at home. One day while I was giving Mariko a bath, she slid her right hand down her leg. Then she looked straight up at me with her big dark eyes and asked, "Why is my skin so dark?" I froze.

"Your skin is beautiful," I said, trying to be calm. "People with white skin like mine lay out in the sun all day because they want to have bronze skin like yours." She looked at me warily, and I knew she did not believe me.

For a long time Mariko insisted on wearing white tights to her nursery school every day, regardless of how warm it was. I felt stupid that I had not understood before that she had been trying to hide her skin. Marie and I had known that the day would come when Mariko would be conscious of our racial differences, but we didn't think that awareness would come so soon. I thought that because I was part Japanese and we spoke Japanese to Mariko, the differences wouldn't seem so important. I was fooling myself.

Marie and I were also slow to understand fully how oddly the Japanese around us regarded our adoption. I remember laughing when two old ladies stopped to exclaim how cute Eric was. I stopped and let them fuss over Eric, who sat comfortably in a snuggly. As the ladies walked away, I overheard one say to the other in Japanese, "It's a real wonder. I guess babies all over the world look the same."

That didn't surprise me, but what did catch me off guard was that even many of our closest Japanese friends would have trouble understanding our decision to adopt. They acted horrified, as if we had just walked into their houses wearing dirty shoes, breaking the most basic rule of civil behavior.

One Japanese friend I confided in about the adoption joked, "Would you adopt me, too?" A Japanese banker acquaintance was slack-jawed: "What? You're joking, right?" An elderly journalist friend who came over for dinner a few months after we adopted Eric said nothing about the adoption throughout our dinner. Then at the end, he formally bowed his head and said, "Thank you for helping to take care of our [nation's] children."

"We didn't do this for anybody else," I told him. "We did this for ourselves. We did this because we wanted to have a family." He nodded, but was clearly uncomfortable.

My Japanese step-grandmother, Shizuka, expressed most clearly what I came to believe was the typical Japanese sentiment toward adoption when she said to me: "Raising children is so much trouble. I can't imagine why you would want to raise someone else's children."

It was difficult to explain to our friends that Mariko and Eric really were *our* children. Our childless Japanese friends would show a flicker of interest in the idea of adoption when we told them our story, but would quickly dismiss the idea, saying their families would never accept an adopted child. Blood lines are considered important everywhere in the world, but perhaps nowhere as much as in Japan. Even adoption in Japan is typically regarded as a way of maintaining the blood line. The idea of adopting not to keep the family name but for the sheer joy of raising children is an alien concept in Japan. One close Japanese friend said she wanted to adopt, but could not because her in-laws would not accept the child. A public relations official I knew well admitted to me for the first time that he and his wife had been unable to have children. When I asked him why he didn't adopt, he asked some rude questions about my children's biological parents, implying somehow that adopted children would not have the appropriate pedigree.

Once, many years later, we visited an inn in the mountains above Nikko. As we were leaving, the innkeeper looked at me and Marie quizzically, then asked, "So you must be the teachers and they are your students?" This was a ridiculous suggestion since Mariko was nine and Eric, six. Yet, this was the only way she could explain our presence together.

I thought of all the children in the orphanages I had visited who were so desperate for affection. At such times, Japan seemed like a cold-hearted place. Much of the support we received during those months came from the many other foreigners who had also chosen to adopt Japanese children. A correspondent for *The New York Times* had adopted two children shortly before we did, as had my brother Chris. And correspondents from the *Chicago Tribune*, the *Christian Science Monitor* and *U.S. News and World Report* were all friends who adopted Japanese children after being captivated by Mariko and Eric. All of us would get together in Tokyo for Easter egg hunts. Our expatriate friends were islands of comfort in a broader society that seemed cold to the idea of adoption. I had lived all my life as a *gaijin* in Japan, but had never felt quite so excluded from Japanese society as I did with adopted Japanese children.

Professionally, too, it felt like I had hit a wall. I had been very excited when I was the only foreigner to be invited in the spring of 1993 to travel with the Japanese press corps on Prime Minister Kiichi Miyazawa's plane—a new 747 that Japan had purchased to be the Japanese equivalent of Air Force One—for a summit meeting with President Bill Clinton in Washington DC. At first it seemed a great privilege to be included in the inner sanctum of this exclusive press club. At the hotel, I sat at a long table with all the Japanese reporters and ordered the same beer they did. In the press room, we snacked on rice crackers as we posted our stories. But I soon learned I would be excluded from the the prime minister's late night session with the Japanese press. When I insisted on attending, the club held a special session to discuss the matter and agreed I could attend as long as I didn't ask any questions about Miyazawa's meeting with Clinton.

It was time to leave Japan. Marie's university was eager to have her return to teach. My employer, the *Los Angeles Times*, would have preferred I stay in Japan, but had generously agreed to transfer me to the Seattle bureau. Marie and I could not be certain of our family's reception in Seattle, but soon we would find out.

NOT LONG AFTER WE HAD settled back into our house in the Magnolia neighborhood of Seattle, I took Eric and Mariko down to the playground next to Blaine Elementary School. Mariko was quickly playing with the other kids. In the next half hour, I met a couple whose daughter had been adopted in China and a Japanese woman who had moved from Japan with her Caucasian husband in part to find a more inclusive community for her son. As I stood there with these mothers, I felt something inside me relax. We had made the right decision. This was the place to raise our children—a city filled with multi-race families. That deep comfort was reinforced not long afterward when I took Mariko to a ballet class and discovered that one of her classmates had a Chinese-American mother and a white father, while another had a black father and a white mother. Among this wonderful mélange, we would not stand out. When our children grew older, we felt ourselves being welcomed by the community as Mariko joined baseball and Eric joined soccer.

Mariko and Eric were also warmly embraced by our extended families. We spent summers with Marie's family in the mountains of Northern California where Marie's grandfather, a Basque from southern France, had once operated a huge sheep ranch in Red Bluff. Each year at a special "Basque" day, there was a large family reunion at which everybody wore red berets, scarves and played Basque music. At their first such reunion, Marie's sister Rosalie spoke of how Eric and Mariko had "slid down a rainbow and splashed into the family." Each

Home in Seattle, 1993.

of the children were declared Basques and given t-shirts with the word "Basque" written across the front in large letters.

On weekends, we often gathered with the families of my brother Chris and my cousin Barbara, both of whom lived in Seattle and had children of about the same age. Chris's children, Marcus and Brendan, were adopted in Japan and became particularly close to Mariko and Eric. Periodically, we would visit the family of my sister Julie in Colorado, or my sister Andrea in Oregon. We felt lucky to have an extended family so supportive of our children.

For the most part, the issue of adoption hardly came up. Once, though, about six months after returning to Seattle, I was shopping in the supermarket as Eric, then eighteen months old, wiggled impatiently in the shopping cart. He kept raising both arms, asking me to let him down. Finally, I pulled him out of the cart and put him down on the floor. "Stay close to me," I warned. Looking me in the eye with a mischievous grin, he turned and took off, running down the aisle, his belly shaking with laughter. I ran after him, scooped him up and put him back into the cart.

When I looked up from the cart, a thin, tough-looking woman was glaring at me, her hands on her hips.

"What are you doing? Put that child down," she demanded.

"What?" I answered.

"That isn't your child. Put him down."

"What? What do you mean? He's my son."

"Can you prove it?"

Proof? I panicked. What evidence did I have that Eric was my son? My driver's license? No, that said nothing about my children. I didn't have Eric's passport with me. And even if I did, I realized, there was nothing on his passport to show I was his father. His adoption papers would have that information, of course, but they were filed away somewhere at home, and in any case the papers were all in Japanese. I felt helpless and humiliated. I knew I didn't look like my children, but I had always assumed that people could see the strong love that connected us. The notion that this woman could not believe Eric was my son stunned me.

Time stood still as my brain tried to process the absurd circumstance in which I found myself: How was I going to show this woman that I really was Eric's father? It felt as if hours passed, although surely it was only a few seconds. When my mind finally cleared, the answer was obvious: I didn't have to prove anything.

"Does he look like he's being kidnapped?" I finally said, raising my voice to embolden myself.

The lady looked at Eric, who was laughing where he sat in the shopping cart. Then she looked at me suspiciously and walked away. My heart was pounding as I wheeled my shopping cart to the cashier. I was happy that Eric was too young to know what had happened, but the incident had shaken me deeply.

When Mariko would periodically say, "I wish I looked like you and Mama; I wish we were a normal family," I had never taken her seriously.

"What's normal?" I always replied. I would point to friends who had only one parent, others who had two sets of parents and still others who had gay parents. In most respects, we were pretty conventional. But now I understood that logic was no comfort. All it took was one comment from a friend or a sidelong glance by a parent, and my entire argument would collapse. Now I understood how Mariko felt—the jarring sense that no matter how close we felt as a family, others would look at Marie and me and assume we were unrelated to Mariko and Eric simply because we were of a different race. Perhaps that was why

Mariko was so close to Eric. Perhaps that was why they never fought the way so many siblings do.

Marie and I felt that our only defense was to make our children feel special by giving them a strong foundation in Japanese culture. It helped that Teiko, our nanny in Tokyo, had agreed to come and live with us in Seattle for a few years to help take care of the children. Since Teiko spoke to Mariko and Eric in Japanese, both grew up speaking the language. Mariko had refused to speak to Marie and me in Japanese once we had returned to Seattle, so she would have otherwise lost her Japanese. To reinforce their Japanese language skills, we barred them from watching television and restricted them to Japanese videos we rented at a store in the International District. There was *Ampanman,* the bean-cake superhero, *Doraemon,* a magical cat, and *Konan,* the brilliant child detective who could kick a soccer ball so hard it would lay any criminal flat on his back. We also had hundreds of Japanese children's books that we occasionally read to them.

All in all, our transition back to the United States from Japan had gone smoothly. I was happy to find a place where my children were accepted and where I could start to make a new life. Grandfather Julie and his family would find it far more difficult to make that move in August 1941, on the eve of war.

13

"PIEDMONT HELMS: JAPS!"

GRANDFATHER JULIE SETTLED WITH HIS family into a small house in Piedmont, California, in September 1941. Just three months later, the news of the Pearl Harbor attack hit him like a punch to the gut. There had been a great deal of speculation that Japan would attack Singapore or somewhere else in Southeast Asia. Never did he dream that Japan would be so brazen as to attack the United States directly. Now Japan—the country of his mother—and Germany—the country of his father—were allies in a war against the country of which he was a citizen, the United States. Julie quietly went through his house, packing and hiding away all the Japanese dishes, dolls and lacquerware he had on display.

Within weeks of Pearl Harbor, Julie was notified that his assets had been frozen by the US government because of questions about Betty's citizenship.

"I have heard that next month, I will be able to draw one hundred dollars per month, the same as the Japanese," Julie wrote in a letter to his lawyer. "Don't you believe it is unfair to treat me, an American citizen, and my wife without nationality on the same footing with enemy aliens?"

The first time I read the letter, I found it odd. Rereading it several times, finally I realized why. "The Japanese" Julie was referring to were Japanese-Americans. In feeling victimized for being treated as an enemy, it had never occurred to Julie that many Japanese-Americans had lived their whole lives in America, while he had only lived in the country for a few years. It did not occur to him that they were classified as enemy aliens simply because, like he and Betty, they were of Japanese heritage.

Frozen assets, as it turned out, were the least of Julie's worries. Betty had come down with pneumonia and could not leave her bedroom. For the first time in his life, Julie had to cook and clean as he did his best to care for Betty. His substantial investments around the world, including a large investment in a Philippine hat company as well as utilities and industrial companies in Taiwan and Japan, were now worthless. There was little hope of ever recovering anything.

Meanwhile, anti-Japanese hysteria was rising to a fever pitch in the United States, especially on the West Coast. "Goodbye Mama, I'm off to Yokohama for the red, white and blue ... We'll soon have those Japs down on their Japa Knees," went one big band tune recorded nine days after the attack. "We've got to slap the dirty little Jap," went another ditty. Much of the anti-Japanese sentiment targeted Japanese-Americans who, columnists warned, could become a "fifth column" for the enemy. "Open hunting season for Japs. No Limit," was among the signs displayed in shop windows. Japanese were portrayed in newspaper cartoons as buck-toothed monkeys.

Julie kept his head down. He didn't correct people when they assumed he was Latin American. When the US government posted notices in January 1942 demanding that all people with Japanese blood register themselves, Julie ignored the notice.

A month later, President Roosevelt signed an order that would lead to the incarceration of 120,000 West Coast Japanese and Japanese-Americans in internment camps across the American West.

"The very fact that no sabotage has taken place to date is a disturbing and confirming indication that such action will be taken," warned General John DeWitt, commanding general of the Western Defense Command, to justify what the US government called its "resettlement" program.

Fortunately, my Grandfather Julie not only managed to keep his family out of the internment camps, but, with the help of his lawyer, was able to get access to his bank accounts. Still, he was under constant fear of being discovered. He knew the FBI had visited his niece Mar-

YOU'RE A SAP, MISTER JAP

garet in Los Angeles and had an extensive file on the family. How long would it take before the FBI followed that trail to Julie's family and arrested him for the crime of hiding his Japanese blood?

The truth remained a secret for more than a year as Julie and his family went every Sunday to the local church, and as his three boys, including my dad, attended the local school. Then one day in early 1943 two men in suits showed up at Julie's Piedmont house carrying little notebooks. Julie told his kids to go to their rooms and then took the men into the living room. When the men had gone, Julie called my dad and his two younger brothers, Larry and Ray, into the living room.

"People may say some rough things," Julie told the boys, as my uncle Ray recounted many years later. "About what?" asked Dad, then sixteen.

"They'll say we are Japanese," Julie said. "It's a lie. Just ignore it. Remember, we are Americans."

Don Helm at army language school, ca. 1945.

Uncle Ray was not sure if the two men were from the FBI or were newspaper reporters, but not long afterward, as Ray recalled, a local newspaper reported a story about Julie. Bold headlines on the front page of the *Oakland Tribune* read: "Piedmont Helms Japs."

I never did locate the article with that headline, but my family's collective memory of the article is so strong I don't doubt its existence. Still, the article might well have been less prominently displayed than my relatives recall.

Wherever that article appeared, it had a big impact on Dad. The first time he mentioned the article to me more than forty years after Pearl Harbor, he shook his head slowly and looked at me with a stunned, deer-in-the-headlights look. Like me, he had grown up in Japan as a *gaijin*. He never doubted he was American. It must have been a shock then to have his family publicly identified as "Jap"—as belonging to the enemy.

At church, Dad and his family were pleasantly surprised to find their acquaintances continued to socialize with them. But at school things were different. Dad's younger brother Larry remembers that a girlfriend's father warned her to "stay away from that Jap."

"They treated us like we were communists or something," my Uncle Larry recalled. "I got into a lot of fights."

If the FBI had learned of the family's Japanese heritage a year earlier, Dad and his family might well have been sent to an internment camp, but by then the war had turned in America's favor. Few now believed that Japanese-Americans were a threat, and so the FBI may have decided it would be pointless to send another family to the camps. It's also possible, as some relatives claim, that the Helms avoided being sent to the internment camps because they provided US authorities with detailed plans of the harbors in Yokohama and Kobe, information the authorities wanted in planning an expected invasion of Japan. In any case, Julie and Betty got off with a light warning. They were told they had to stay within a ten-mile radius of their home. They were forbidden from crossing any bridges or traveling in the vicinity of any port facilities.

Years later my Uncle Leo, Betty's nephew, revealed that Betty did violate that order at least once. Leo and his brother Ed lived with their mother Gretchen, Betty's sister, in San Francisco. Leo, then fifteen, remembers being told by his mother to put all the family's Japanese heirlooms, including a Japanese sword, into a footlocker and to bury it in the yard. Leo struggled over whether to do his patriotic duty and reveal to the authorities the terrible knowledge that his mother had been born in Japan and that he was part Japanese. He asked for advice from the school counselor.

"You never have to volunteer personal information," the counselor said. "But if you are asked directly, you must not lie."

Leo's brother, Ed, had been accepted to the Naval Academy at Annapolis. Gretchen was so proud of her son she wanted to show him off to Betty, but since people of Japanese heritage weren't allowed into Annapolis at the time, her son would have been expelled if the family connection to the Helms had been revealed. So Gretchen persuaded Betty to come to San Francisco one day and sit at a table by the window of a certain restaurant at precisely half past noon. Then Gretchen took her son, dressed magnificently in his white cadet's outfit, and held his arm as they paraded proudly on the sidewalk in front of the restaurant, walking slowly so Betty could get a good look.

As a teenager, Dad hid his mixed heritage and set out to remake himself as an all-American boy. He joined the swim team and the glee club and played softball. Perhaps he even attempted to do what a relative had once advised: "If you keep your eyes wide open, people won't notice that you're slant-eyed." But even as he was welcomed into the church youth group and was admired for his skill at dancing to the swing music of the time, there was always a part of him that was afraid of what people said behind his back.

In June 1943, after graduating from high school at age sixteen, Dad enrolled at the University of California, Berkeley. As soon as he turned eighteen, he enlisted in the US Army. By then, the Germans were weakening in Europe, but American forces were still fighting the Japanese in bloody battles in Iwo Jima and the Philippines and capturing many prisoners. There was heavy demand for Japanese-speaking officers to interrogate the prisoners, so Dad was sent to the Army Language School at the University of Michigan.

I was always curious about Dad's years in the army. At the dinner table when I was growing up, Dad constantly barked at us about our table manners. "In the army," he would say, as if there were no better authority on matters of etiquette, "if you stuck out your wings [elbows] like that they would get slapped down." Only now do I understand that the army was the crucible that shaped his notions of what it meant to be an American.

198

I received valuable insight into Dad and his time in the army some years ago when my Uncle Ray gave me a black, three-ringed binder full of Dad's letters that his mother, Betty, had saved.

In those letters, Dad did not describe the hard knocks of army life he related to us at the dinner table. Instead, the letters revealed a sense of excitement and adventure and an emerging self-confidence. The letters introduced me to a man I had never known, and I felt close to Dad as I read about his coming of age in the army.

"ARMY LIFE AS I SEE IT is just a glorified Boy Scout camp," my eighteen-year-old Dad wrote on March 21, 1945. "Yesterday we finished our processing and then they worked us like cows. That's right, we were picking weeds around the barracks sunning ourselves: about fifty guys doing a job two men could do in a couple hours of hard work ... For the Laveda show (couple of girl entertainers) I wore full uniform for the first time. Fits fine. Tomorrow I leave California for Michigan."

The Army Language School had originally been located at the University of California, Berkeley, but moved to the University of Michigan at Ann Arbor in 1941. The *nisei* (second generation Japanese-American) instructors were no longer allowed to live on the West Coast because they were considered a security risk. Dad's older cousin David had enlisted two years earlier, and Dad was thrilled to find himself in the same advanced Japanese class as his cousin. David was Jim's son, the baby who had narrowly escaped being crushed by a wardrobe during the 1923 earthquake. Dad was at once impressed and intimidated to learn David was a "brain" who usually placed first or second in the class of 145 students. Dad's Japanese reading and writing skills were weak, but he was good at speaking. "The way some of the fellows chew up the Japanese language is highly amazing," Dad snickered in one letter.

The students took four hours of class each morning and then were expected to study at least eight hours a day after class. They had to memorize fifty kanji characters a day, learning in one academic year a language program designed to be taught in college over three years.

There were a few students like Dad and David who spoke good Japanese because they had been raised in Japan. Most of the language class, however, was filled with students who had been assigned to the program because they had scored high on intelligence tests. Dad was in awe of these "geniuses." He often spoke enviously of one classmate in particular, a man who had a photographic memory and could memorize hundreds of kanji by merely glancing at the complex ideographs.

Illustration for Army Language School graduation dance, December 1945.

For Dad and most of the other students, learning kanji meant making flash cards and studying them at every spare moment, whether they were waiting in line for a movie or eating at the mess hall. Dad's eyes grew so tired reading the characters that the eye doctor ordered him to go easy on the studying. What the eye doctor didn't know was that Dad had no choice: Students were warned that if they scored lower than a B in two consecutive tests, they would be sent to the battlefront. For decades after World War II, many professors of Japanese studies including Donald Keene and Edward Seidensticker, as well as many Japan experts in the US State Department would be drawn from among the graduates of those Army and Navy language schools.

With so many men at war, Dad found himself meeting women who

were both smart and beautiful, and he was inspired to improve himself. "I am on a campaign to educate myself in the line of aesthetics," Dad wrote to his mom. "Art, music and literature."

He was thrilled to be placed in positions of responsibility. "Tonight I'm in charge of quarters, the whole company is sort of resting on me for the whole evening," wrote the eighteen-year-old soldier on embossed United States Army letterhead. "Taking in reports from the various sergeants, making reports to the headquarters etc. My ego just soars to the ceiling and even higher."

When some of his classmates learned Dad had a black belt in Judo and asked him to teach them, Dad organized a class that attracted 150 men. "We did a lot of rolls, and then I taught them some hand tricks," wrote Dad. Cousin David was shy and refused to be the one to demonstrate the various throws. Consequently, Dad wrote, "We have come to be known as the throwing Helm (me) and the falling Helm (David)."

In the spring and summer of 1945, as American troops fought bloody battles in the Philippines and Okinawa on their way to the main islands of Japan, Dad was tucked away in a world of his own. As he wrote home, "Mother dearest, with a wonderful buddy and a swell girlfriend Rita and schoolwork OK, I feel as if I were on top of the world and am very happy."

14

A BITTERSWEET HOMECOMING

JAPAN'S SURRENDER IN AUGUST 1945 was greeted with great joy in Ann Arbor, Michigan. "The dead little town went wilder than I'd ever seen," Dad wrote his mother. "People acted as though they were drunk—everything was just so wonderful. How did you celebrate v-J day?"

Dad's joy was dampened by his concern about Yokohama, which he knew had suffered from fire bombings. How were his friends and relatives in Japan? Had his house survived? What about the Helm business his father and grandfather had worked so hard to build? When he learned that General Douglas MacArthur landed in Japan and established his office in the Hotel New Grand in Yokohama, he stayed close to the radio. "It's good to hear the name of the New Grand mentioned so often," Dad wrote home. "They say the surrounding few office buildings are the only ones left standing in Yokohama. That may mean the Helm House could be still standing."

If Helm House survived, perhaps Dad's many relatives and friends in Yokohama were also safe. But he was right to be concerned. On December 7, 1941, not long after the attack on Pearl Harbor, military

OPPOSITE: Japanese parliament during US occupation, ca. 1946.

General Douglas MacArthur's wife Jean goes shopping in Tokyo.

police had fanned out across Yokohama. Police stood at the train stations and picked enemy nationals out of the crowd. British, Dutch and
Americans were sent to a prison camp on the site of the race track on
the edge of The Bluff where horse races had been held the day Great-
Grandfather Julius first arrived in Yokohama in 1869.

Those suspected of spying were handcuffed and marched off to
prison. Among them was Mike Apcar, Julie's Armenian friend who
police suspected because he was an official of the Masonic Lodge in
Yokohama, which the Japanese authorities considered a subversive
foreign institution.

Unlike World War I, when German prisoners had been treated well
by Japanese authorities, this time many prisoners faced torture. In-
terrogators sometimes pushed wood splinters under their prisoners'
fingernails and lit them on fire. Apcar, tortured and imprisoned for
over a year, remembered how dogs licked their wounds, and did the
same to his own wounds to help them heal.

Walter Helm, Julie's nephew, was also imprisoned and tortured.

Although he held Japanese citizenship like his father Charles, he was suspected of spying because he had had American friends and relatives, and his home in Honmoku overlooked the sea. The Japanese government took control of much of Helm Brothers' assets. Helm House was rented to the German Navy, which used it as its regional headquarters. Willie and his nephew Walter managed to transfer some of the Helm family's assets to a new German company called Gebruder Helm (the Brothers Helm), which he continued to operate throughout the war.

DAD ASSUMED HE WOULD BE shipped to Japan following the surrender, but was crestfallen when he was ordered to spend three more months in class and a month in boot camp for basic training. The University of Michigan campus that fall was transformed by returning soldiers. "There are more men than women for the first time in nearly five years," Dad wrote home. "It seems so strange to see so many husky, good-looking fellows going to college again."

A few weeks later, in mid-October, Dad received the first of three letters from Yokohama that his mother had copied and forwarded to him. They revealed what conditions had been like in Yokohama during the war. The first was from Dad's former French teacher at St. Joseph College, Brother Xavier Bertrand.

Sept 15, 1945

Finally the World War has ended and we are still alive … In the fall of 1943, the police came to tell us that all the foreigners on The Bluff must evacuate. We decided to move St. Joseph (school) in early 1944 into the Park Hotel at Gora in the Hakone Mountains. It took 30 trucks to transport the most necessary and important things. The hotel had no furnace and all were cold. One of the best things about the hotel was the warm baths of mineral water coming from one side of Big Hell [a famous hot spring].

In Nagasaki, the Kaisei School was damaged by the atomic bomb. In Kobe, Father Fage was caught in his burning church and trapped by falling debris. He was burned to death while trying to save the Blessed Sacrament. What a beautiful death for a missionary … Our school in

Yokohama was spared but our neighbor, the sisters [St. Maurs], were burned out …

You did well to leave for America because the [American prisoners of war] were not well treated, especially towards the end. One man, Emery Jones, died there of hunger. [At the end of the war] American fliers let fall forty sacks of supplies for us. One sack went through the window of the old confession room.

Dad was overjoyed to hear his old school was still standing. About two weeks later, he received a copy of a second letter, this one from his Uncle Willie, who could stay in Japan because he was a German citizen.

Oct 24, 1945

Dear Folks,

… In March 1944, authorities ordered all foreigners on The Bluff and Honmoku to clear out. We went to Karuizawa. The good furniture as well as baby grand, phonograph, Frigidaire, washing machine, sun lamp, were placed in our go-down [warehouse] No. 90 in the settlement, which later burned down.

Bud [the nickname for Charles's son Walter] purchased [Julie's] house, which was not in the fortified area and therefore did not have to be evacuated by foreigners. We thought it a good idea instead of any Nip getting it. But on the morning of the 29th of May, practically all of (Yokohama) went up in smoke up to former Miss Ross's house. In the excitement, Bud only rescued his tuxedo, swallow tail suit, still with New York laundry labels, and 85 cents alarm clock. Bud and Willie moved to Helm House.

Although (Japanese) soldiers are back, the Nips seem to be dazed that they lost the war. They ought to work since they have no food to eat; but even if they had money there is no food to buy. On the 24th of August, Nip authorities gave orders for all people living in Helm House to clear out to make quarters for US officers.

I wonder if Dad was disturbed that Willie called the Japanese "Nips" or had he heard such terms so often in the army he had also begun to look on the Japanese in that way? What had it been like going through language school and basic training hiding from friends the reality of his Japanese heritage? In the same letter, Dad learned that his cousin Walter injured his leg at the time he was imprisoned and it became infected. He would have died of gangrene if the war had not ended when it did. Charles Bernard, a British tea merchant whose son married Lillian, Walter's sister, had spent the entire war in a prisoner-of-war camp and would have died of starvation if not for the food his Japanese wife brought to him.

Dad was happy to hear his relatives had come through the war safely and that Helm House had survived. But he was saddened to hear that the Yokohama home he grew up in had burned down.

In January 1946, Dad headed for Fort McClellan, Alabama, for basic training. It was his first time in the South, and he found it surprisingly like Japan with its "pine forests, small farms, marshlands instead of paddy fields and hilly cultivated grounds." The only difference, he noted, was the red dirt and the untidy farmsteads.

At boot camp, Dad was made hut leader, "responsible for all the actions of the new recruits, therein being father, mother, slave driver, servant, timekeeper, referee and guide."

Dad wrote, "You have no idea how raw these recruits are, Many of them talk so tough you'd think they were strong enough to beat Joe Louis." Dad was a skinny boy of nineteen at the time, yet he wrote of how he whipped the new recruits into shape with "a lot of yelling, swearing as I had never sworn before, threatening, encouraging and all the tricks of the trade."

In Alabama, Dad experienced for the first time the tough physical training and irrational demands that are a staple of boot camp. He would take his rifle apart and thoroughly clean it only to be screamed at a few minutes later because dust had already covered the rifle again. He would be sent off on long runs with heavy packs on his back.

I wonder if Dad wasn't a little embarrassed for complaining about the treatment after receiving a letter from John Schultz, a slim, sixteen-year-old mixed-race boy with wavy brown hair and freckles who had been a schoolmate of Uncle Ray and Dad's at St. Joseph College. Had he stayed in Japan, Dad could have suffered John's fate.

John lived with his Japanese mother and sister, about a fifteen-minute walk from Dad's house in Yokohama. His American father had left the family and returned to the United States shortly before the war. John sent his letter from the home of his aunt in Renton, Washington, written in broken English.

John had been close to starvation when American troops found him and put him on a boat to San Francisco. "I'm eighty-five pounds, about three times the size of turkey," he wrote. Schultz described how food grew scarce in Japan as the war dragged on. "In 1942, even the fish and vegetables were rationed. In 1943 they gave us half of the food what we need. In 1945, we could not get anything. The fishermen did not go out to fish because they were afraid of the submarines and seaplanes. The government even tell the people to throw out all the jazz records or be punished. They said that they cannot fight against America when they are listening to the American music."

One day, when John was still fourteen, a Japanese policeman arrested him for walking near a beach considered a security area. John was beaten so badly he was bedridden for more than a week.

Then on May 29, 1945, the B-29 bombers roared over his house. John wrote: "The air raid began at nine o'clock in the morning and finished at eleven o'clock. Two hours after, there is no more Yokohama left. Americans dropped average of two bombs for every people of Yokohama. For me I got one extra bomb. We got three of the hundred pounds incendiary bombs into our house. I think you know how small my house was."

In the chaos, John lost sight of his mother and sister, and spent the whole night looking for them. He found their bodies the next morning in a canal where they had gone to escape the fire, only to be asphyxiated by the smoke.

"That day, I can't even understand what the people are talking about, because I lost my mother and sister at once. The word that I cannot forget was the neighbor who told me that 'Your mother and sister must be glad because they were killed by the American bombs.'"

I wonder how Dad reacted to that letter. He used to tell us as children that America's firebombing of Japan's civilian population ranked with the dropping of the atomic bombs on Nagasaki and Hiroshima among the most heinous acts ever committed. The American forces used weather forecasts and detailed maps to calculate the best conditions for creating a firestorm that would kill the most people. They knew Japanese houses of wood and paper would quickly burn. But for maximum damage, they waited for dry days when the winds were heavy before sending out the B-29 Superfortresses to drop their giant drum cans.

"The drums would crack open in the sky, and it looked like tin cans were falling out," said one of Dad's friends who lived through the bombings. Those "tin cans" were the size of steel milk jugs and packed with jellied gasoline. It was napalm, later heavily used in Vietnam. The napalm was dropped in a circle around heavily populated areas so that the wind and heat drove the people to die in hellholes in the center.

Everyone who lived in Yokohama at the time has stories about what they did when the firebombs fell. Mori Taro, an old Japanese man whose family had worked for Helm Brothers for generations, remembered how he and his sister, as teenagers during the war, were forced to work in a Toshiba factory near Yokohama assembling balloon bombs that were then filled with helium and set adrift, on air currents, to America's West Coast. (Six people in Oregon would be killed by the bombs.) He and his sister were working at the factory when they heard the "death wind" created by the American bombs as they screamed toward the earth. They and the other children in the factory linked their arms while a *yakuza* labor boss led them through the burning city to the safety of a riverbank. He was lucky. Those who hid in their backyard shelters baked to death. The fire was so hot it vaporized the asphalt on the streets. In Tokyo, a witness wrote of "a borealis of horrible beauty that hung over the city and turned the night to day," a description that resembled descriptions by witnesses of the firestorm that followed the 1923 earthquake in Yokohama.

In addition to Yokohama and Tokyo, sixty-five other Japanese cities were burned to the ground. Somewhere between 200,000 and half a million civilians burned to death in what Brigadier General Bonner Fellers, who served under General MacArthur, called "the most ruthless and barbaric killings of noncombatants in all history." General Curtis Le May, the architect of the bombings, later admitted that had America lost the war, he would have been convicted as a war criminal for the people that he, in his own words, "scorched, boiled and baked to death."

WHEN DAD FIRST ARRIVED IN Yokohama in the summer of 1946 after a long voyage from Seattle, the city looked peaceful as seen from the

Grounded battleships still dotted Japan's coastline in 1946.

bridge of the USS Mitford Victory. "At the entrance to Yokohama Bay, we saw ten or so wrecked ships lying idly in the beautiful green waters. A little further on, we came across the cholera fleet, a bunch of ships carrying Japanese soldiers who had been quarantined when disease struck them."

As the ship entered Yokohama harbor, Dad saw the coastline where he had spent his summers. "The sun was in my eyes, but I still could make out the roofs of our [summer] house on the hill and Uncle Charlie's. The trees there looked as pretty as ever and the cliffs were a very familiar sight."

Past the first breakwater, the ship took on an old Japanese pilot who guided it safely into the harbor. Dad could see the Hotel New Grand, the American Consulate and, just behind them, the familiar façade of Helm House with smoke rising from its chimney.

Dad had mixed feelings about the scene he encountered as the ship docked at the pier. "The Japanese coolies, most of whom seemed young boys and old men, swarmed on the quay. The GIs threw cigarettes and candy, and they jumped for them like animals," he wrote. Returning now as an officer in the conquering army, it must have been easier for him to regard these defeated people as less than human.

The following morning, when Dad's unit took a train to a nearby base, he saw for the first time the power of the firebombs. "All around Yokohama station, up through the outskirts of Yokohama and Tokyo where we passed, there wasn't one pre-war building standing—nothing but these huts that had been cleverly put together from the wreckage."

A week later, Dad took leave to visit his German Uncle Willie and his Japanese cousin Walter at their homes on Helm Hill in Honmoku. The area had somehow survived the fires. On his way up, Dad spotted his former cook. "She didn't recognize me even after I called out to her," he wrote his mother. "In fact, I had to convince her and then she cried to beat the band."

It was an emotionally confusing homecoming. Dad was happy to find his German aunts Louisa and Elsie well, but was disturbed by reports that his Uncle Willie had operated a lucrative black market out of the basement of Helm House, where the Germany Navy had been headquartered during the war. Word was that Willie was one of the wealthiest men in Yokohama near the end of the war as a result of his black-market activities.

Then Dad went to see the ruins of his old house, a ten-minute tram ride away. "Bits of pottery and porcelain are scattered all over, my bicycle is twisted and mangled by the fire but somewhat recognizable," Dad wrote his mother.

Thinking of Dad's first days in war-torn Yokohama, I wondered, *Did Dad harden his heart to what he witnessed because he had to believe that America was justified in its actions?* Although he didn't like what had happened in Yokohama, it was easiest to blame the Japanese militarists who had launched a war that had ended in so many deaths. Since the war had begun, Dad had sought to separate himself from Japan, and that must have made it hard for him to feel compassion now for its difficult plight.

Perhaps somewhere deep down, Dad was aware that, but for a quirk of fate, he might have been in John Schultz's shoes. I expect Dad would have resisted that thought. He would have told himself that John was different. He was not *really* an American. John's mother was Japanese,

TOP: Helm House occupied by German navy officers during WWII.
BOTTOM: Helm House occupied by US army officers after the war.

and he lived in a Japanese house. He had that stilted way of speaking English so common among half-Japanese kids.

I believe that was Dad's reaction because, I am embarrassed to admit, it was my reaction, too, when I first read that letter. But in successive readings, it soon became clear how absurd it was that we Helms, because we had the wherewithal to leave Japan before the war, considered ourselves to be different. Dad, who was also mixed blood, could have been John. And John had suffered at least as much as the Japanese. The huge gulf I had always felt existed between me and "the Japanese" was an illusion that generations of Helms had created for our own comfort. It is the knowledge of how long I had deceived myself that makes me cry each time I reread John Schultz's letter.

BETTY, WHO RETURNED WITH JULIE much later in 1949, as soon as the Occupation forces would allow them to enter the country, would suffer from a different realization. She walked amid the rubble that was once her house, picked up a shard of pottery and wept. She understood that it wasn't just her home and her collection of old pottery that she had lost. She lost the Yokohama she had come to know and love with its dance clubs and old-world charm. These were gone forever. In its place was a desolate landscape, a defeated people. Armies of women had been pressed into prostitution to serve their new masters, the US Occupation forces. But in those first years of the Occupation, Betty's son Don would rekindle his love for Japan in a place far from colonial Yokohama.

Looking down on (SASEBO) HARIO REPAT
CENTER FROM LOOKOUT POINT

横浜

LOVE &
OCCUPATION

日南 銀嘯

15

参拾五銭

ALONG THE WESTERN COASTLINE OF the island of Kyushu at the southwestern edge of the Japanese archipelago are craggy promontories that sink their rocky claws into the rough waters of the East China Sea. From that shore extends a chain of tiny islands that seems to exist in a world of its own. The locals call it Kujukushima [the "Ninety-nine Islands"], which is another way of saying "infinity" in Japanese. Perhaps it is the sheer number of uninhabited islands peppering this coast and calming its waters that gives Kujukushima an odd sense of timelessness.

Or perhaps the goddess Izanami, when she created the Japanese archipelago by dropping bits of brine into the ocean from her heavenly spear, gave the spear a final flip at the end, like a calligrapher with a paintbrush, to create this fine spray of emerald islands.

There is an amorphous quality to the landscape: The blue-grey sky, the dark green sea and the dense bluish canopy over the islands all seem to blend one into the other. That posed a challenge for me on a summer day in 2002, when I sat in a motorboat roaring past the islands, scanning the landscape for a familiar landmark. I was looking for an island paradise my father had discovered after World War II and described in long letters to his mother.

As I searched, I was reminded of the haunting Japanese fairy tale about the fisherman Urashima Taro who was carried on the back of a turtle to the undersea palace of the dragon king, where he fell in love with the king's daughter and lived a life of beauty and splendor. Somewhere among these countless islands was such a paradise. There was a palace crowned by an elegantly sloped tile roof perched on a private lake stocked with fish that the palace cook prepared for his fabulous feasts. The island's vegetable gardens produced gourds the size of watermelons, and wisteria blossoms hung from arbors like purple clouds, giving off a fragrance sweeter than lilacs. I knew that on this island paradise lived a beautiful girl of noble birth. I knew all this because my father had taken pictures of that island paradise. He had written letters to his mother about his love for that princess.

I was looking for that small island and the girl who had captured the heart of my father, then a young lieutenant serving in the US Occupation of Japan. Now she would be an old woman, but perhaps we could talk about my father as a young man as we sipped tea and gazed out over the sea. Or so I imagined.

Those post-World War II years were strange times. The Japanese, a people who had once vowed to defend their island to the last man, had unexpectedly welcomed American soldiers onto their soil, if not into their hearts. For Dad, and for Japan, it was a time of glory and of humiliation; joy and heartache; devastation and renewal.

BEGINNING IN JANUARY 1947, DAD spent two years living in a Quonset hut on Hario Island, a speck of land in a large sheltered bay about twenty miles south of the Kujuku Islands. A handsome, dark-haired man with a winning smile that made him look a little like a young Frank Sinatra, Dad had been sent to this distant outpost to interrogate the Japanese soldiers who had been released from Soviet prisoner-of-war camps and brought to this port for processing.

On the day Dad arrived in Hario, he hiked to the highest point on the island to take in the breathtaking views of the bay edged by flats where salt, so precious in those days of scarcity, was harvested from the sea. Rows of barracks along the shore held thousands of Japanese soldiers who had just arrived from the Soviet Union and were waiting to be processed. Dad wrote that the unpainted buildings with their elegant tiled roofs were "like a woman who worries more about her hat than her clothing."

Repatriated Japanese soldiers are transported to shore, 1947.

Dad made his way down to the water's edge and watched as the repatriated soldiers, looking thin and tired, trudged off the rusted die-
sel boats that brought them from the Russian freighters anchored in
the bay. They were the tattered remains of a mighty army that had
conquered most of China. When the Japanese army was already on
the edge of defeat, the Soviet Union, violating its neutrality agree-
ment with Japan, had swept into Manchuria and captured more than
600,000 soldiers, putting them to work in labor camps across Siberia. Now, eighteen months later, they were on their way home.

The job of Dad and his dozen or so fellow officers, as described in
intelligence files declassified in 2002, was "to uncover Soviet agents

Don Helm with actress Takamine Hideko.

among Japanese repatriates for exploitation as double agents." The men were usually quick to admit they had been trained as spies. Some claimed the Soviets had coerced them at gunpoint; others said they pretended to be spies so they would be better fed. They described how the Soviets taught them to hide their radio equipment in the large ceramic pickle jars most families have. Another mission for Dad and his fellow officers, called Project Stitch, was to gather information about the Soviet Union's industrial and military buildup in Siberia.

Perhaps it was during this period that Dad developed the imperious voice that could make policemen tremble. When a Japanese sergeant refused to answer a question, finding it difficult to take seriously this baby-faced boy, Dad would humiliate the battle-hardened veteran with his acid tongue and thunderous voice.

Today, American soldiers, even officers, are often looked down upon in Japan. But during the Occupation, even low-level officers had social status. Dad could order policemen to buy rice and soy sauce for him on the very same black market that American military police were trying to shut down. He could ride the trains free by standing in the front cab with the driver.

The officers often had important visitors. "The other day a couple of movie actresses came into town and of course we had them come over to our place to shoot the breeze," Dad wrote his mother. "Never thought that a Japanese girl could look so pretty. Takamine Hideko by name, quite an eyeful I can assure you." Takamine's fame in Japan at the time was on the order of Doris Day in the United States.

Dad also adopted some of the racist attitudes of his colleagues. In letters to his brother Ray, he referred to Japanese as "gooks." In one of his letters, he mentioned that he was being asked to teach English to his Japanese-American colleagues. He said they spoke "St. Joseph-style English," a reference to the scrambled English and Japanese spoken by many children of mixed parentage at his Catholic high school in Yokohama.

One day in March 1947, Dad must have felt as if he had opened one of those ugly oysters the region was so famous for, only to find in a thousand-to-one odds a perfect pearl. Exploring the coastline, he was invited by a boatman to tour a gem of an island with "cherry trees and large, stately, well-shaped pines." The island had a large inner lake and was owned by a family with a beautiful daughter named Miki. "I went crazy about her toute-de-suite for she was a beauty and her personality developed from a Shanghai life was terrific," Dad wrote his mother.

Miki had been a newspaper reporter in Shanghai and, after the war began, had become a nurse. Dad had craved female company, yet the only women available to him were prostitutes in the nearby port of Sasebo. Most respectable Japanese women disappeared when they saw an American soldier coming.

More than fifty years later, I ventured to Kyushu to find this particular island and Miki. I rented a car in Sasebo and drove north until I saw a sign for the Saikai Pearl Sea Resort, which advertised ferryboat tours through the Kujuku Islands. I pulled into a large parking lot and asked shopkeepers if they knew an island called Fukurogaura, the name my father had mentioned in his letters. Nobody had heard of the island, but one lady suggested I talk to the director of the nearby aquarium.

The director was a young man full of energy. He laid out a large, detailed map on the table and pored over it, but could not find an island of that name. I pulled out a copy of a picture Dad had taken of the place. It showed an island shaped like a horseshoe with the two narrow peninsulas connected by a bridge that looked like a Roman aqueduct with a dam below it. Behind the dam was a beautiful inland lake. On its right was a large, elegant villa. The caption in my father's writing said, "Miki's island."

"Hmm, this looks familiar," the director said. He often went diving in the area to collect sea life for his aquarium. He recalled seeing something that reminded him of the picture. "I'm curious," he said. He had an hour before he had to pilot the next ferry tour and said he would take me to the place in his speedboat.

This area escaped major development, the director told me over the roar of the outboard motor, because it had been a naval base. During World War II, the Japanese navy bombed the smaller islands, many of which are shaped like battleships, for target practice. After the war, the area became part of the large US naval base nearby at Sasebo.

As we approached the island, we came upon thousands of white floats bobbing in the water, and the speed boat slowed. The aquarium director explained that the nets below were filled with oysters into which perfectly spherical grains had been implanted to cultivate pearls. Before the technique was invented, girls would dive down as much as a hundred feet into those dark waters in search of wild oysters and their naturally grown pearls, learning to swim underwater as long as five minutes at a time.

"Look! Over there!" the director said pointing to the tip of a peninsula. He accelerated the boat in that direction, and soon we could see remnants of a Roman aqueduct-like bridge, now in ruins. On the northern shore where the mansion should have been, however, there was only jungle.

We tied up the boat and made our way up the embankment and into a thick jungle. As we walked, it became clear that this vegetation was part of a garden grown wild. Wisteria vines as thick as my thighs wended their way like snakes through ancient cherry trees, chest-high azaleas and massive rhododendrons. Soon we came upon a sunken outdoor bath made of rock and tile. And just beyond that, we could see the house that was in my father's picture, now hidden by overgrown trees. When we slid open the glass front door and looked in, we stood silently for a few minutes. There was something very sad and haunting about the place. The elegant sweep of its massive tiled roof had caved in at several places. The wood floors, once polished to a shine by the soft shuffling of *tabi*-socked feet, were now covered with shards of glass and tile. Broken *shoji* doors were scattered across a rock garden in the

224

Don with Miki.

THE SHINOHARA'S & MIKKI

MIKKI SHINOHARA

OYSTER DIGGING

MRS. SHINOHARA - SHE RAN THE ISLAND

HIKARA DESUNE

OFF LIMITS AYASHI TOKORO RASHII

small courtyard. I wondered what terrible thing had happened to make the inhabitants of this beautiful island leave.

IN THE SPRING AND SUMMER of 1947, Dad fell in love with Miki, a woman who had the oval face, the full mouth and the well-shaped nose of a classic Japanese beauty. Dad's photo album was filled with pictures of her: Miki rubbing suntan lotion on his back at the beach; Dad and Miki standing on a hill, the wind blowing through Dad's *yukata;* Dad in uniform next to Miki in front of a large rock memorial; and Miki in wood clogs gathering oysters. There were also photos of Miki's stern-looking mother with the caption: "She rules the island." Other pictures depicted the friendly cook, the vivacious sister and the happy boatman with his three apple-cheeked children. There were no pictures of Miki's father. It seemed as if Dad were a young prince, brought there to fill the throne as lord of the island.

Periodically, however, the army sent Dad to other parts of Japan, so he could take a hand in America's mission of building a democracy. In May 1947, Dad and a couple of his buddies were sent to a small town near the port to supervise a local election. "Of course we had to meet the mayor and the chief of police and all the town officials," wrote Dad. "They treated us as though we were the emperor himself. They gave large feasts in our honor, geisha parties and so on." Dad wrote of beautiful sulfur springs and the blind masseuse who would work his back for an hour in exchange for half a pack of cigarettes. Dad spent a few days supervising the polling booths and reported that everything was in order.

After the war, the US military kept largely intact the pre-war Japanese political system and bureaucracy in order to make it easier for the US to rule the country. Japanese officials quickly learned that if they kept American officials happy, they could still run Japan pretty much as they wanted. In the villages, democracy was used to give legitimacy to old village leaders.

In the city, Japan used cruder means to keep the Americans happy. Just days after the emperor announced Japan's surrender, the Japanese Home Ministry established a "Recreation and Amusement Association" which, in the name of patriotism, recruited tens of thousands of Japanese women to work as bar hostesses and prostitutes serving

American soldiers. The association established dance halls, cabarets, hotels and brothels. In Maizuru, another port where Dad was sent to interview repatriated Japanese soldiers, local officials established a dance club for the soldiers. On opening night, the authorities invited officers along with some of the city's young women. "They were all from good families, danced well on the whole, were very pretty, and we all had a jolly good time," Dad wrote. "The chaperones were even worse than American ones but we sang the girls 'Goodnight Ladies' as they were carted away on the bus."

Dad found it difficult interacting with everyday Japanese the way he had done growing up as a child. His American uniform identified him as a member of the Occupation—someone who was a potential source of valuable cigarettes and whiskey, but could also be a source of trouble. Once when he was on duty, Dad heard the faraway sound

of drums. It was a dance celebrating the *obon* festival of the spirits. He wanted to join the ring of dancers making their way around the platform on which the drummers performed. He wanted to dance as he used to as a child, but he was sure the Japanese wouldn't feel comfortable having an American soldier in their midst, and so he quietly went home.

Dad was happiest back in Hario, where he could retreat to his island paradise. He loved the lavish feasts Miki's cook always prepared. "Fresh because the fish were alive one hour before. Tasty because the cooks were formerly engaged in serving these things at a big restaurant in Shanghai." And to top it off, there was the pleasurable company of Miki. "Might I say that I am slowly but surely falling for her? She is a corker in every way," Dad admitted to his mother.

When Miki told Dad one day that her family was related to the Japa-

Kusai Kusai

nese Imperial family, he was impressed, but not surprised. Although Miki's mother had the square jaw and tough eyes of a sergeant, she had exquisite manners, always wore elegant kimono and spoke in a highly stylized manner befitting a person of high birth. Dad was also impressed by Miki's sophistication. "Miki discusses the problems of the world intelligently ... all of which is very much opposite to the average protected Japanese girl."

WALKING THROUGH THE DILAPIDATED OLD mansion with the aquarium director, I could easily imagine its former splendor. I could picture servants shuffling up and down these hallways, carrying trays of elegant dishes filled with delicacies from the sea. I could imagine Miki's mother directing the household with a quiet nod here and an occasional frown there. When I told the aquarium director that Dad's letters had spoken of the island family having ties to the Imperial family, he was skeptical.

But on the way back to the boat we came upon a stone monument about twelve feet high that was all but hidden by shrubs. I held the branches back while the director read the inscription carved into the stone: "This is to memorialize the visit of his highness ... of the Imperial family." The aquarium director looked at me with excitement.

"Who would have dreamed you would find a house connected to the Imperial family on this remote island?" he said. "We can make this a stop on our ferry tour of the bay!"

I shared his excitement. I felt as if I were getting close to finding Miki and to learning more about my father as a young man. When we returned to the Sea Pearl Resort, I thanked the aquarium director for his help and gave him copies of my father's photos. Then I drove to the village where the boatman used to pick Dad up to take him to the island.

"The island was abandoned sometime in the 1950s," said an old fisherman who was putting away his gear in a small shed. "They didn't have electricity and running water, you know. It was very inconvenient." I tracked down a woman in a small village who had worked on the island in the early 1950s, but nobody could tell me about Miki.

It was clear from Dad's letters that he was head over heels in love with Miki that fall of 1947. He was writing to his mother asking her to send him books on dancing. He was learning the tango and taking Miki with him to the dance halls in nearby cities to try out new steps. Spending so much time with Miki, I imagine, must have made Dad feel warmer toward Japan. He became more engaged with the Japanese men he was interviewing. In his letters home, he expressed empathy for the returning soldiers and what they endured. Some had been starved and treated as slaves in Dutch-ruled Indonesia. Others had been forced to fight on both sides of the civil war in China.

BEING JAPANESE — COMFORTABLE

The next time Dad came upon an *obon* festival, he joined in the dancing. "It was loads of fun," Dad wrote his mother. "For once the Japanese people are out of their shells and act more like themselves. There were four hundred people around three *taiko* [drums] and several *shamisen* [stringed instruments]. Not drunk, but yet as gay as ever."

During the long winter months of early 1948, Dad found himself more and more disenchanted with the army. He couldn't relate to his army buddies and more frequently succumbed to the magic of the island. He felt at home and happy when he was there. "She is the kind of girl that I would want to marry if she wasn't Japanese," Dad wrote his younger brother. Dad knew that his mother and father would not approve of his marrying a Japanese girl. They did not want Dad and his children suffering the discrimination they had faced.

By the spring of 1948, the Soviets had started treating their Japanese prisoners better and were having better success at indoctrinating them. When the Russian ships came into the harbor, the soldiers would be singing *The Internationale,* the revolutionary workers' anthem. During interrogations, they would refuse to answer questions. The US Army hired Japanese men who had been intelligence agents in the Japanese army and smuggled them aboard the freighters. The agents mingled among the soldiers and singled out the communist ringleaders. Once they were removed and isolated, the rest of the men were compliant. The men were often quick to renounce the Soviet Union, and many became double agents serving US interests.

Dad's assignment would come to an end that summer of 1948, and he was beginning to get impatient. He wondered if he shouldn't be preparing for life after the army. When he was at the island, it was as if his ambition was drained from him. He just wanted to take walks and talk nonsense with Miki. But when he was not with Miki, he dreamed of Paris and all the other places in the world he wanted to visit.

Perhaps it was to keep himself away from the island that he volunteered to be one of six men sent to deliver food and medical supplies to Fukui City, which had been hit by a major earthquake on June 28, 1948. They were trucked overnight to the city where they dug out survivors. "We never had to look far. They were always there—crushed chest, broken spine, broken limbs and flesh wounds," Dad wrote in a letter home. "One became numb to it all working methodically, quickly, but carefully."

Nearly two thousand people were caught in an inferno that engulfed two adjoining theaters; only four hundred people made it out alive. Their charred bodies were pulled out by local firemen and thrown onto carts to be carried away. Everywhere there were cracks in the streets, and broken water mains flooded sections of the city. There was a story of a woman who was walking home from the paddy fields when the earth swallowed her up to her chin. The ground closed again, crushing her. The story, only a day old, was already told as if it were just one more tale in the long chronicle of tragedies the town had endured.

Fukui had suffered more than any city should. Five years before, the city's main shopping district had burned down in a fire. In 1945, the city had been destroyed again by American firebombs. Now this earthquake. Yet each time, the people cleaned up and went on with their lives.

Dad admired the people of Fukui for their strength, but it seemed to him that their lives were a hopeless struggle. He wanted to get away from Japan. His plan was to finish college, enter the Foreign Service and travel the world. Miki and the island would not fit into those plans.

MANY YEARS LATER, I TOLD my mother about my visit to the island and about Miki.

"Oh, her?" Mother said. "She must be the girl that Dad used to talk about. Whenever we went to see *Madame Butterfly*, he would always cry. He always felt guilty about making her get an abortion."

An abortion? I felt disoriented. The child, if born, would have been my brother or sister. Dad was twenty years old at the time. How would he have reacted to the news of the pregnancy, and why had they chosen to abort the child?

Perhaps he was concerned that his mother would disapprove of Miki. Or perhaps he concluded that she did not fit into his life's plan. In either case, his father, Julie, had always spoken about taking responsibility for his actions. I suspect Dad was ashamed of himself for taking the easy way out.

Dad escaped to Paris. He fell in love with another girl, this time a blond Swede who refused to follow him to the United States. By the time he returned to college at UC Berkeley, he had lost much of his early swagger.

Dad's broken relationship with Miki may have also colored all his views of Japan, for in some strange way, the island had come to represent everything that he loved about Japan. On the island he had experienced the joy of a Japan not consumed by the horrors of poverty and humiliation. There was the elegance of the house and the people, the simple happiness of the boatman's family, the wonderful fruits of the sea. With the abortion, Dad may have felt he had besmirched the island, and in doing so, his image of the nation and its people.

As I thought about the tragedy of Dad's relationship with Miki, I was reminded of the end to the old folk tale about the undersea palace. Urashima Taro, growing tired of his long stay in that undersea kingdom, decided to go home. When he left, the princess gave him a box.

"Do not open this box," the princess said. "For as long as you have this unopened box you can return to this kingdom." The turtle took Urashima Taro back to the beach from which he first came, but he no longer recognized anybody in the village. Feeling lonely and forlorn, he sat down, untied the silk cord around the lacquer box and removed the lid. A cloud of pink smoke came out. When he next looked at his reflection in a pond, he discovered he had turned into an old man. During his life of pleasure in the undersea palace, three hundred years had passed. The lacquer box had preserved those memories, frozen in time. Now that he had released them, he could never return. I wonder if Dad didn't feel he had lost his innocence on that island, his sense that anything could happen if only he let it.

Sometime after my visit to the island, I received a magazine clipping from the aquarium director. It was an article about the island and its Imperial connection. There was a sidebar about my search for the island "following in his father's footsteps." The article was illustrated with my father's picture of the island.

Soon afterward, I received an e-mail from Tomimura Hideaki, a young man who had just graduated from a junior college in Seattle. His family had once owned the island, but they had no pictures of it. He wondered if I would send them a copy of the picture. I was intrigued. I asked him if he knew anything about Miki and her family. He said he would look into it.

That summer, a year after my first trip to the island, I flew with Hideaki to meet the Tomimura clan in Sasebo, a half-hour drive from the Kujuku Islands. Hideaki found cheap, luxury accommodations at Huis Ten Bosch, a $3 billion replica of a Dutch town that had been completed five years earlier to help boost the local economy, but was having trouble attracting tourists. It had a life-sized clock tower, a brewery and a cheese factory—all made of stone like the buildings in the original Dutch town. There were canals and windmills, acres of tulips and an authentic nineteenth-century ship that had sails as well as a steam-powered side wheel, like the *Golden Age* on which my great-grandfather had first traveled to Japan in 1869. There were hundreds of houses for sale built along Venice-like waterways in this fake Dutch town.

At an exhibit showing the history of this town, I saw something that set my head spinning. There was a picture of a series of huge barracks in an otherwise beautiful valley at the edge of a bay that looked exactly like one of my father's pictures. Suddenly it struck me: This fantasy town had been built on the site of one of Japan's saddest and most humiliating events: the repatriation of Japanese soldiers. It was near here that my father had worked for nearly three years, interrogating soldiers. This strange effort to revitalize Kyushu's ailing economy seemed to me like an expensive attempt to erase a past nobody wanted to remember.

That night, I was invited to a banquet at a Chinese restaurant where twenty or so members of the Tomimura clan gathered in my honor. They thanked me for bringing the family together by rediscovering the island. They were an eccentric family. They had made their riches running a soy-sauce brewery. Hideaki's grandfather took ballet lessons in a studio he built over the soy-sauce factory and later moved to Tokyo because he felt he didn't fit in the little village. I asked everyone I met about the family that lived on the island when my father was there, but nobody seemed to know anything.

Many cups of sake later, I was talking to an elderly man when he looked at me coolly and replied. "Sure, I knew them."

During the war, the Tomimura family had used the island as a summer home, the old man explained. They often entertained members of the Japanese Navy's top brass, one of whom was an admiral, a member of the Imperial family. The stone monument on the island was erected in his honor. Toward the end of the war, Sasebo was fire-bombed and virtually the entire city burned down. The Tomimura family lost their home. By some strange fate, there was a woman, recently returned from Shanghai, who lived in a house that survived the bombing.

"The woman was a geisha, you know, a woman of the floating world, the entertainment world. She was very good at business," the man said. "I assume she heard about how we used the island to entertain Japanese naval officers and decided it would make a good business for entertaining American soldiers. She made this deal with us. We would move into her house in the city. In exchange, we would let her use our island."

"What about the daughter, Miki?" I asked.

"The daughter? I don't know. Maybe she was the geisha's daughter. Maybe she was the cook's daughter. Maybe the cook and the geisha were married. They were running a fancy restaurant in Shanghai when the war ended. They must have come with the first boats that brought refugees from China. When the Occupation wound down, I guess their business on the island fell apart. One day they disappeared. When we went to inspect the house, we found they had stolen all the copper gutters. They probably sold them for scrap."

Later that night, a few of the men took me to a nearby bar. The owner, a woman with a heart-shaped face who looked twenty-five but was clearly older, served us whiskey and water. Her enchanting smile and easy conversation pulled us into a cozy circle. She flattered me in a gentle way that relaxed me and made me feel smart and witty. I felt as if she were an old girlfriend who knew my deepest secrets. The way she moved her hands gracefully as she talked, her musical laugh when someone made a joke, put me in a trance. She was no geisha—but she had the alluring talents of a woman of that world.

I wondered what it must have been like for my father to have a woman like this catering to his every desire. Dad said Miki had so much in common with him. Perhaps Miki, like a chameleon, had merely adjusted her personality to match his. She had made herself the kind of sophisticated woman she knew Dad would love by claiming to have been a newspaper reporter and a nurse. Miki turned the island into a paradise in which Dad truly felt like a lord. Dad never learned that the island paradise was as ephemeral as Urashima Taro's undersea palace.

16

MOTHER &
THE BLIND
PROFESSOR

IN THE FALL OF 1950, after studying in Paris on the GI Bill, Dad returned to classes at the University of California, Berkeley. He was part of a small group of students in Professor Robert Scalapino's class on Japanese politics who hung out together that included Hans Baerwald, who later taught at the Univesity of California, Los Angeles, and Ogata Sadako (nee Nomura), who would later serve as the United Nations High Commissioner for Refugees. At coffee shops they railed against the McCarthy-era loyalty oaths their professors were being forced to sign. They played pingpong at the student union and ate noodles at a Japanese restaurant. They established "The Society for the Preservation of Parlor Games," a fancy name for the parties where they played charades. Most were BIJs (Born in Japans), but there were also several who had attended the Army Language School during the war.

Among them was my mother, Barbara Schinzinger, an attractive twenty-four-year-old German with dark, frizzy, shoulder-length hair, high rounded cheekbones and an infectious laugh. Her English was so good the others never thought of her as German.

Mother was particularly attracted to two of the men, both BIJs. One was a blonde, gregarious boy who had been raised in Japan by mission-

OPPOSITE: Robert Schinzinger and daughter Barbara.

ary parents. The other was a shy boy with dark, baby-faced good looks. When the blonde boy came down with mononucleosis halfway through the semester and was forced to stay in bed for a few weeks, it was left to the shy one to drive Mother home from a dinner at Professor Scalapino's house. That was when he finally gathered the courage to ask her out. The shy one was Don Helm, my father.

Mom found Dad smart and urbane. He was interested in art and literature. She loved the fact that she could speak to him in French as well as Japanese and English. But what she found particularly alluring was something sensitive, even vulnerable, about him. She liked how, on their first date to a symphony concert, Dad placed his hand over hers, as if by accident.

When Dad brought Mom home to have dinner with his parents in Piedmont, where he was still living at the time, she liked the way Dad and his two brothers sang in harmony as they washed the dishes. She liked his parents, Julie and Betty, and was impressed by how well-read Betty was, even though she had never gone to college.

Betty loved Mom, too, and for Dad that was the best endorsement. My dad saw my mom as an intoxicating concoction of the innocent and the intellectual, the humorous and the adventurous. Charming and articulate, Mom represented to Dad the best of his new American life. Mom loved to tell stories of the world around her that she found ironic or amusing. She loved to talk of the two young women she worked for in Santa Barbara when she first arrived in America. They claimed to be close to the Eisenhower family and insisted on formal dinners each night at which Mom had to serve them dressed formally with a white towel hanging over one arm. Her laughter was never at the expense of another. If Dad teased Mom, she didn't take offense. She simply laughed with him and Dad felt witty instead of mean.

There was something at once endearing and naïve about Mom. The ear for speech that helped her pick up so many languages also led her to adopt some of the slang Dad had picked up in the army. One day, Dad was looking over Mom's shoulder as she played a game of solitaire when he was shocked to hear her say to herself: "This son-of-a-bitch goes here, and this son-of-a-bitch goes there."

In less than two months, Barbara and Don were engaged to be married. They were similar in many ways. Both were of German heritage and both were born and raised in Japan. And yet, Barbara's experiences in Japan could not have been more different. Where the Helms, over three generations, had built a successful business and grown up regarding Japanese as their employees and servants, Barbara's family lived among the Japanese as neighbors and friends. Her father, Robert Schinzinger, whom I called Opa, interacted with Japanese intellectuals both as a student of Japanese philosophy and culture as well as a teacher of German philosophy and literature. He wrote a German-Japanese dictionary that came to be widely used both in Germany and in Japan. Whereas the Helms had consciously separated themselves from Japanese society and often felt alienated from it, Robert, as a teacher and scholar, found a comfortable place in society and was respected for it. Novelist Mishima Yukio was one of his students. Many students, among them Nakayama Shozen, the head of Tenrikyo, one of Japan's largest Buddhist sects, would continue to send Robert gifts for decades after they had graduated from his class. As a journalist traveling through Japan, I constantly ran into people in important positions who had been students of Robert's, and without exception, they loved and respected him. I took special pride in Robert being my beloved Opa.

I remember Opa as a tall, thin man whose shoulders always seemed hunched over, perhaps from having to bend down each time he passed through a doorway or perhaps because of the many tragedies he had experienced: He was virtually blind as the result of a childhood disease; had lived through two world wars; lost three homes, one each to flood, bombs and fire; and suffered through the early death of his wife. Opa had a bottlebrush moustache that turned downward with the corners of his mouth, and it always made me think he was a little sad. During his lifetime, he had seen mankind engage in horrible deeds. It seemed to me that his philosophy was simple—if you didn't expect too much of the world, it was less likely to disappoint you. He had a quiet confidence I envied. His laugh was so warm and infectious, and so lit up his dour face, that I always wanted to say something funny just to hear it.

Robert Schinzinger arrived in Kobe from Germany by ship via the Suez Canal on September 3, 1923, two days after the Kanto earthquake had destroyed most of Yokohama and Tokyo, 260 miles to the east. His tropical tan silk suit, which he had just had tailored in Hong Kong, looked smart on his tall, thin frame. His blue eyes were the color of the sky and his blond hair was brushed straight back. In a photo, his long arms were wrapped around his wife, Annelise, whose

Robert Schinzinger with wife Annelise.

unruly, dark, frizzy hair was tied in a ponytail at the back. Annelise had always been a self-assured young woman, but the separation from her family in Germany had been hard on her and she often brooded, as Opa recalled in his unpublished reminiscences, *The Mosaic of My Life*. Annelise now tilted her head back to look up at Opa. She smiled and Opa kissed her on the lips.

They looked down from the ship's deck onto the bustling pier below: coolies loaded bags onto handcarts; rickshaw men wended their way through the crowds; a uniformed chauffeur helped a kimono-clad woman into an automobile; men in Japanese garments wore bowler hats.

Opa had taken his doctorate in philosophy, studying under such luminaries as Karl Jaspers and Martin Heidegger. Opa's father, an attorney, married the daughter of a wealthy industrialist, but he himself rarely had money because he looked down on his rich merchant clients, making it hard for him to retain their business. When Opa needed money to print three hundred copies of his dissertation, a requirement for getting his Ph.D., he turned to his rich Uncle Albert. This eccentric man had made a small fortune representing Krupp, the German arms company, in Japan. On his return to Germany, Albert had become the honorary Japanese consul general in Berlin. It was while visiting Albert's three-story mansion in Freiburg named Villa Sakura and seeing his Japanese antiques that Robert first became enamored of Japan. When he was unable to find a job in Germany's inflation-wracked economy, it was Uncle Albert who found him a job teaching German in Japan.

Opa and Annelise found a Japanese house far from Kobe's foreign settlement. Their large shipping crate, which contained a brass bed, a brand new Junker & Ruh coal-burning stove, dishes, table linens, bed sheets and dozens of boxes of books, arrived on the back of a horse-drawn wagon. The name on the side of the wagon amused Opa because it was a German name: Helm Brothers Ltd.

Opa had intended to follow a career as a serious philosopher, so it must have been hard for him during those first few weeks teaching at an elite high school for the sons of the wealthy. They talked incessantly and refused to listen to what the teacher had to say.

I learned about those tough early days for my Grandfather Schinzinger at an unusual gathering I was invited to in 1992 by an alumni group that called itself "The Association of Those Who Sing the Songs

Taught by Professor Schinzinger." They paid my way from Tokyo to Osaka so I could attend the fiftieth anniversary of the closing of their elite high school, which had been shut down at the end of the war. The reunion was a lavish one held in a giant ballroom. Many of the men wore their old school uniforms: the stiff, full-length skirts once worn by samurai, black capes and black caps. They gathered around an artificial bonfire and sang old military songs. Later in the evening, the whole ballroom fell silent as the master of ceremonies called on a very special association to come to the stage: It was the association that had invited me. The men who walked to the stage included retired doctors, lawyers, professors and chief executives. The youngest was 82. When they started to sing, the power and sweetness that came from those aging vocal chords took my breath away. The men sang, in good German, old folk songs about apprentices traveling in the countryside, bird songs and sweethearts left behind.

"Your singing was wonderful," I said to one of the men when he came down from the stage. Then I asked him what he remembered of Opa, who had died a few years earlier.

"When he first came to teach us, we were unruly. Nobody listened to him. The professor never raised his voice. One day, he stopped talking and just started to sing softly. We quieted down because we were curious. The songs were so beautiful, we asked him to teach them to us.

"The songs I learned from Professor Schinzinger were my lifelong treasure," said the student, who, half a century later, had helped found the association to sing those songs again and to remember those good times with Opa.

As a teacher and philosopher, Opa found his identity in translating Japanese philosophy for German readers and explaining German philosophy and culture to his Japanese students. Over time, he found it increasingly difficult to express pride in his country. Annelise learned in 1933 that her brother had been denied a job in the German government because of his Jewish heritage. Annelise's great-grandfather, Ludwig Binswanger, had been born Jewish before he converted to Christianity when he migrated to Switzerland from Germany after the revolution of 1848 and started a sanatorium to treat nervous disorders. Annelise's uncle, also Ludwig Binswanger, took over the sanatorium and maintained an active correspondence with Sigmund Freud. Binswanger offered Freud a place to stay when it became clear in 1938 that Jews would be targeted in Austria as they had been in Germany. When Annelise's father, a longtime government official, learned that his son could not enter the German civil service, he committed suicide by jumping into the Rhine.

Opa's brother had also suffered under the Nazi regime. He had been a leader in a German youth group, and when he complained of the way the group was being politicized, he was accused of being a homosexual and imprisoned.

By the spring of 1934, Nazi influence pervaded the German community in Japan as well. Opa was forced to resign from the board of the Association of Foreign Teachers when Nazi colleagues were offended by an article he had written.

Yet, as much as he hated the Nazis, Opa felt it was his duty to continue to teach his students about the "true" Germany, the home of Kant and Goethe. Opa and Annelise decorated their Japanese house with valuable heirlooms from Germany and invited Opa's Japanese students so they could experience what a good German home was like. For Annelise, the house represented a piece of the old Germany she once knew. She served her Japanese guests with china she received as her dowry and linens from her mother-in-law and old Rhineland wine glasses inherited from Opa's mother's wealthy family. A philosopher visiting Opa from Germany compared the home to Goethe's *gartenhaus*.

In 1938, toward the end of the rainy season, it poured for three days and three nights ceaselessly until the earth and mountains above Kobe were saturated with water. The little stream next to Opa's *gartenhaus* became a turbulent river.

A few days later, an old lady who lived nearby knocked so violently on their kitchen door that the glass window broke.

"Come out quickly, the water is already underneath your house!" the old lady shouted.

Annelise and Opa grabbed a few clothes and evacuated to the old shrine nearby. Their maid, fearing the worst, quickly threw the silverware in a tablecloth and brought it along. Fortunately, the children were at school. Suddenly Annelise realized she had left behind the dog and the children's new shoes. She ran back to the house before Opa could stop her. She retrieved the shoes but the dog was nowhere to be found. Then she ran back to the shrine. She had barely reached her husband's side when he saw the first wall of their house collapse under the power of the rising water.

Opa didn't think the shrine was safe enough, so they climbed over fallen trees to higher ground. On the way, they met a teacher from the Catholic middle school.

"How is your house?" the priest asked.

"It is sailing away toward the ocean," Opa replied.

The rain stopped as suddenly as it started. It wasn't until the children had located their parents and had learned that the dog was dead that they started to cry.

Everybody was supportive. Japanese and foreign friends put the Schinzinger family up in their cramped homes and offered them blankets and second-hand clothes. Annelise found one brown dress that seemed in particularly good condition, but she mourned the loss of all her German belongings, the things that connected her to her family and home, which she missed every day. For Opa, the biggest loss was all the files he had carefully compiled for a challenging translation of the works of Nishida Kitaro, a leading Japanese philosopher.

The flood was just the first of worse things to come. Not long afterward, Opa was standing in front of the post office when he read the bulletin: "Hitler marches into Poland." Although many of his German colleagues in Japan were excited at the prospect of war in Europe, Opa had seen the horrors of World War I. He was seventeen when he was drafted, and because of his blindness, sent to work as a medical orderly at a big military hospital in Frankfurt. "One of my duties was to take the corpses of the dead soldiers on a black pushcart to the dissecting room where the attendant didn't treat them any better than a butcher treats slaughtered cattle," Opa would later recall in his memoir.

Although Opa and Annelise hated the Nazis, they did not want their children to be isolated from their friends, so they allowed Barbara (my mom) and her younger brother, Roland, to take part in the German Youth, the local variant of the Hitler Youth. In deference to their host country and ally, Japan, the organization allowed part-Japanese members. In Germany, only pure Aryans were permitted in the Hitler Youth. Mom loved the youth group with its handsome uniforms and camp trips. Her father tried to counteract the propaganda taught by the leaders of the German Youth. If the children repeated something they had heard about "evil Jews," their father would say: "Our friend so and so is a Jew. Do you think he is evil?"

Years later, Opa would reflect on that time and ask, Was that enough? Anybody who outlived the war had somehow found a way to save his own skin. "As Karl Jaspers had once suggested in his book *The Question of German Guilt*," Opa wrote, "it may simply have been impossible to live through Hitler's horrible regime and not share in the guilt." At heart a pragmatist, Opa did not believe in sacrifice for the sake of sacrifice. And the full horror of what the Nazis were doing in the death camps may not have yet reached Japan.

And yet I cannot escape feeling Hitler's evil touched my mother. There is a picture of her at age fifteen that appeared in the May 1939 issue of the *Berliner Illustrierte,* the German equivalent of *Life* magazine, next to a picture of a young Princess Elizabeth (later Britain's Queen Elizabeth II) in a swimsuit.

Mother had just won the gold medal for the hundred-meter sprint in the Kobe Junior Olympics. Her dark, wavy, shoulder-length hair was pulled back and tied in a thin ribbon. She had a small rounded chin and a prominent, but nicely-shaped nose. She wore a carefree smile as she leaned forward, arms outstretched, to receive a large glass case containing a Japanese doll. Mother was wearing dark shorts and a white, polo-style shirt buttoned up to the neck. Prominently printed

Die Siegerin im 100-Meter-Lauf: eine Deutsche — der Siegespreis: eine japanische Puppe.

In Kobe fand ein Jugend-Olympia statt, an dem Jungen und Mädel von 31 Nationen teilnahmen. Nach feierlichem olympischem Zeremoniell wurden die Sieger verkündet und die Preise verteilt. Statt der Gold-medaille gab es aber für die Siegerinnen .. kunstvolle japanische Puppen.

on the center of her shirt, between her youthful breasts, was a swastika. Mom had unknowingly become a poster child for the Nazis.

In Japan, my mother insists, the German Youth was like Girl Scouts. But one of my mother's friends recalls singing "Deutschland Uber Alles" ("Germany Over All") and giving the Hitler salute during German Youth meetings.

In 1942, Opa was offered a position as a professor teaching German at two of Japan's top institutions, Gakushuin and the University of Tokyo. Annelise worked as an editor for *The 20ᵗʰ Century*, a German journal published in Shanghai that avoided Nazi propaganda. As a teenager, my mother attended the German school in Tokyo. One day, she heard sounds in the sky and looked up to see unfamiliar planes. "Those are American planes," a classmate said knowledgeably. They were B-25s engaged in the Doolittle Raid, a strike that would cause little damage but was a psychological blow to Japan, which believed its homeland was invulnerable. Afterward, Mother's family was asked to participate in the neighborhood group responsible for putting out fires in the event of a bombing. When a boy from the neighborhood was sent to war, they were asked to put a stitch in a Japanese flag, one of a thousand stitches which, worn under the shirt, was supposed to protect the soldier.

One weekend, there was a knock on the door of their house in Tokyo. It was a young soldier on leave from China. The soldier had come to thank the family for sending its good wishes along with the stitched flag.

Opa invited the young soldier in for tea, as he recalled in his memoir. The boy entered shyly and sat on the chair at the dining room table. He was not much older than my mother, who was seventeen at the time. When Opa asked him about conditions in China, the boy fidgeted with his hands and rubbed his spine against the back of the chair as if he had an itch he couldn't reach. Then he answered with surprising frankness: "The newspapers say that every soldier dies shouting, 'tennoheika banzai!' (long live the emperor!), but they all die crying for their mothers."

As the war progressed, the schools where Opa taught became military facilities and he was asked to leave. My mother was sent to a family to do her compulsory six-month service as a housekeeper, as required of all German girls when they reached age twenty. Her brother, Roland, was sent to Hakone, a mountain resort where the German school had been relocated. This decision was made by Josef Meisinger, the Gestapo chief in Japan, according to Opa's reminiscences, because he wanted the children isolated from their parents and "educated by a uniformed campus leader." Meisinger had been transferred to Japan by submarine because superiors were unhappy with the atrocities he committed in Poland that had earned him the moniker "the butcher of Warsaw." At their new mountain school, Roland's teacher chastised the students for not shouting "Heil Hitler!" with enough vigor. "I want you to say it so loud that the rafters shake!" the teacher commanded.

The next day, when the students shouted "Heil Hitler!" the teacher was shocked to see the lamps begin to sway back and forth. Roland was expelled from the school when a classmate reported that Roland had attached a fishing line to the lamps and had pulled the line just as the students were shouting their salute. Roland was happy to rejoin his family.

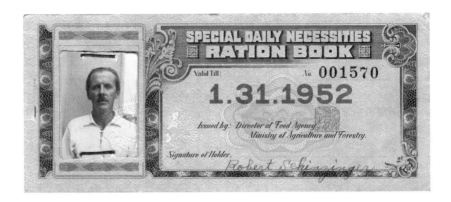

Robert Schinzinger's ration card during the US occupation.

In the middle of 1944, American pilots began dropping leaflets in major cities announcing that massive air attacks were planned. The Japanese government ordered a mass evacuation of children, women and foreigners from the city to the countryside. Children were put to work farming the land. The Schinzingers moved to Karuizawa, a mountain resort.

In the early years of the war, Mom and her family ate relatively well. Shipments of sardines and tuna that Germany had ordered from Japan, but which could not be exported because of the British naval blockade, were distributed among the German community in Japan. Similarly, when Japanese or German battleships intercepted Allied freighters at sea, the coffee, sheep tongue, lard and other Western food they captured would be passed out to the Germans.

But as the war continued, food began to run out. Mom and her brother Roland would bicycle from farm to farm exchanging clothing and various household items for fruits and vegetables. Once they came across a farmer who supplied canned fruit to the Japanese army and they came home with several weeks' worth of fruit. They picked up horse dung in the streets and night soil from the family's outhouse to fertilize their garden. As winter approached, they dug root cellars to store their winter provisions. The cabins in which they lived had not been winterized, and the cold was penetrating. The only stove was a small tin box. Mom wore a wool hat and gloves as she swept the kitchen and did her chores.

By early 1945, food was scarce. The rations from the Japanese government, which once included rice, miso and soy sauce, were now

Robert Schinzinger and Barbara teaching German on NHK, Japanese public television.

down to a head or two of cabbage every few weeks. Mom collected edible weeds like dandelions that her mother made into soups. What neither Opa nor his children had noticed was the gradually declining health of their mother Annelise. She had been starving herself so she could give extra portions to her husband and children.

One day in March 1945, a man from the German Embassy appeared at their cabin door with a bottle of wine to tell them that their house in Tokyo had burned down in the Allied bombings.

Mom, then twenty years old, drove back to Tokyo with the embassy official to see if there was anything worth salvaging. After they had descended the mountains and begun making their way through paddy fields, they saw in the distance a huge dust cloud. As they approached the cloud, Mom understood. It was a mass exodus of people from Tokyo.

"At the head of the procession were cars, trucks, buses and motorcycles that stretched for miles," Mom later recalled. "Then came the thousands of bicycles; then there were men pulling wooden carts; and finally the refugees on foot, a mass of humanity that extended for as far as I could see." During those months, Tokyo shrank from seven million residents before the war to a city of less than two million, as people relocated to farms in the countryside.

One day my mother was at a friend's house listening to the radio as the emperor, in his thin voice speaking a strange, otherworldly dialect, declared surrender. She remembered afterward a deathly quiet in the town. On August 28, thirteen days later, she celebrated her twenty-first birthday.

The end of the war did nothing to end the food shortage. Mom moved into a hotel in bombed-out Tokyo to work for a US Army PX, a kind of supermarket used by GIs where, one day, she found herself serving General Douglas MacArthur's wife and son (page 204). Later, she found a job translating into English documents that had been flown in from Germany which would be used in the Tokyo war crime trials of Japanese leaders. She lost each job when her superior learned she had been part of the German Youth.

One evening, Opa telephoned his daughter and told her to find penicillin for her mom who had come down with meningitis. Mom spent all night contacting her friends, desperately searching for medicine. Finally, the next morning, she found a US Army doctor who had a small supply of the rare antibiotic. She rushed onto a train with the medicine. But when her train pulled into Karuizawa Station that evening and she saw her father's hunched figure standing alone on the platform, she broke into tears. She knew she was too late.

Roland, then nineteen, built his mother's coffin and, with his father's help, put Annelise's body in it and nailed it shut. Mom helped Opa and Roland push the cart through the snow to the cemetery. The three of them watched in silence as the cemetery caretaker lowered the coffin into the grave and, without ceremony, began shoveling dirt over it.

Sixty years later, when I was visiting my mother in her apartment at the senior home where she was then living, I discovered the stack of diaries she had been keeping since she was a little child, I asked her to read the entries from the war, which she did, effortlessly translating the German into English I could understand. Tears streamed down her cheeks when she began to read a poem her father had written after her mother's death:

I still hear your sad, quiet words:
"It would be good to die in spring, when May flowers bloom and birds sing."

But before May came with its shine to the woods
I had to put flowers on your grave.
The ground was still frozen.
Now today, from the south, comes a whisper of warm air.
It brings the memory of spring.
The forest wants to turn green.
"Spring is a good time to die," you said.
But I am left alone in the autumn.

"She was too young," Mom said to me as she wiped her eyes. Annelise was forty-nine when she died, the age I was that afternoon as I sat with Mom. Mother's eyes were red, and her hair was whiter than I remembered. But as I sat beside her, holding her hand and holding back my own tears, I felt that forty-nine was also too old—too old to be coming across, for the first time, this window into her heart. I felt privileged to see it now, but also cheated that she had closed herself to me for so long. I had waited too long to take the time to sit beside Mom on her bed, as I did that afternoon, to listen to her story.

17

DON & BARBARA

MOM AND DAD MARRIED ON the three-day weekend of George Washington's birthday in February 1951. How strange it is to think that if California's anti-miscegenation laws, which banned inter-racial marriage, had not been struck down by the California Supreme Court in 1948, my father would not have been allowed to marry my mother because of his mixed-Japanese heritage.

It was also ironic that Mom had been a beneficiary of America's racist laws. The United States had a quota of immigrants for each country. Mom had had no trouble getting a visa to enter the United States because she was born in Japan and fell under the Japan quota. The Japan quota of immigrants was always undersubscribed because, under US law, people of Japanese blood could not immigrate to the United States. To enter America under the Japanese quota, you had to be born in Japan, but because of the exclusion laws, you could not enter with Japanese blood!

One of the few surviving photos of the wedding shows Dad and Mom looking out the side window of their car. Mom has her head on Dad's shoulder and is looking up at the camera with a big smile. With her dark, shoulder-length hair curled up and her lipstick shining, the

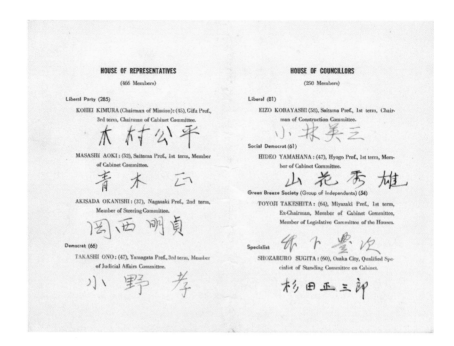

black-and-white picture made her look like a Hollywood star. Dad, with his arm around her, looked out the window with a shy grin, as if a little surprised that he was the one driving away with the prize. A poster taped on the car door read, "Brand New Mr. and Mrs."

Mom was wearing the brown dress her mother had picked out for herself from among the second-hand clothes offered to the family after they had lost everything in the Kobe flood.

The war had decimated the assets of both of their families, so they started their married life penniless. Mom and Dad had to choose between spending their scant savings on renting an apartment or buying a car. They chose a Studebaker, and Dad moved into Mom's room at a UC Berkeley professor's house where she did housework in exchange for room and board.

From the beginning, my parents were like two volatile chemicals: she, smart and opinionated; he, arrogant and insecure. Not long after they were married, they were invited to a bridge party. Dad began sniping about Mom's poor playing. At first, Mom ignored him, but when his comments turned nasty, she lost her patience.

"Stop it, Don!" she finally said, gritting her teeth and glaring at

260

him. Dad couldn't resist delivering a final barb with a self-satisfied grin. Mom grabbed the card table and lifted it up, tipping drinks, cards and all onto Dad's lap. Everybody was stunned. She looked at Dad's shocked face and broke into laughter.

JAPANESE CONGRESSIONAL MISSION ON ADMINISTRATIVE ORGANIZATION

JULY 1951

They had been married less than four months when Dad was offered a job interpreting for eight members of Japan's parliament who were on a three-month tour of the United States. They were coming to study US democracy at the invitation of the US Department of Defense. As an officer in the Occupation, Dad had had great authority. Now he saw his role as a kind of guide, helping these men understand the US system of civic engagement. The Japanese politicians didn't see things that way. They regarded Dad first as an interpreter and second as a servant. The task would call on Dad's skills as an interpreter developed in the Army Language School and as an officer in the Occupation, but it would also ignite the worst of his prejudices and insecurities.

Dad often found himself embarrassed by the Japanese politicians, his "herd," as he began to call them. "Previously I had respected the Japanese people as being modest, well-behaved, understanding and clear thinking," Dad wrote Mom.

Now Dad discovered the politicians were intolerant and self-centered. They were rude to the bellboys, secretaries and bartenders who served them, and particularly toward their own countrymen of lower standing. For example, one day the group was attending a lecture on education. Also attending that lecture was a group of Japanese teachers and principals who happened to be visiting Washington, DC. Much to Dad's consternation, his entire "herd" stood up right in the middle of the lecture and walked out.

It was simply too demeaning, the politicians later explained to Dad, for Japanese members of parliament to be put in the same lecture hall as a group of Japanese teachers. In any case, they added, they were sick of all the boring lectures. They wanted to meet President Truman

and General MacArthur. They also wanted to do more sightseeing. Dad was furious. In that commanding voice that once brought veteran soldiers to heel, he told them that the US government was paying for their trip and they would do what they were told. With two thousand dignitaries visiting Washington, DC, at any given time, he said, they shouldn't expect special treatment.

"They are as low a breed of humanity as I have ever met anywhere," Dad wrote. "God help Japan if [they] should ever reach any important positions."

Dad was also frustrated by the patronizing attitude of the American politicians who met the Japanese. One US senator said to the Japanese: "Y'all just put away your samyuraii swords and we'll git along just fahn." Dad chose not to translate that line.

The group was pleased when they got to meet Joseph Dodge, the hard-nosed Detroit banker who helped put Japan's inflation-wracked economy on the path to recovery, although Dodge proceeded to give the men a tongue-lashing for the role of the Japanese government in coddling big corporations with subsidies and protectionist tariffs. They also met with John Foster Dulles, who was representing America in peace treaty talks with Japan. Dean Rusk, the assistant secretary of state for the Far East, held a reception in their honor. Dad was always embarrassed when the Japanese men would crowd around these important men asking for their autographs.

Dad's Japanese politicians called him at odd hours to negotiate problems with the hotel staff or arrange for private weekend trips. When one of the men asked Dad to help arrange for a prostitute, it was the last straw. Dad moved out of the hotel and into a boarding house nearby.

Dad was clearly lonely. He wrote long letters declaring how he yearned for Mom "like a modern man thirsts for civilization, moths are drawn to the light, fish to water, man to air, anarchists to freedom." Years later, Mom would say that their relationship might have lasted longer if she had communicated more with Dad through letters. When he wrote, Dad opened himself up in a way he never could in person.

In one letter, Dad promised to argue less and listen more. But there was intensity to his love then that I never saw at home. In one letter he wrote: "I want to see you so much, to touch your hair, to kiss your lips, to lie with you through the night, to talk to you of our life and plan and think, to quarrel with you and even make you cry—just to make up afterwards—that feeling of relief, a crisis past. I would like to shower with you, scrub your back, wash dishes—if you would wipe them, go out dancing with you, dine with you—look at you and see you near, so close as to be a part of me, my life, my world, my thoughts."

Dad's Japanese improved daily and he was proud when he stood before the US Senate to translate a speech by the senior Diet member in the group. "It was my most wonderful victory yet," he wrote.

But the more confident Dad grew, the more condescending he became toward his group. In one letter, he refers to the senior Diet member, a man more than twice his age, as "my boy Kimura." Dad told Mom: "They have no finesse, warmth, *savoir faire* and anything but a kind-hearted peasant's heart with a nouveau-riche accent on their power, prestige, money and position."

Dad increasingly acted like a representative of the group rather than an interpreter. When he appeared on an NBC radio talk show with some of the men in his group, he not only translated what the Japanese had to say, but also took up much of the scarce time expressing his own opinions.

At the end of July, when their stay in DC was over, Dad took the group of Japanese politicians on a whirlwind tour of the United States. They met with police chiefs, prisoners, county clerks and reporters. They took the Empire State Express to visit a farm in Syracuse. In Mt. Vernon, Ohio, which the State Department had used for a widely distributed public relations film about "typical America," there were lavish dinners and luncheons in their honor. Crowds followed the Japanese politicians everywhere, asking for their autographs. Their every activity made the local newspapers. "Tired Japanese Take Day Off, Will Leave for Chicago Tonight," *The Mt. Vernon News* reported on the day of the group's departure. In Kansas City, the reporters picked up on their comments about communism in Japan. "Japs Fear a Red Surge," blared the *Kansas City Times*. "Modern Kitchens Interest Japanese Diet Members," *The Salina Journal* reported, quoting one Japanese politician who noted: "If a housewife has time for nothing but housework, she can't take an active interest in government."

JAPS FEAR A RED SURGE

COMMUNISTS COULD CAPITALIZE ON A DEPRESSION.

Members of Diet Are in U. S. to See How Democratic Methods Can Be Applied to Their Nation.

Seeing the respect the American reporters gave Dad made the Japanese men also treat him better. "My group treats me now, without exception, as their equal," he wrote. Now he began to indulge the men. He took them to a burlesque show in Chicago and frequently stopped at nickel-and-dime stores where the men liked to walk down the aisles amazed at the incredible variety of goods for sale.

By the time the Japanese politicians bid farewell, the men were emotional and Dad felt close to them. He would later agree to take other groups on tours.

Many decades later, the mayor of a midsize city, would recall how, when visiting California's Central Valley Project on one of those tours, Dad went out of his way to show his group the shacks of the Mexican "wetbacks" who toiled in the fields. "He wanted to show us the dark side of the American dream," the mayor said. That tour, guided by Dad, had changed the mayor's life. He had returned home determined to introduce real democracy to Japan. But Dad would never know the deep impression he had made on many of the Japanese visitors.

By January 1953, Mom was studying for a master's degree in library sciences while Dad was finishing a master's in political science at Berkeley. Mom was then pregnant with her first son, Chris, and the family finally moved out of the professor's house and into a small apartment. Their bedroom was so small Mom and Dad had to sleep separately in bunk beds. They could hear the train as it barreled through town, a stone's throw from the apartment. Even so, Mom remembered that time as the happiest years of her marriage.

One day, upon returning from a picnic, Mom and Dad came down with severe cases of poison ivy. They were moping around trying to get sympathy from each other when they found themselves face to face: each was as white as a geisha because of the calamine lotion they had slathered all over their faces and bodies, and they just burst out laughing.

On graduating, Dad passed the Foreign Service examination and applied for a job at the US State Department. When early promises of a job never panned out and his father, Julie, asked him to return to Japan to head Helm Brothers, Dad felt he had no choice.

Mom, Dad and their son Chris thus found themselves, one sunny, windy afternoon, on a freighter in San Francisco bound for Yokohama. I have a home movie that shows Dad passing around a bottle of Scotch among his friends. Later, when his friends leave and the ship pulls away, Dad tosses the empty bottle far out into the Pacific Ocean. He would dearly miss his American friends; most of them would go on to become professors. While they would envy Dad for the money he would make as managing director of Helm Brothers, Dad would envy them for the carefree, intellectual life he assumed they continued to live. His mother, Betty, had always warned against getting involved with Helm Brothers, but it was a fate he could not avoid.

18

BETRAYED AT WORK AND AT HOME

FOR DAD, THOSE FIRST DAYS back in Yokohama were thrilling. His father had built a house for Don and Barbara's family to move into, and the daughter of a Helm Brothers carpenter was hired as a nanny. Since Dad was the first college graduate in the family to manage Helm Brothers and worked hard to learn the ropes from Julie, his colleagues were impressed. They had never seen a foreigner who could not only speak formal Japanese but could also read and write the language. Although Don knew nothing about business when he started, he learned quickly.

But in February 1954, just as Dad was beginning to feel comfortable in his new job, Julie announced that he and Betty had decided to return to Piedmont, California, to retire. Since the war, Julie said, Yokohama no longer felt like home. Dad was terrified. "Just ninety days he gave me to learn the business," Dad would recall decades later. Perhaps Julie, who had worked for Helm Brothers since he was fourteen, didn't realize how difficult it would be for Dad, at twenty-seven with no business experience, to suddenly take over a company. Though far smaller than before the war, the company still had dozens of employees and several lines of business. The employees were loyal and honest

OPPOSITE: Tsuru-*san* holds Leslie. Brother Chris with nanny.

with Julie. They respected him. But would they transfer that respect to Dad, a man who had only just learned how to read a balance sheet?

At first, Dad was exhilarated by his newfound power and responsibility. Yokohama was emerging from the postwar recession and Helm Brothers was well positioned to benefit from its recovery. He plunged into the task, promoting capable young men and winning their loyalty. He consulted with his father by letter, detailing the problems and offering solutions.

Dad's first recommendation was to shut down the stevedoring operation, which had been supplanted by Japanese companies in the postwar years and was now losing money. He wanted to focus instead on developing the extensive real estate that Helm Brothers still owned in Yokohama and Tokyo. Dad set out to build new apartments and duplexes on land left empty by the firebombing. He rented apartments not only to businessmen and US servicemen, but to the soldiers' girlfriends, sometimes called *onrii wan* (only one) because, unlike prostitutes, they had a relationship with only one soldier.

Building was not easy. At a time when capital was scarce, the Japanese government discouraged Japanese banks from lending money to foreign companies such as Helm Brothers. To get around this financial roadblock, Dad had to draw from the company's meager savings, which included money the company had received from the Japanese government in war reparations, in order to pay for the new construction.

Dad was also convinced real-estate prices would rise, and he searched for new land to buy. Although Japanese property owners seldom sold their homes, he could usually find property that the US Army or some departing foreigner was eager to sell. Dad's early real-estate transactions were all in cash, and he once found himself walking several blocks to the bank carrying an athletic bag filled with fifty million yen, the equivalent of about twenty years' worth of his salary.

While Dad intuitively understood real estate, his youth, his impatience and his brutal honesty left him ill-prepared for straightening out the business messes left from the war years. The property titles to some Helm land had been transferred into the names of German relatives to avoid appropriation during the war. There was Helm Brothers cash that had disappeared with no explanation. The fifty-five-ton floating crane, the pride of the Helm company, had ended up in the hands of a Japanese employee who got the contract to load onto Soviet freighters all the locomotives that Japan was handing over to Russia as part of its war reparations.

Then there was Walter, the Helm cousin who had been accused of spying by the Japanese military police during the war and imprisoned. Walter had borrowed money from Helm Brothers during the war and now wanted to return the money in worthless yen. Dad was sorry about the tough times Walter had experienced during the war, but business was business. Dad began to deduct some of the money Walter owed from his Helm Brothers' pension.

Dad also had to contend with cousins who wanted him to give them jobs and board members who wanted to sell their land to Helm Brothers at inflated prices. Dad was less than diplomatic in handling these issues, calling the board director a "crook" and telling his cousins to look "in the wanted ads" for a job. Then there was Dad's godfather, Uncle Jim, who constantly complained that Dad was taking too many risks. Still, Dad gradually learned the business, weeding out ineffective employees while promoting those who worked hard. With Mom's help, he managed to keep peace with the relatives.

Some Japanese employees were unhappy. "Your father didn't understand the soul of the Japanese like your grandfather," said Mori Taro, whose family had worked for Helm Brothers for generations. "He didn't understand that sometimes you have to spend 100 yen in entertainment expenses to get 100 yen in business."

When I was born on October 30, 1955, at a small, two-room clinic on the edge of Motomachi, a shopping street at the foot of The Bluff, the nurse placed me in a tub of hot water and I screamed. Dad popped his head in long enough to make sure everything was okay, gave Mom a quick kiss and rushed off to the Yokohama Country & Athletic Club for his Sunday soccer game.

"Leslie has the happiest and broadest smile of any baby anywhere," he wrote to his mother Betty. "[Leslie] lifts his left hand, palm up in the air, beckoning me to pick him up. He is a very strong-minded child with a tremendous fiery temper and I fear that we are going to have trouble with him in the future."

Not long after I was born, my Opa announced at age fifty-seven that he would marry a twenty-four-year-old Japanese woman he had met at the Cabaret Chicago, a Tokyo bar where she worked as a hostess serving drinks and dancing with customers. He called her Shizuka, the quiet one, because she seldom spoke. Shizuka, with her country upbringing, was simple and always good humored. Opa would never know that Shizuka's father had knocked her across the room when she told him she would marry a foreigner more than thirty years her senior. "Until he hit me, I wasn't sure if I would marry him," Shizuka later wrote in her reminiscences. She had run away from her family because of the boredom of farm life and had ended up at the cabaret after first working at a sushi shop and then a pachinko parlor. At the Cabaret Chicago, her job was to dance with the patrons and persuade them to order drinks. Robert had come in to the Cabaret Chicago with a group of professors and he had asked Shizuka out after dancing with her. She found it exciting to go on dates with Robert to the Imperial Hotel for dinner or for coffee and cake at a nice Ginza shop. She had been impressed to see him on television teaching German and once attended one of his lectures wearing a beret so people would think she was a student. One sunny day, however, when Shizuka was walking in a park with Robert, she looked up at his beautiful smiling face with his perfectly white teeth and realized with a start that she was about to marry someone with false teeth.

A week before Christmas 1955, Dad took the whole family to attend Opa's wedding at the Imperial Hotel. When Mom arrived, Shizuka, who wore a beautiful kimono, asked to hold me. I was then six weeks old. "I remember the look on the faces of all these respectable people when they saw me holding you," Shizuka told me many years later. "They thought the blond baby was my baby and that this was the reason the professor and I were marrying."

The wedding was reported on the evening news. Nomura Koichi, the chamberlain to the crown prince (now Emperor Akihito), gave a toast in Opa's honor. (Earlier that year, when Opa received the Distinguished Service Cross of the West German government, the crown prince's younger brother had sent him a box of cigars imprinted with the Imperial Crest.) The master of ceremonies read a congratulatory telegram from Tanaka Kotaro, the chief justice of Japan's Supreme Court.

As my dad watched the ceremony, he was envious of the respect accorded Opa. He thought of his own job. He was happy at Helm Brothers, but it wasn't the life of culture and intellectual stimulation he had imagined for himself.

In February 1956, Dad received the letter that would change the trajectory of his life. Julie was dying of kidney cancer, Betty wrote.

Within a week, Dad was on a freighter with his family headed for San Francisco. Dad found his sixty-nine-year-old father at their Piedmont home looking frail. He took over from his exhausted mother the job of emptying the bedpan his father used and giving him morphine shots to ease his pain. I imagine father and son greeted each other stoically, with a handshake. They did not talk of death. They did not hug each other.

While he cared for his father, Dad wrote long letters to his Helm Brothers employees giving them detailed instructions on how to carry on the business. When he took a brief break from nursing his father on March 29, 1956, to visit friends, he returned to find his father dead. Just a few weeks later, even as he grieved for his father, Dad received a letter that shook him to his foundation. His cousin wrote that he and another cousin had held a meeting of the Helm Brothers board of directors and decided to appoint their seventy-year-old Uncle Jim as the company's managing director. Dad would be fired and replaced by his Uncle Jim, the very man who, at Dad's baptism had signed a pledge to his godson "to care for, and protect him, in event of anything happening to his parents."

Reading that letter many years later, I could understand the bitterness Dad felt toward his relatives. Dad quickly dashed off a letter to the Helm Brothers accountant telling him he intended to fight the family decision. Then he booked passage for himself and his family on a ship headed back to Yokohama.

Dad stood on the sheltered bridge of the ship one April day in 1956 at the Japanese captain's side, capturing a stormy scene on his home movie camera. "I've sailed for twenty years, but I've never seen anything like it," said the captain. Dad had left Mom and his two sons in the family's small cabin and had joined the captain on the bridge to film the Pacific in all the splendid fury that reflected so well the rage my father must have felt as he pondered the coming battle with his family. How would he make the rest of the family understand what a terrible mistake it would be to put his aging Uncle Jim in charge of the company? How would he win the support of his Aunt Louisa, who now controlled almost a third of the shares in Helm Brothers and would be crucial in his coming battle?

In the next shot on the home movie, the ship was anchored in the calm waters of Yokohama harbor. Mom held a leash, at the other end of which was my brother Chris in a leather harness. The camera fo-

cused on me. At six months, I was bundled up and lying on my back, laughing at the sky. Then there's a shot of a tugboat flying the HB logo of Helm Brothers. There were a dozen people on board who began walking up the gangplank. Opa was the first to reach the deck. He held a bouquet of flowers rolled in a paper cone for my mother. Then came Dad's cousin Walter and Uncle Willie. Last up the gangplank was Aunt Louisa. When she pressed her lips together and straightened her back, Dad must have known with chilling certainty that he had already lost the battle.

As the launch pulled away from the freighter, Mom put her arm through her father's arm and laughed. From the home movie, it was clear that she was oblivious to Dad's despair. When she later discovered the source of his humiliation, she tried to get Dad to understand the situation from the extended family's point of view, which Dad found disloyal and made him furious.

Dad's sorrow over his father's death turned into bitter resentment toward his relatives. In letters to his mother in California, Dad described how he pretended to make his peace with the relatives while he waited for the right time to strike back. He agreed to help Uncle Jim, taking a job with Helm Brothers that paid only half his previous salary.

Seven months after Dad had been demoted, he finally resigned. He taught English for a while, exported Japanese *tansu* (chests) and looked for a new line of business. That's when Dad received a call from a mysterious man in the US Central Intelligence Agency with an offer: If Dad would allow his office to be used as a drop-off point for the CIA, the government would give him some money to help launch his own real-estate company. As part of the deal, Dad would be asked to return briefly to the United States to study Russian. Japan had become a major front in the Cold War. Dad rented a small office, while keeping his plans secret from his relatives.

Betty was worried about her son's hostility. "Above all, please remember your father's name comes first. What would he do if he were alive?" she wrote to Dad. "Don't hurt people deliberately to accomplish this—we do not need revenge, we want fair play."

Dad was in no mood for fair play. He intended to compete with Helm Brothers head on. But just as he was about to launch the business, about a year after his father's death, his mother, Betty, fell ill. Once again Dad found himself back on a freighter headed for California. This time he asked Mom to stay in Yokohama with us kids and

Don Helm Realtors office in Yokohama, ca. 1962.

help supervise the opening of his new business. Dad would take care of his mother, and while in California, take a course in Russian. Mom would join him in America with the kids once she had launched the business.

If Mom and Dad's first separation right after their wedding strengthened their relationship, this period pulled them apart. Since his father's death, Dad had begun to drink more. He played less tennis and more golf. He began having the occasional affair.

Mom confronted him about his affairs. She wrote, "I would not condemn you if you should sleep with another woman—you really can do as you please—but I can't help my emotional reactions, and the knowledge or even the thought of your sleeping with another woman repels me."

With Dad away, Mom discovered she enjoyed her newfound independence and happily wrote to her husband, "My days are so full and

busy that I have little time to miss you. In making yourself independent of me, you made me independent of you, and I guess I should be
thankful for that."

Dad was apologetic for straying but then rationalized his behavior
as "a question of appetite." He said he was happy his wife had grown
more independent, but then sent letters with long lists of what she
had to do: "Rent the next door house furnished for $175; bring my
real-estate books, summer, autumn, spring clothes and our important
papers in the safe; give up your English teaching, there is too much
else to do; sell our Studebaker."

His Uncle Jim soon found out that Dad was going into competition with Helm Brothers. "It seems that Uncle Jim's voice was shaking
when he talked about this situation," wrote Mom. "I can just see how
he, in his sentimental way, is terribly upset about this 'treachery' on
your part."

But there was also good news: "Our ad in the paper about the new
business has drawn many exclamations of surprise and many have already noticed your new sign. We've got a lot of friends, and I think
they'll help get business for us."

Mom joined Dad in California with the kids for two months and
then brought the whole family back to Yokohama. Dad's new business
was a success. "Pad? Hut? Chalet? Don Helm Realtors," declared an
advertisement Dad placed in newspapers, school programs and club
bulletins around Yokohama. The Helm family, concluding that Dad
was now working in open competition with Helm Brothers, threw him
off the board. But Dad and Mom's relationship improved. My mother
loved to be pregnant, to have children, and so she was happy when
my sister Julie was born in 1958, followed by my other sister, Andrea,
in 1962.

MOM DID HER BEST TO raise us as good Americans. Every Sunday
morning she left Julie, still a toddler, with the maids, and drove my
brother Chris and me to the American Consulate in Yokohama on the
Bund for lessons on American citizenship. Chris and I walked into the
imposing stone structure with its tall Greek columns and walked up the
broad white marble staircase in the middle of a large atrium that led
to the American Cultural Center on the second floor. It was a grand,

Leslie Helm, center, with brother Chris and sisters Andrea and Julie.

almost church-like structure that always made me think America must be a cold but powerful place.

The American Cultural Center was taken up, in large part, by a library intended to help educate Japan on American democracy. It was in this library that I learned to draw pictures of bronze-skinned American Indians shaking hands with pilgrims in strange black outfits. All of this made me wonder what kind of country I belonged to. I learned that my heart was on the left side of my chest and that I should put my right hand over it as I recited the Pledge of Allegiance, wondering each time why it was "one nation, under God, *invisible* with liberty and justice for all." I learned to sing "My Country 'Tis of Thee" and the "Star Spangled Banner." But it was really at home, watching American television programs like "Father Knows Best" and "Gunsmoke," dubbed into Japanese, where I drew my notion of America as a society of close-knit families, wise fathers and justice-enforcing gunmen. I got a different view of America from Japanese television programs I watched, including a cartoon about a Zero pilot who outfoxed American fighters, a tall Japanese pro-wrestler who pummeled short and fat American wrestlers and a nuclear-powered boy robot named Atom (known outside of Japan as Astroboy), who was kidnapped by unscrupulous Americans and forced to work in a circus. My favorite Japanese programs were about swim teams and kendo clubs in which even the toughest obstacle could be resolved through perseverance, self-sacrifice and a few kind but strict words from the coach.

During the school year, I had Japanese lessons once a week and took judo, archery and karate. These disciplines taught me the importance of patience, persistence and self-control. But my most memorable times were the weekends spent at the Yokohama Country & Athletic Club (YC&AC), a country club for foreigners in Yokohama on a hill overlooking the sea that was a world apart from the crowded city. When Yokohama was hot and humid, there was almost always a breeze and cold lemon squash to cool me, and friends to keep me company. The swimming pool was deep blue and the lawn bowling greens perfectly trimmed. The bowlers in white shorts and polo shirts chatted as they waited their turns sipping from tall glasses of cold beer. Inside, nicely air conditioned at a time when that was still rare in Japan, was a four-lane bowling alley.

After a swim, my friends and I would order cheeseburgers with French fries that we paid for by signing little pink chits. On Sunday evenings there was always an American movie like *Chitty Chitty Bang Bang* or *Swiss Family Robinson*. Looking back now, I realize that at the time I was happy to live the insular but comfortable life of a *gaijin*.

The YC&AC was also an escape from what had become a nightmare at home. In bed at night I could hear my parents arguing loudly. One evening, when I was nine or ten, I woke up to a commotion and walked downstairs to our dining room.

"You stupid goddamned German," Dad was yelling at Mom, spittle flying out of his mouth. Dad's tie had been pulled loose. His white dress shirt, unbuttoned at the top, set off a neck blushed red from drink. He gripped Mom's arm tightly and pushed her from the dining room into the kitchen. Mom, dressed in a nightgown, looked frightened.

"Don, you're hurting me! Stop it!" she cried. I stood by the dining-room table, frozen.

"Just get out of my life," he said, teeth clenched, eyes dark and cold. "I don't need you."

He pushed Mom toward the back door. She stumbled at the *genkan*, the sunken entryway, and, when she caught herself, she saw me.

"Don, the children!" Mom said, nodding to me.

Dad barely gave me a glance. "Get out!" he commanded, holding the door open.

Mom walked out, and as I ran after her, I heard the kitchen door slam shut behind me. I was cold in my bare feet and pajamas. It was dark, and Mom held my hand as we walked along the deserted road that ran through The Bluff, our foreign enclave. We sat on a low brick wall across the street from the Foreigners' Cemetery.

Mom cried quietly, her head bowed down. I sat beside her, helpless, still trembling from what had happened. I had frequently lain in bed listening to my parents argue. Occasionally, Dad would take off his belt and hit me or my brother with it, caught up in his rage. But I had never before seen him so rough with my mother.

"What are we going to do, Mommy?" I finally asked.

My mother shook her head. The street in front of us was dark and empty, like a stage set long after the play was over and everyone had gone home. After what seemed to me like hours, Mom stood up and took my hand. "Let's go home." Dad wasn't there when we entered the house. Mom quietly tucked me into bed.

Decades later, my mother told me it had happened to her many times before. People would ask her about a bruise and she would tell them she had taken a fall. But for me, that night was the turning point. I could no longer trust Dad. I feared and hated him. I stopped looking to him for approval. For years afterward, whenever Dad turned his gaze toward me, I averted my eyes. Not until I began to write this book did I begin to understand what had made him such a difficult man.

HELM BROTHERS FOUNDERED UNDER ONE manager after another until the family finally asked Dad to take over the company again in 1967, nearly a decade later. Helm Brothers agreed to purchase Dad's business. Now he was happier, and for a while, peace returned to the household. Dad took us on a long trip through Europe, bought a new car and hired a contractor to put an addition on the house. He treated Mom better and their relationship seemed to improve.

Energized by the new challenge, he immediately began planning Helm Yamate Residences, a ten-story apartment building for foreign residents on a large piece of company-owned property on The Bluff. He came home with stories of carpenters who were unaccustomed to building Western-style houses and put the doors on the bathrooms so they opened inward, bumping into the toilet bowl. But he was enjoying the work.

He tried to bring modern management to Helm Brothers, hiring an accounting firm to go through the books so he could release a report to shareholders that, for the first time, revealed the true value of the company. "Don was too honest," an accountant who worked for Helm Brothers told me decades later. Although Helm Brothers was worth many times what shareholders had previously believed, none of the shareholders had the money to buy out other shareholders at those high valuations. And since Japan's strict regulations on the flow of capital out of the country made it difficult for the company to increase dividends, many shareholders wanted to unload their shares. It was only a question of time before some disgruntled shareholder would seek an outside buyer.

I remember sitting at the dinner table in 1972 when Dad came home and threw the prospectus on the table. A Hong Kong company was offering to buy Helm Brothers at exactly the price Dad had said the company was worth in his report several years earlier. Several relatives in the United States had already agreed to sell their shares without consulting Dad, and he felt betrayed for a second time. He knew the company's value had skyrocketed since his last report, and a better price could have been negotiated if the relatives had contacted him first. For a second time, he decided to fight. He called all the relatives in Germany, New Zealand and the United States and asked them to hold off. He would get a better deal. It was a stressful time. Dad began drinking again. He often stayed out overnight. I would come home to find my mother crying. "Why is he doing this to me?"

Ultimately, the Hong Kong company doubled its offer and there was little alternative but to sell.

"The family has grown too large and diverse and more distant from Japan for it to remain as a cohesive unit. Now done is done," one cousin told Dad. He had retired early on his Helm inheritance and advised Dad to do the same: "It gets easier when you pass fifty," he said.

Dad was only forty-seven, but he saw no way out. On May 2, 1973, he convened the last board of directors meeting of Helm Brothers, bringing to an end family involvement in a company that Great-Grandfather Julius had started in 1891. The board agreed to sell the 210,000 shares outstanding of Helm Brothers for 2.1 billion yen, about forty million dollars today adjusted for inflation. Split among dozens of shareholders and after paying heavy Japanese taxes, it was no fortune. Over the next ten years, both the yen and land prices would soar, pushing the company's value up almost tenfold.

Dad turned down the Hong Kong company's offer to keep him on as manager, a decision his employees blamed for the company's later collapse and the loss of so many of their jobs. Dad had decided it was time to start a new life. That meant making a clean break with the company; it meant divorcing Mom and marrying Toshiko, who had worked in his office for many years.

AS MY PARENTS DRIFTED APART, I knew my mother was suffering, but it was something I could not face. Years later, I read a fable that Opa, my grandfather, wrote. It helped me understand her pain. It was about a "Golden Bird" who loved to soar through the sky and to sing out her happiness but decided one day that she wanted to be human.

"You don't know what you ask for; you don't know what sorrows really are," the old architect of the universe told Bird in Opa's fable. But he granted Bird her wish and she became a beautiful maiden.

Many young men saw the beautiful maiden and heard her joyful singing. Every one of them wanted to marry her so he could keep her in his house, where she would sing when he wanted her to sing and would be silent when he wanted her to be silent.

Bird found her world narrow and so she went out across the great ocean, where she fell in love with a man who was handsome, smart and joyful and came from the same land as she. Bird faced many sorrows, including her mother's early death. Each time she cried all night and in the morning her old father told her, "Human beings must have the courage to live and say good-bye."

After the birth of her fourth child, Dr. Death came to Bird's door. (This part was about my mother's battle with breast cancer.) *Bird looked into Dr. Death's cruel eyes and drove a hard bargain. "I have four children to take care of; and my husband, though he doesn't show it, needs me too." Bird offered Death a part of her body, promising him the rest when her children were grown. The architect of the universe, seeing her sorrow, shed tears that fell upon Bird's forehead and, shining like diamonds, blinded Dr. Death, who finally agreed to Bird's offer. But Bird extended her life only to be confronted with a husband whose misery had turned love to pain. When her children were grown, Dr. Death returned for her. Bird was ready. She left her body, returned to her original form and flew away.*

Although mother would continue to live for decades more, Opa's fable wove the raw pain that I couldn't bear to see in my mother into a sad but soothing fairy tale in which joy and sorrow are just part of the endless cycle of human life. I wish I could have had that perspective when Mom turned to me for comfort.

Instead, when Dad stopped coming home one day and chose to be with Toshiko, I was relieved. At least the fighting would cease. And with my parents preoccupied, I was free. It was my senior year, one of the happiest years of my life. Looking back, it seems odd that this should have been so, given that my family was coming apart. But the planets of my universe had aligned for me in a way they would not again for many years. At the Yokohama International School, where I had been enrolled since nursery school, I was involved in theater and karate and soccer. After school, I walked down the hill to a neighborhood I now know is close to where my Great-Grandfather Julius first lived, to take karate. After being a terrible student most of my life, I suddenly found I enjoyed reading and writing. Most of all, I found a perverse pleasure in embracing my *gaijin* identity and rejecting the straightjacket of Japanese society.

One weekend, two good friends and I decided to take a trip north across the main island of Honshu to the Japan Sea—a trip that would change my relationship to Japan. Marco was a Dutch national who had been my best friend since fifth grade, with a Chinese-Indonesian father and Belgian mother. My other close friend was Joji, a black belt in karate who had been raised by his Japanese mother after his Irish-American father abandoned the family.

As we waited for the train, Marco and I sat cross-legged on the concrete platform. I pulled a bottle of sherry out of the pocket of my large army surplus coat. I had won it at a school fair booth a few days before and had been carrying it around with me ever since, waiting for the appropriate occasion. Joji stuck his hand in his pocket and, with a flourish, produced two small wine glasses. I poured the sherry.

We sat and drank our sherry as a train whooshed into the station a few feet away. We didn't budge as it screeched to a halt, the doors sliding open and thousands of commuters pouring out. When one man bumped into Marco and mumbled something in disgust, we laughed. What a joy it was not to be "them," to be free spirits in a world of conformity. When our train finally arrived, we jumped on. When the ticket conductor came around, the three of us crammed into one of the tiny bathrooms on the train to avoid paying the fare.

It was dusk when we got off the train eight hours later with a vague notion of finding a hot spring where we could take a bath. We walked down a narrow street that cut through rice paddies toward the resort town, holding our thumbs out hoping to hitch a ride. It was our private joke; we didn't expect anyone to stop. People didn't pick up hitchhikers in Japan—particularly not foreigners. We had barely walked a hundred yards from the train station when a car pulled over in front of us followed by a second car. The two drivers happened to be friends, and we piled into the two cars.

"Where are you going?" the first driver asked.

"We want to take a bath," said Joji, laughing as if it were a good joke. When the driver pulled up in front of a large, expensive-looking inn, we got nervous. We had brought little money.

"Don't worry," the driver said. "My mother works here as a maid. She can get you in for free." The mother, a middle-aged woman wearing a white apron, came out and led us into a waiting room where she poured us some green tea.

"You can go in the bath when the guests are finished," she said kindly.

It was nine o'clock when she handed us a stack of crisply starched and ironed *yukata* and a few small hand towels and led us to the baths on the top floor. We stripped down, dumped our clothes and *yukata* into a wicker basket and walked into the large, steamy bathing area.

We washed, rinsed off and then lowered ourselves gently into the hot, milky water that had the pungent sulfur smell I had come to love. The tile bath was the size of a small pool, and I couldn't resist swimming the butterfly stroke across its full length before relaxing at the other side next to an artfully arranged rock waterfall, where the water poured into the bath.

Afterward, we donned our fresh *yukata* and walked out onto the hotel roof. The evening breeze felt cool against our steaming bodies. We leaned against the low concrete wall and looked out over the black tile roofs. It was a quiet night with no cars on the roads. There were few lights, and in the sky above was an ocean of stars. That's when we heard it. *Ka-kop, ka-kop.* It was a woody, hollow sound.

"What is that? It sounds like a horse," said Marco. But no, there was a different rhythm to it. As we listened, the sound seemed to multiply until the whole village was echoing with the sound: *Ka-kop, ka-kop, ka-kop.*

Suddenly it was clear to me. "Everyone's wearing wooden *geta* (clogs)."

As we looked down into the narrow alleys between the rooftops, we could see that the streets had filled with men and women in their *yukata* returning from their baths.

The *geta* had a certain leisurely sound accompanied by shuffles and strange street echoes that seemed to harken from a pre-industrial era. Later it would occur to me that this was a sound Great-Grandfather Julius must have heard when he first arrived in Wakayama.

When we changed back into our clothes and left the inn, our friends drove us to our next stop, an *ochazuke* restaurant owned by one of their fathers. It was arranged like a sushi bar, with one row of six bar stools. Townspeople liked to stop by for a bowl of rice and a piece of salted salmon that you sprinkled with seaweed and covered with green tea.

We slurped down the meal and bowed our thanks. The father brushed off our efforts to pay. Our last stop was the home of another one of the young men whose father, a carpenter, was building an addition. "You can sleep here," the carpenter said, leading us to a room only partially completed.

As we lay down, it struck us that we had not drunk a drop of alcohol or smoked a single joint, and yet we were on this incredible high. We had thrown ourselves at the mercy of the road and something wondrous had happened.

The next morning, the carpenter took the day off and guided us around Noto Island, a short ferry ride away. He led us on narrow paths through tall bamboo forests that reminded him of his experiences as a soldier fighting in China when every day they had to scrounge for food, often stealing it from Chinese villagers. He now felt guilty about what he had done and seemed to feel better after sharing the experience with us. It was the first time a Japanese man had ever spoken to me about the war, and I felt as if I had glimpsed a deep wound that had never healed.

As we walked through the bamboo forest, we noticed rustling sounds behind us. "Could be a wild boar," the carpenter said. "You can still find wild boar in these parts." But when we came to a clearing, we could see a gaggle of boys following behind us. One brave boy came out from behind the foliage. He pointed at us, shocked by our non-Japanese appearance, then screamed and ran for cover. We pretended to be scared. The boys laughed and followed at a distance. As we made our way back to the ferry boat to leave, the boys finally came out from their hiding places and waved to us. "Come again," they yelled. That night we ate curry and rice cooked by the carpenter's wife.

"Thank you so much for your hospitality," I said to the carpenter and his wife after dinner. "We feel so lucky to have met you. I don't know what we would have done if your son and his friend hadn't picked us up."

"It wasn't luck," said the carpenter. "Somebody would have helped you. Noto is famous for its hospitality. There is a well-known story about a thief who ran away from Tokyo to hide in this region. People gave him a place to sleep. They fed him every day. Everybody was so kind to him that he began to feel ashamed of his life. He left a note thanking the people of Noto and then committed suicide."

The story silenced us. Confronted with the goodness of these people, we felt ashamed. What right did we have to make fun of the hardworking Japanese men while we sat on the platform in a crowded train station drinking sherry?

The next afternoon we headed home. We paid full fare for our train tickets and sat quietly in our seats. I had a new respect for Japan, for the beauty of its rural towns and the generosity of its people. I am reminded today, as I think back on that experience, that for every time I have been made to feel like as an outsider, there have been a dozen times I have been treated as honored guest. They are two sides of the same coin.

DAD, BY CONTRAST, WANTED NOTHING more to do with Japan. The summer after my senior year, he and Toshiko set off on a year-long honeymoon trip around the world. The goal was to take walks on the beach, have drinks at sunset, scuba dive, dine at the world's best restaurants and find a beautiful place in which to spend the rest of their lives.

But from the very outset, he was uneasy. Years later, I would find a box full of old notebooks. One gray notebook revealed just how troubled Dad had become. On one page he had made a list of the things he feared most: "Parental type commands; loud voices; physical punishment; making and keeping new friends; parties and social functions; public speaking; effects of divorce on children and Barbara; friends' response to divorce and Toshiko."

On another page was a list of "Dos" and "Don'ts." Under "Do" was: "Stay relaxed, wake up and live." Under "Don't" he listed: "Dwell on failures; be preoccupied with self."

Here was Dad, at the turning point of his life, at a time when he had plenty of money and had just remarried, listing his hopes and fears like the numbers in an accounting ledger. On a page written shortly before he left Japan on his trip was his "To Do" list: "Pay Harry for stereo; dentist; traveler's checks; review will; get married; sell typewriter." Number twenty-two of the thirty-four items on the list, and the only one not crossed out, was the item that read: "What can I do for the children?" That one had stumped him.

In the first few entries on his round-the-world trip, things seemed promising. "Enjoyed Toshiko. Missed my family," he wrote. He bought Toshiko a long green dress in a colorful market and ate fabulous oysters. In Singapore, the two feasted on spicy fish and satay with peanut sauce. In Thailand, they saw elephants lifting logs, snake handlers playing with cobras, and exotic Thai dancers.

GOAL ORIENTED BEHAVIOR. (to think about)
1. Drinking
2. Sex
3. Marriage
4. Keep your cool
5. Children
— 6. Fear of negative response
— 7. Fear of parental type commands, voices (loud) physical punishment
— 8. Fear of making and keeping new friends. Remember Names.
9. Expressing clearly
— 10. Fear of public talking
— 11. Fear of effects of divorce on children, Barbara
— 12. Fear of friends' response to divorce + Toshiko
— 13. Fear of consequences of past mistakes in tax problems
14. Decision on: occupation "what to do". Goals
15. Where to live
16. Mental Image of self
— 17. Fear of parties + social functions

Dad had hardly been away from Japan for three weeks when things started turning sour. "Bad dreams. Up in the night and wake up early," he reported. At a houseboat in Kashmir, he smoked hashish and asked for career advice from a Pakistani saleswoman also staying on the houseboat who advised him to remain in real estate. He missed Mom so much that in Paris, he went to the post office and spent two hundred dollars to telephone her. In Paris, he jotted in his diary: "The constant shopping is driving me mad … Death to shoppers!"

He and Toshiko rented a car and drove over the Pyrenees toward Spain. "How I miss my family," he wrote in Torremolinos.

Dad enjoyed paella in Spain; the rugged cliffs in Malaga reminded

Don Helm and Toshiko (Hondo) Helm.

him of the Japanese shoreline. While in Gibraltar, he learned that our family home, 236 Yamate, had sold for 120 million yen, about twenty-five times the price he paid for it ten years before. Although most of the money would go to pay Japanese taxes, it would be enough for the divorce settlement. He was happy about the sale, but he already missed his old life in Yokohama.

While Dad traveled around the world that summer, I was going through the house with my mother getting rid of stuff. It didn't concern me that Helm Brothers had been sold after almost a century in the family, Dad had lost his job, my parents were divorced and my childhood home would soon be knocked down. I should have cared, but I didn't. I just wanted to move on.

WHEN I LEFT JAPAN FOR college in 1973, I was unaware of the country's powerful hold on my life. I assumed I would never return. However, when I left Japan in 1993 after the adoption of my two children, I knew I had lots of unfinished business and would often return. Even so, it was a surprise to me how quickly I would be pulled back to the country and the unexpected window I would soon get into my family's past.

On January 17, 1995, when a great earthquake leveled Kobe, my editor asked me to fly to the city to cover the disaster. I contacted the reporters who were already covering the story. One was sleeping on the floor of the city hall. Others were staying at hotels in Osaka and taking taxis in, a two-hour ride because the trains weren't running while the elevated expressways had collapsed. I scanned my mind for people I might know in Kobe with whom I could stay and remembered a visit my father had received in 1983 from Tsunemochi Atsushi, a retired furniture distributor from Kobe who claimed to be a relative. Dad told me at the time that Atsushi's great-grandmother might have been the mistress of his Grandfather Edmund, his mother Betty's father. I had met Atsushi briefly at a train station coffee shop many years before, but had never understood our relationship. I tracked his phone number down and telephoned him in Kobe, asking if his family was safe.

"We don't have water," said Atsushi. "But we are safe." Then I told him my assignment and asked if I could stay with him. "My father-in-law lost his home and is living in the basement, but of course. I can make a bed for you in the office," he said. I knew it would be an imposition, and I felt bad, but I had no alternatives.

I flew into the new Kansai airport built on a man-made island in Osaka Bay and took a hydrofoil to the ferry terminal on the city's waterfront. It was past eight o'clock at night when I stepped off the boat onto the concrete pier, walking along wooden planks that had been placed to bridge large cracks in the concrete. The streets nearby were deserted, and an eerie silence blanketed the city, periodically shattered by the wail of an ambulance siren.

I walked through the dark streets, dragging my wheeled carry-on bag behind me as I searched for a taxi. The first scene that gave me a hint of the devastation was a fifteen-story concrete building that had been ripped cleanly from its foundation and was lying on its side, otherwise looking completely intact.

I knew this Kobe earthquake had been a mighty one. The temblor, which struck at 5:46 AM two days before, had measured 7.3 on the Richter scale. At the time, it was the worst to hit Japan since the Great Kanto Earthquake that had leveled Yokohama in 1923. The earth moved as much as a yard upwards and as much as twenty inches sideways. In twenty seconds, 67,000 buildings had completely collapsed, 3,900 people died and more than 200,000 were left homeless. Total damage was estimated at $200 billion.

As a child, I had experienced dozens of earthquakes. At school, we were taught to hide under our desks when the earth started to shake. At home, we would stand under door frames as the house shook. Sometimes we ran out to the bamboo grove in our garden. Bamboo, we were told, had roots that would hold the ground together and keep it from splitting open.

Growing up, I had heard many of the Helms' stories about the 1923 earthquake and the firestorm that followed. I had read Dad's description of how he had dragged bodies from the rubble after the Fukui earthquake in 1948. But it wasn't until I saw that building in Kobe lying on its side that I really understood the destructive power of an earthquake.

As I walked on, I saw concrete telephone poles strewn across the sidewalks, their cables wrapped around trees and buildings. Cars had been flattened in their collapsed concrete garages. One big office tower had collapsed floor by floor like a giant accordion.

As I reached the center of town, I finally flagged a stray cab that took me as far as Rokko, a train station about a mile from Atsushi's home. At the deserted train station, I found a telephone and called Atsushi. He said he couldn't drive, but would send his wife, Yoshiko, to pick me up.

Yoshiko was an attractive woman in her sixties. She waved for me to get in the car. As she drove, taking a roundabout way home to avoid collapsed retaining walls, she gave me a quick rundown on the situation. Most of the earthquake damage had been in the flatlands that consisted of landfill. Her father, who lived in that area, had lost his home and was staying with them at the house, so things would be a little crowded.

"I'm so sorry to be bothering you at a time like this," I said, acutely conscious of the huge imposition.

"No, we are happy you thought of us."

A few minutes later, she pointed to a large modern complex on her left that took up an entire city block. "That's the headquarters of the Yamaguchi *gumi,* a large *yakuza* organization," she said. "During the day, when they distribute food and water to the residents, there is a line that extends all around the block."

I smiled to myself. I knew the Yamaguchi *gumi.* The *yakuza* boss I had interviewed with the gold-plated, Kennedy-coin belt buckle had been from that organization.

At the house, Atsushi, now an elderly man with graying hair and gentle eyes, led me to his small office, where a futon had been laid out on the floor. "Feel free to use the telephone," he said. "Then get some sleep."

As soon as I was alone, I sent my editor an e-mail telling him I would file a story the next day on the *yakuza* relief efforts. The Japanese government was being criticized for its slow response to providing food and shelter for the hundreds of thousands left homeless by the disaster. This was a unique angle on that story. Atsushi had given me shelter. Yoshiko had found me my first story. I felt very lucky.

In the morning, Yoshiko made me toast and coffee. While I ate, she told me she had made some telephone calls; she had found a neighbor willing to lend me a bicycle, so I could get around the ravaged city. She had also found me a city map.

With map in hand, I took my borrowed bicycle and headed for the *yakuza* headquarters. There, sure enough, residents were already waiting in line. Some were walking away with large bags of diapers and toilet paper. I talked to a guard at the gate but was told the boss would not see me, but residents in the line told me the story. Only hours after the earthquake struck, trucks sent by affiliated gangs across the country began arriving with relief supplies, quickly filling the large compound. The boss had so many supplies that he began giving stuff away to neighbors. The relief effort was so well received in the neighborhood, the boss sent word to his associates around the country to send more supplies.

As I was walking away, I saw half a dozen posters plastered on the concrete walls. "Let's chase the gangsters out of our neighborhood," they said.

For the rest of the day, I bicycled all over the city. I visited tent cities where refugees sat stony-eyed, warming their hands over small fires. I talked to an old man who collected rags and then sold them as scrap. His tiny shop had suffered minor damage and he was making repairs. He remembered how the firebombs had destroyed his shop during World War II. "There will always be some disaster," the old man said, shrugging his shoulders.

When I returned home, I helped Yoshiko collect water from the well at a shrine nearby. Much later, I would learn that the shrine was the same shrine Opa and Grandmother Annelise had evacuated to after the flood of 1938. Atsushi's house, it turned out, was just blocks from where Opa's *gartenhaus* had been. Yoshiko was concerned about her dog that hadn't stopped barking since the earthquake. Every tiny aftershock made the dog shake and yelp with fear. That evening, she prepared a delicious feast from the various canned goods she had around the house. After dinner, I insisted on helping with the dishes. Most Japanese women don't like having other people in their small kitchens. Yoshiko, after some reluctance, allowed me to do the dishes. I felt as if I had become a part of the family.

Afterward, we moved to the living room, and Atsushi pulled out his scrapbook. It was time to talk family. At his mother's death bed, Atsushi told me, he learned from his uncle for the first time that he was part German. Curious, he looked through his family registry. There it was: His grandmother's father was listed as Edmund Stucken. He went to a German priest, who took him to the Kobe foreign cemetery.

"It was a grey day in 1975," Atsushi recalled. "The caretaker showed us where the grave was on a map. As we reached the area, the clouds parted, and a shaft of sunlight fell on a gravestone shaped like a large natural rock." When Atsushi approached the rock, he saw the name on the gravestone: EDMUND STUCKEN—my great-grandfather, Betty's father. Although Atsushi was far older than me, we shared the same great-grandfather.

Perhaps I gave a skeptical smile at that moment because Atsushi pulled a picture from his album and showed it to me. There it was, a spot of sunlight on the gravestone, as if the photo had been overexposed on that spot.

Atsushi became obsessed with his German heritage. All his vacations were spent in Germany. With little English and no German, he tracked down relations around the world. He was invited to a reunion in Germany that included 110 relatives from twenty-one countries. His family's photo was included in a beautifully bound volume of genealogy distributed to everyone who attended. He left the Catholic Church into which he had been baptized and became a Protestant so he could attend the Kobe Union Church that his Great-Grandfather Edmund had attended.

Atsushi learned, much to his delight, that our common great-grandfather came from an illustrious family. When Edmund's sister married the Baron of Mansberg, her father gave the couple as a dowry the castle Pichl. Atsushi discovered that his German ancestors had been international wool traders who had settled all over the world. Edmund's mother was born in Cuba to diplomat parents. One of Edmund's uncles was Adolf Bastian, one of the founders of modern ethnography, a man credited with having inspired both anthropologist Joseph Campbell as well as the creators of the movie *Star Wars*. Atsushi visited the massive Chateau Stucken outside Paris where the wealthy Russian branch of our family had lived in exile after the Russian revolution of 1917. He even visited a distant relative who was the head of a large multinational in South Africa called Stucken and Co. I was envious of Atsushi's adventures, maybe even a little jealous, but I was excited by all he had learned. These people around the world were his relatives—but they were mine too.

Atsushi began to visit Edmund's grave regularly. One day when he went to ask for Edmund's blessings before departing for the big family reunion in Germany, he was shocked to find a gravestone on Edmund's plot, disturbing the harmony and beauty of his ancestor's grave.

He had assumed he was the only living relative to Edmund in Japan

Leslie Helm with Japanese cousin Atsushi Tsunemochi by the grave of Great-Grandfather Edmund Stucken.

and had adopted the grave as his own family grave. He could not ignore that new gravestone that lay so impertinently in his great-grandfather's plot. Finally, he went to the caretaker and asked him who had the authority to put the grave there. The caretaker went through his notes.

"It was a man named Donald Helm from Yokohama," the caretaker said. Atsushi asked for Dad's address, and one rainy evening in 1983, he visited Dad at his home on The Bluff. Dad received him hospitably, but Atsushi could tell he did not share his enthusiasm for family history. Dad told Atsushi that he had put his Aunt Gretchen's ashes in her father's grave.

Edmund was Gretchen's father? This could only mean that Edmund had married twice: Atsushi was the descendant of Edmund's first wife. Gretchen and Betty, Dad's mother, were children of Edmund's second marriage.

"After all my travels in Europe," Atsushi said to me as I sat there on his couch, "I learned that my closest relatives were not Germans after all, but Yankees who lived in Yokohama."

It felt odd, just days after Kobe's devastating earthquake, when so

296

many people were homeless and living in misery, to be talking family history. Yet there was something about seeing how our past was woven together, how our meeting revealed so many new connections to the world, which was comforting in the midst of such destruction.

Later, when we were closer, Atsushi would tell me details he left out of the story that day. For example, one of his mother's childhood friends recalled that when Atsushi's mother acted uppity, they would say: Who are you to talk like that? You are just the daughter of a half-breed, and that would make her quiet."

When Reggie Life, an American producer, approached Atsushi about being interviewed for a documentary that suggested people of mixed blood should not be called "half" American and half Japanese, but instead be called "doubles," Atsushi was hesitant to participate in a project that would announce to the world his own mixed-blood status. He ultimately agreed, he said, hoping others would feel better about revealing their secrets. As Atsushi and I grew closer in successive trips, Atsushi even shared the story about how his Japanese grandfather, as a medical student, had cured the daughter of a powerful *yakuza* boss and had been rewarded with the most beautiful woman from among his brothels, a woman his grandfather made his receptionist when he started his clinic.

I came to feel a strong bond with Atsushi that went beyond kinship. Not only did we share the same German great-grandfather, but both our families had been ashamed of their heritage and had sought to hide it. We even shared grandfathers who had dealt with gangsters. I felt as if we had become soul mates. His quest was the mirror image of my own.

FROM SHAME
TO PRIDE

AS MARIKO AND ERIC GREW older, their ties to Japan weakened. They stopped watching Japanese videos and reading Japanese comic books. Every year it became more of a challenge to keep them interested in Japan. Still Marie and I did our best. They enjoyed Japanese food and we frequently had Japanese visitors. Marie was chair of Japanese Studies at the University of Washington and editor of *The Journal of Japanese Studies*. Periodically, we took trips to Japan. When I had the time, I continued my family research, connecting with a vast network of relatives in Japan, Germany, New Zealand and across the United States.

By 1999, our nanny, Teiko, had been gone for two years, and Mariko, now ten, and Eric, seven, were rapidly forgetting their Japanese. Marie and I decided it was time to return to Japan to renew those ties. I would also have time to conduct research on my family. We each received an Abe Fellowship, which supports US and Japan-based researchers focusing on contemporary issues. We settled into an apartment for foreign scholars just outside the campus of Hitotsubashi University, on the outskirts of Tokyo, where Marie would be based. I commuted into Tokyo to The Center for Global Communications (GLOCOM), a think tank where I would study the evolution of the Internet in Japan.

Although the Hitotsubashi campus looked run down in places with its abandoned hulks of rusting bicycles and its untended shrubbery, we knew the kids would be safe in this small town, and so we allowed them a great deal of freedom. They loved to bicycle to the hundred-yen store on the other side of the campus where they could buy everything from toys to school supplies for less than a dollar each.

Japan had changed since we had left six years earlier. Name-brand clothes and handbags that sold for hundreds of dollars apiece were less in evidence. Popping up instead were funky stores that sold second-hand clothes and cheap imports from China and India.

To get Mariko and Eric speaking Japanese again, we placed them in a Japanese public school. Initially, everything went smoothly. We were impressed when the city government paid for interpreters to stay with each of our children every day for the first week in school. It concerned us that school regulations would not allow us to walk our children to school. Strangely, they were also forbidden from riding their bicycles. But we were thrilled when we discovered that the classroom teachers had appointed "friends" to walk with Eric and Mariko to school.

Every morning, Yumi would call up from the road to our second-floor apartment, and Mariko would run down to join her friends as they walked to school. Mariko quickly became close friends with Yumi. Mariko loved finding herself in a class full of Japanese. In Seattle, she had been disturbed and angry when her class talked about the US bombing of Hiroshima. The only other Japanese-American in her class was a boy, and she didn't feel like she could share her feelings with him. In this class, everyone was Japanese; everyone knew how to pronounce her name. For the first time, she said, she felt like she really belonged.

Eric was also initially enthralled by Japan. He loved to visit temples. I would light the incense and he would stand quietly staring at the gilded Buddha that glowed from within the dark recesses of the temple hall. He had always been fascinated by religion and, at age five, while attending pre-school, once asked me about the crucifixion. When I explained to him about what the Romans had done, he was disturbed. "They should have used their words."

Eric's teacher, an energetic woman with hair dyed red and a mouth full of glittering silver crowns, did a good job of including Eric in the class. Just a few days after school started, she assigned Eric to work as a server at lunch. Stainless-steel carts loaded with rice, stew and miso soup were rolled into the classroom. Eric beamed as he stood behind one cart, wearing a white apron and white paper hat and using a ladle to fill the kids' soup bowls as they came through the lunch line.

The teacher also assigned Eric a role as tadpole number ninety-nine in the class play. The play was about a mother frog who ventured out in search of a lost tadpole, only to be captured by an evil crayfish. The tadpoles gathered around and discussed what to do.

"We must save our mother!" Eric bellowed, his only line in the play. The only dramatic instruction the children received was to shout out their lines as loud as they could. The tadpoles then broke into song as they marched off to rescue their mother. When Eric returned from school, he would march around the living room singing that martial tune.

One morning, Eric's classmate, Yuuta, knocked on our door while Eric was finishing his breakfast.

"Hey, Eric! Are you *still* eating?" said Yuuta in Japanese. "Come on. Let's go."

Eric grabbed the boxy black leather backpack that has been the standard issue school backpack in Japan since World War II and headed out with Yuuta. Less than ten minutes had passed when Eric came home in tears.

"I'm *never* going back to that school again," Eric thundered as he strode into our little apartment and slammed the heavy metal door behind him. "It's stupid!"

Then Eric's eyes brimmed with tears as he burst into a staccato of mournful cries. An older Japanese boy had made fun of Eric's name. Then he had taken his backpack and swung it, hitting Eric in the face.

I looked at Marie, wondering if we had made a tragic mistake in bringing our children back to Japan. I gave my son a hug and held him tight. I felt his shaking stop and his body relax. Only then did I begin to feel the tightness in my own chest ease.

I could have done one of many things that morning. I could have signed Eric up for a martial-arts class. That's what Grandfather Julie had done when Dad was teased by Japanese kids as a child in Yokohama. I could have sent Eric back out there and told him to be tough. That's what Dad often said to me. But I had read enough about bullying in Japanese schools to know that minor incidents could become major problems. This issue had to be resolved immediately. I took Eric's hand and walked him to school.

"Did you know the boy who teased you?" I asked Eric as we walked.

"No. He was from another class." Eric's voice was shaking.

"Where did your friends go?"

"I don't know."

I noticed then that his tears had left dirty streaks on his cheeks. I knelt down in the street to wipe his cheek with a paper tissue. I could imagine how it felt to have this new world he had been so taken with, suddenly turn on him.

The elementary school was a cream-colored, two-story concrete block of a building much like every other school I'd seen in Japan. Inside the entryway, we took off our shoes. Eric changed into the clean inside shoes he kept in his backpack. I put my shoes on a large shoe shelf and took a pair of green slippers I found in a basket. Holding Eric's hand, I walked down the polished wood hallway and knocked on the door of his classroom. I explained to the teacher what had happened. She nodded. Eric let her take him by the hand and lead him to his desk.

Then I went to the school office and asked for the principal. She was not there, but the vice-principal came to the door. He was a hand-some, stern-looking man. His looks reminded me of the kind of men who always played the role of the wise sports coach in Japanese television shows. They were tough but fair, and they always had the answers to life's most difficult questions.

"My son, Eric, was bullied by one of the Japanese boys this morning," I said.

"Oh? What happened?"

"He made fun of Eric's name and hit him in the head with his backpack."

"Well, that's unfortunate," he said, sounding concerned.

But when I looked him in the eyes, I saw that he was annoyed. I felt myself blushing as it suddenly became clear that he considered my problem too trivial to warrant attention.

"Perhaps it wasn't a big deal," I conceded. "But I think you should talk to the kids."

"Shouldn't the kids work things out for themselves?" asked the vice-principal.

"Maybe," I said, trying to stay calm. "But if things get worse, it will be your responsibility."

The vice-principal's eyes narrowed. He knew exactly where I was

302

going with this. Bullying had become a major issue in the Japanese press. There had been a spate of suicides by children bullied by their peers, often with the complicity of teachers, an informal way to enforce conformity. Once a teacher presided over a mock funeral in class for a junior-high boy who was often bullied by classmates and so stayed at home complaining of stomachaches. The boy committed suicide soon afterward by hanging himself in his bedroom. It was Japan's conformist schools that made Japan disciplined, but also intolerant of diversity, unable to produce the creative thinking that its post-industrial society demanded. In that moment, it seemed to me that all of Japan's problems could be reduced to the attitude of this one vice-principal.

Finally, the vice principal gave me a brief nod. "I will talk to the teachers."

A few days later, Eric's teacher called me at home. "About this incident," she said. "I talked to the boy involved. He was only trying to be Eric's friend."

"Isn't that an odd way of trying to make friends?" I asked.

"Well, in any case," she added, "I think everything will be okay." And sure enough, Eric was never excluded again.

THAT FALL, I LEARNED THAT the think tank where I was studying was hosting a conference in Kyushu, the island where Dad had spent much of his time in the Occupation interviewing Japanese soldiers. However, this conference was on the northeastern side of the island, the opposite side from where Dad was stationed, and not far from a mountainous region where Grandmother Betty's Japanese mother, Koshiro Fuku, was born. Fuku was the woman Edmund married after separating from Atsushi's great-grandmother. I decided to attend the conference and then take a trip to the mountains in search of Fuku's origins.

I knew little about Fuku, who died in 1901 at age twenty-four. When the city of Kobe moved the foreign cemetery into the hills above Kobe to open up space in the downtown area, they found Fuku's skeleton buried together with the skeleton of a small baby. Fuku had borne four children in six years, and, it seemed, had died trying to give birth to a fifth.

Relatives had told me that Fuku had come from a family of disgraced samurai whose feudal lords had lost their domains in war or who had somehow lost favor with their lords. My newly discovered cousin At-sushi did some research and discovered that in the mountainous area north of Oita, there was a village called Egomori that was thought to have been founded by disgraced samurai. After the conference ended, I rented a car and headed for the mountains.

By the time I got on the road, it was already dusk. I passed a number of little towns including one called Usa. I wondered if that was the town we used to laugh about in my childhood. In the days when Japanese products were still of low quality, the town used to stamp on its manufactured goods "Made in USA." A car dealer in the town had a large model of the Statue of Liberty in its car lot.

For several hours, I wended my way through the mountains. It was nearly ten o'clock and dark when I realized I had lost my way and en-tered a little village to ask directions. When I got back on the highway, I stepped on the gas, eager to reach my destination. As I sliced through the dark paddy fields, I saw headlights in the distance. As they got larg-er and larger, I suddenly realized with horror that they were from a truck that was fast bearing down on me—on my side of the road.

Is this guy nuts? The truck was now less than one hundred yards away, blasting its air horn. *What am I supposed to do?* To my right, the road had no shoulder. I suspected that on the other side of the flimsy railing was a cliff that dropped off sharply into a river gorge. Adrenalin rushed through my veins. I had nowhere to turn.

Then it came to me in a flash. *Oh, my God! I'm the one who's crazy. I'm driv-ing on the wrong side of the road!* As the front grill of that giant truck loomed above me, I swerved over to the left lane. My car shook as the truck shot past me just a few feet away, its air horn still blaring. My heart was pounding violently, so I pulled over to the side of the road and put my head back against the headrest. It was time to find a place for the night.

The white-haired innkeeper was a friendly woman who brought dinner to my room on a tray and then knelt on the floor by the door to talk while I ate hungrily.

"Have you come to teach English at the high school?" the innkeep-er asked.

"No. I'm here to look for my great-grandmother's hometown. She married my German great-grandfather in Kobe, but I think she may have come from Egomori. Do you know that town? I can't seem to find it on my map." I took my map out of my bag and gave it to her.

The innkeeper put on her reading glasses and pored over my

304

map. "I know of the place. It's not far. I have a former classmate who grew up there." She got me a map and circled the town with my pen. Egomori was written with rarely used kanji characters for "house" and "seclusion."

"If your great-grandmother was from Egomori, she must have had a tough life," said the innkeeper. "My classmate said they had to walk twenty minutes down the hill from the village to fetch water. To get to school by eight thirty every morning, she had to leave her village at five, while it was still dark. She would carry a paper lantern to guide her on the steep mountain paths. When day broke, she would blow out the candle and leave the lantern by the side of the path to pick up on the way home.

"Life was so hard in those villages. Trainloads of girls, most of them barely thirteen, went to work in the textile mills in the big cities. Maybe that's how your great-grandmother ended up in Kobe."

The next morning, I headed into the mountains, following a small river before turning left into a narrow tunnel. When I came out the other side, there were tall maples whose leaves had turned a bright scarlet and white-barked birch trees with leaves so yellow they looked like patches of sunshine.

After winding through rolling hills and valleys, I reached a broad plateau where there were hundreds of rows of little teepees made of pine logs drilled with holes from which sprouted shiitake mushrooms. About ten miles later, there was a small temple on my right and a mound of gravestones on my left, placed on either side of the road as if to protect the small cluster of homes just beyond.

"I think my great-grandmother may have come from this village," I said to an old woman who was hanging clothes on bamboo poles in her small yard next door. "Do you know of any families named Koshiro?"

"Well, there used to be a Kono in town until not long ago, but they left," said the old lady. "Only ten households live in the village now. There used to be thirty, but with the cheap mushrooms coming in from China, it's hard to make a living."

The woman turned her back to me and continued to hang her clothes. I grabbed a box of bean cakes from the backseat of my car. Thanking her profusely, I pushed them into her hands. Then I walked about the small village taking pictures. A dog slept in a sunny spot in the middle of the dirt road. The houses were unremarkable, but most had well-tended vegetable gardens. Just outside the village was a bamboo forest that seemed to be pressing in, waiting for the opportunity to retake this almost deserted village.

I wandered into an old mill filled with wooden gears and pulleys the size of bicycle wheels that seemed to date from the age of the steam engine. Inside, I spotted a small grinding stone about the diameter of a steering wheel. "Do you think anybody would mind if I took this grinding stone?" I called out to the old lady who was still hanging her clothes next door.

She came beside me to take a look. She was ghostly thin and not much more than four feet tall. "Go ahead. We used to use those stones to grind rice and barley to make soba [noodles]. The people who owned that mill just left all that trash there and took off years ago. But be careful, the building could collapse." I lifted the stone, feeling a little guilty as I put it in my car. Nobody would miss it, I assured myself. And it could have been here when Fuku lived in the village.

"Is it true that Egomori was founded by fugitive samurai?" I asked.

"Sure it is," she said with a twinkle in her eye. "We were Heike."

"Heike?"

I thought back to my Japanese history. The Heike ruled Japan briefly in the twelfth century. As recounted in "The Tale of Heike," a famous epic poem composed in the thirteenth century, a Heike warrior named Kiyomori, the bastard son of a former emperor, became Japan's most powerful minister. He sought to cement his rule by marrying his daughter to the emperor and putting his grandson on the throne. This was hundreds of years before the Tokugawa Shogunate was established.

So absolute was Heike's power in those days that it was said: "If you are not [Heike], you are not a human being." Brothers from the rival Genji family, which had been crushed by Kiyomori, gathered an army and rose up against the Heike, launching one of the bloodiest civil wars in Japanese history. After five years, the Heike forces were routed at the decisive battle of Dan-no-ura. Hundreds of warriors took their own lives. A few surviving members of the Heike clan, legend has it, clambered to shore, shed their samurai garb and ran for the hills. The Genji soldiers fanned out across the countryside, determined to hunt down and kill every last Heike. Even women and young children were slaughtered.

"There's a cave back there in the woods where I used to play as a child. We called it the Heike cave," the old lady said. "My father told me that his ancestors hid in that cave and watched as the Genji soldiers came through these hills to hunt them down. We have a memorial for the thousand Heike soldiers killed in the great sea battle. It's that mound on the side of the road by the temple."

"If you are interested in this, I have something to show you," the lady said and disappeared into her house. As I waited, I thought about the famous Heike-Genji battle. Recently, I had read up on the history in connection with an *inro,* a palm-sized, lacquer case that my father had left me when he died. The design, made in bold relief with numerous layers of powdered gold, was of a warrior on a horse charging down a steep hill. It was a beautiful piece signed by a famous nineteenth-century artist. But with all its gold, it was gaudy, not the kind of design I would have chosen for myself. I had wondered at the time why Dad had chosen that particular piece for me.

The *inro* depicted the famous Ichinotani battle scene in which the legendary warrior, Yoshitsune, the most famous and revered of the Genji brothers, led a surprise attack on the Heike. Yoshitsune was

later given credit for defeating the Heike forces in the final sea battle. How odd that the memento from Dad depicted a battle in which the hero was vanquishing Heike, the samurai family from which Fuku, Dad's grandmother, may have descended.

When the old lady came back, she had a crumpled, stained paper that had printed on it the words of a song, written during World War II by a school principal who had helped the village through a period when many villagers nearly starved to death. It was clear the principal had written the song—in the style of a traditional Japanese dance—to help the villagers find pride in their Heike heritage.

"Would you sing me the song?" I asked.

She smiled and sang in a voice that was so weak, it sounded like a faint whistle. *When the morning fog clears, the sun shines through this plain of dreams. There is the Heike cave and the memorial for the thousand fallen in the Heike–Genji battle.*

The old lady's eyes started tearing. Suddenly, she stopped herself. "I don't need this anymore," she said, folding the piece of paper on which the song was written and putting it in my hand. "You take it."

I was never able to determine if Great-Grandmother Fuku really did come from Egomori. There were other small villages in the area that claimed to have been established by Heike survivors and were still known as villages of disgraced samurai. I've since learned that there is little historical evidence to support the notion that any of these villages were really founded by Heike soldiers, but it didn't matter to me. There was something about the image of the Heike soldiers running from battle and seeking shelter in these mountains that touched me. Like my family, they were not heroes. They were survivors. These villagers, whose clan might have once ruled Japan, chose to live in disgrace rather than to die with honor. My family, too, did not always choose the honorable path. We took different nationalities to protect our assets through two world wars. But if we had been outsiders in Yokohama for over a century, what was that compared to the inhabitants of this village who had been treated as descendants of disgraced samurai for 815 years? Even then, these villages had transformed that shame to pride.

BACK IN TOKYO, ERIC OFTEN played with his friends. Mariko enjoyed spending time with Yumi, whose parents ran a Japanese restaurant.

They would run around the large restaurant, sometimes watching the elaborate meal preparations. Within a couple of months, Mariko and Eric were both once again chattering away in fluent Japanese.

Perhaps it was the college town we lived in, or the trip to Egomori, or perhaps it was the fact that I was looking at Japan as a researcher rather than a cynical journalist, but I, too, found myself enjoying Japan more than I had since childhood. I wasn't looking for the dark side of Japan, but rather trying to re-establish a connection. When friends invited us to traditional dances or music performances, I didn't complain of boredom, as I once did, but sought instead to savor Japan's unique charms the way Great-Grandfathers Julius and Edmund, and Opa might have when they first experienced them.

Those final winter days of 1999, before we left Japan, were glorious. I had almost forgotten how bright and clear the sky could be in December. Marie and I took long bike rides with Mariko and Eric along the nearby Tama River. On New Year's Eve, the night before the last year of the second millennium, while some of my colleagues at the think tank had retreated to their country homes in fear of the millennium bug's impact on computers, we went to Jindaiji, an old temple on the outskirts of Tokyo. We painted little clay figurines of dragons to celebrate the year 2000, the year of the dragon. We stood in line before the temple bell for our turn to ring in the New Year. Mariko and Marie went first. Then Eric and I stood right below that thirteen-hundred-year-old bell, the size of a Volkswagen Bug. We grabbed the hemp rope that was attached to a large log, pulled that bell ringer as far as we could and then swung it forward so it hit the bell hard.

At first, the sound was deep and faint, as if it had come from far away. I imagined the sound beginning in the distant past and then gaining power as it reached the present, ringing so powerfully that my whole body vibrated. And as it did so, I somehow knew that the chasm I had once felt was no longer there. In its place was something new, something real that I could not quite define but had something to do with who I was and how I was connected to my past and to my children and to my future. Then the sound faded, as though it were sinking again into the past. I put my arm around Eric's shoulder and we followed Marie and Mariko into the New Year's crowd.

In the lazy days of the New Year, when most businesses in Japan shut down, we made a final round of visits to our friends. I felt a noticeable change in their attitude—or perhaps I was just more receptive.

One Japanese couple gave our kids the traditional pocket money given to children by relatives at New Year's. They asked the kids to call them aunt and uncle. "I can see your hearts have connected to your children," said the mother at the end of our stay.

When we told the school we were leaving, Mariko's and Eric's classes gave them a warm send-off. They each came home with scrapbooks filled with pictures and farewell messages. Yumi wrote Mariko that she was her best friend and that she would never forget her. Eric's classmates gave him a scrapbook filled with drawings by each child. Eric and Mariko had come to love Japan and their new friends, but they were happy to return to Seattle. I was also happy to be going home, but for the first time I also felt sad to leave Japan. Back in Seattle, I placed the grinding stone by our back door under a Japanese camellia bush.

一〵〱〴〵可五枝〱〱

外二
せんす〱堂　横井朝治

横〱

外二
金武円ヤ　小宮ひろ

横〱

外二
〱〱〱円〳　羽山〱三〱

LOOKING FOR HIRO
& MY JAPANESE
ROOTS

WE HAD ONLY BEEN IN Japan for four months, but it had a big impact on our family. Eric and Mariko both came home speaking Japanese fluently. They missed their friends in Japan. Soon immersed in their American schools and sports, they gradually drifted again from Japan, but Eric had developed a strong sense of his Japanese heritage. He was twelve when he came home one day mystified that some of his friends didn't believe that I was Japanese. It had never occurred to him that I didn't look like him. For Mariko, by contrast, being adopted remained a sore point all through high school.

"How did it go?" I asked Mariko hesitantly when she returned from school one day.

"What do you think? I can't believe you made me do this! I felt like I was walking around all day with a sign on my head that says 'I'm adopted.'"

It had been grandparents' day at Mariko's school, when students were asked to take their grandparents on a tour of their high school. When my mother had received the invitation from The Northwest School and expressed an interest in going, I had told her Mariko would be happy to take her around. I had been wrong, but I didn't have the

OPPOSITE: Record of Hiro's large gift to Komiya relative at funeral.

heart to tell my mother that her granddaughter didn't want to be seen with her and I had insisted Mariko agree to guide her *Babachan*, as our children called their grandmother, around the school.

"I'm sorry sweetie, but I didn't want to hurt *Babachan's* feelings." I told her.

"What about my feelings?" she wailed.

"Everybody has some cross to bear."

Mariko refused to talk to me for a week. I should have known better than to force the issue. Although Mariko's closest friends knew her parents were white, she hated having to explain to everyone else that she was adopted.

I continued to plod along with my family research. I learned much about myself and the Helms. Yet deep down I still longed for some public recognition of my family's long presence in Japan. So when I received a copy of a book about Yokohama landmarks in the spring of 2001 and saw featured on its jacket cover a picture of Helm House, the five-story building Grandfather Julie had built in 1938, I was thrilled.

The slim volume contained a chapter on Helm House written by Mukuyoshi Saburo, a young reporter for *The Yomiuri Shimbun*, Japan's largest daily newspaper. Mukuyoshi quoted experts who admired the building as an early example in Japan of "modern" architecture and called it a harbinger of the "Western lifestyle." So when I traveled to Japan with my family later that summer, I visited Mukuyoshi at his Yokohama office. Our meeting that morning would launch me on one of the most unexpected and rewarding parts of my family journey.

"Have you seen the Helm House site yet?" Mukuyoshi asked after we had finished our tea. "Let me take you in my car."

I was not prepared for what I saw when I got out of the car. The massive concrete building that my grandfather built in 1938—and which had anchored my family to Yokohama for three generations—was gone. In its place was a large dome of stretched white plastic, the kind of temporary structure so common at trade fairs.

I felt sick. Growing up in Yokohama, I had never thought much of the building. But after years of research I had become attached to it. I thought of the German navy officers who stayed there during World War II and the US Eighth Army brass that replaced them afterward, during the Occupation. Then I thought of the time capsule Grandfather Julie buried under the building. Now we would never know what it contained.

"A lot of people wanted to preserve the building," said Mukuyoshi. "They gave several tours of the building, and hundreds of people came to see it."

"What is that?" I asked, pointing to the plastic dome.

"It's a Kabuki theatre. An official of the prefecture was a big fan of Bando Tamasaburo [a Kabuki actor famous as a female impersonator] and built this new stage so he would perform in Yokohama." After his first performance, Tamasaburo declared that the street noise made it a terrible location.

"Now the theater is unused," said Mukuyoshi. "But there's something else I want to show you." He led me to the far corner of the block where there was a small stucco building the size of a neighborhood post office.

"When they started to knock down this little storage building, they were surprised to hit brick," said Mukuyoshi. "People thought all of the city's brick buildings had collapsed during the 1923 earthquake. An architectural historian determined that this is probably the oldest building in Yokohama."

The building's address, #48, appeared above the door in stone. I knew my family had owned this property for half a century. *Perhaps Great-Grandfather Julius himself had built it?* I wondered. Mukuyoshi revealed, however, that a local architect had identified the structure as the surviving wing of what had once been the headquarters of Mollison, a British trading company.

Back at the Yomiuri office, Mukuyoshi could tell I felt dejected. "What are you going to do now?" he asked.

"I want to track down my Japanese Great-Grandmother Hiro who was married to my Great-Grandfather Julius," I said.

"Oh? What do you know about her?"

Some years before, I had found a genealogical chart that my Great-Uncle Willie had filled out, perhaps as part of an effort to join a Nazi-affiliated association. It included the names of Hiro's parents, her grandparents, her siblings and even their spouses. I had also heard that Hiro's father had been mayor of Hiratsuka, a city of a quarter million west of Yokohama. I went to the Hiratsuka City office to look at birth records, but was told my search would be impossible since birth records were filed not by name but by address. I was directed to a scholar who worked in the library next door.

The scholar offered little encouragement. "Your great-great-grandfather couldn't have been the mayor of Hiratsuka," he said. "This city didn't even exist until the early 1900s. This area was just a handful of small villages."

The scholar led me to the reference section and pulled out a book. "Read this. It contains the names of villagers who served in official posts over the past century."

I sat at a nearby desk and flipped through the book. I was crest-fallen. The book had no index. It was packed with thousands of names, most of which I could not read. I knew that Hiro's last name, Komi-ya, was written with the kanji for "small" and "shrine." But I had no idea how her father's name, Shichizaemon, would be written. My eyes glazed over as I scanned page after page packed with kanji characters I could not recognize.

I was ready to give up when my thumb stopped on a page with sever-al Komiyas. I could not read the first names of the first two Komiyas, but the kanji in the third name were quite simple. The first character was 七, which means "seven" and is read as *shichi*. The second character was 左. It meant "left" and is read as "*sa*" or "za." The third character was 衛. It meant "protect" and read as "*e*." The final character was 門. It meant "gate" and was pronounced "*mon.*" *Shichi sa e mon.* Shichizaemon. *This could be my Japanese great-great-grandfather!*

I had finally tracked him down, or so I thought. The name, I learned later, means "guard at the seventh gate," suggesting it was the name of a low-ranking samurai. Shichizaemon was identified in the book as a "neighborhood leader" in the village of Yokouchi.

I returned to the scholar's office filled with excitement, but the scholar shook his head. Pulling out a local phone book, he showed me there were hundreds of Komiyas living in Yokouchi, a neighborhood on the eastern edge of Hiratsuka. "You'll need to check the Buddhist temples," he advised. "There are only two in the Yokouchi area. They might have a record."

In Japan, people tend to have their weddings at Shinto shrines and their funerals at Buddhist temples. Shrines avoid funerals because the native religion associates death with pollution. Buddhism, on the other hand, with its belief in rebirth, puts a great emphasis on rituals related to death.

At the first temple I visited, a priest kindly waded through a large stack of scrolled rice-paper records with names listed in bold black brush strokes. He found many Komiyas recorded, but none with the

316

first name Shichizaemon. At the other temple, which had recently been rebuilt, the priest's wife looked at me scornfully. "We threw away all those old records," she said. "We have nothing."

I told Mukuyoshi, on finishing the story, that my next step was to start telephoning all the Komiyas who lived in Yokouchi. "Maybe someone will know something about Hiro's marriage to a foreigner."

Mukuyoshi was skeptical. I wanted to explain to him how Hiro was this remarkable woman who had stopped a sword with her bare hand, how she had single-handedly led her young children across the Pacific Ocean and the continental United States to join her husband in Virginia in 1886, at a time when few Japanese had set foot on American soil. But I said nothing.

"Do you mind if I write a story about your family search?" Mukuyoshi asked, as if he had been reading my mind. The article, which was prominently displayed in the *Yomiuri* the next morning, included a picture of Hiro and a second picture of me under the large headline: "Great-Grandmother Komiya Hiro. Do you know her?"

The next day, Mukuyoshi called me at my hotel room with excitement. He had received a phone call from a woman who thought she might be related.

I met Yoko and her husband Katsuaki in the lobby of a hotel near Yokohama Station two days later. In her mid-30s, Yoko had the poise, the perfectly coiffed hair and the formal speech of an upper-class lady. Katsuaki was dressed more informally and had kind eyes that were big, dark and shiny like the eyes of a deer. He seemed uncomfortable when I handed him a bottle of Chivas as a gift.

We sat on a stone bench in the hotel lobby, while I showed them the family scrapbook I had put together. Katsuaki's face fell when he saw my photocopy of Hiro's family crest—two eagle feathers crossed.

"Are you sure that is accurate? This is not our family crest," Katsuaki said. "Our family crest shows three wisteria blossoms." We were all disappointed, but Katsuaki had already arranged to have me meet his parents.

As we moved slowly through heavy traffic headed for Hiratsuka, about nineteen miles west of Yokohama, Katsuaki filled me in on his family history. "The Komiyas were one of several families that descended from a powerful lord who ruled the Yokohama and Tokyo area in about 500 AD. There was a Komiya who was a senior retainer in 1192 of the Shogun Minamoto Yoritomo [the Genji leader who triumphed over the Heike]. In the 1400s, there had even been a Komiya castle, although it burned down when the Komiyas were defeated in battle."

Then Katsuaki bowed down as if in apology. "You know, we are not samurai. In the old days, many families, including the Komiyas, were both farmers and samurai. They worked their fields from spring to fall, then went out to fight as samurai in the winter. When Toyotomi Hideyoshi established the caste system in the late 1500s, everybody had to make a decision. Some of the Komiyas became full-time samurai, but our family decided they could have better lives as farmers."

When I told the Komiyas about the dead-end I had reached trying to track down my Great-Great-Grandfather Shichizaemon at the temples, Katsuaki said he was not surprised.

"The local temples would not have had records of Shichizaemon," Katsuaki explained. "The practice of having funerals at Buddhist temples is a relatively recent phenomenon of the past few hundred years. The ancient Japanese believed that ancestors became gods who protected their family. Older families like Shichizaemon's therefore kept their family cemeteries close to their homes."

I was mystified by the depth and breadth of Katsuaki's knowledge. "I've never met anyone able to explain Japan's history and customs as well as you do," I told him.

"That's my job," said Katsuaki. "I studied history in college. Now I'm a Shinto priest at the Hachimangu Shrine."

My jaw dropped. *A Shinto priest?* The only Shinto priests I had ever seen wore long white robes and tall black hats, and chanted with voices and faces devoid of emotion. It seemed impossible to me that Katsuaki, so young and engaged, could be such a priest. And not just any priest, but a priest at Tsurugaoka Hachimangu, one of Japan's largest and most famous shrines. It was located in the old capital of Kamakura, about eleven miles outside Yokohama.

Later, I learned that Yoko's father was also a priest. Her family owned three shrines that had been passed down through the family for generations. Since Yoko had no brother, it was always understood that Yoko would marry a priest. He would be adopted into the family and take her family name as well as her father's priestly duties at the family shrines.

Japanese are typically tight-lipped about their private lives. Yet Yoko and Katsuaki, from the beginning, were unusually open. At one point,

318

I asked Katsuaki how long it would have taken my Great-Grandmother Hiro to walk from Hiratsuka to Yokohama.

"About seven and a half hours," he said. "I know, because once I walked the whole way."

"You walked from Yokohama to Hiratsuka?" I said in disbelief.

Katsuaki looked back at Yoko, and I saw her nod.

"Yoko and I got into a fight, so I left the house, but since I didn't have the keys to the car I had to walk all the way to my father's house."

Yoko chuckled softly. "I told him that next time he stomps out, he should remember the keys."

At Katsuaki's parents' house, a typical two-story Japanese residence with brown stucco walls and a tiled roof, Katsuaki's mother served me cold barley tea. The house was warm and humid, and the cold tea was refreshing. Katsuaki disappeared and returned holding the elbow of his frail grandmother.

I greeted the grandmother and then showed her my photo of Hiro and Julius with their seven children.

"My, what a fine family Hiro had," the grandmother said, stopping to clear her throat. "My husband gave me a foreign leather purse that he said came from Hiro. I used to keep all my valuables in it. I always hid it in the futon closet. I lost it when my house burned down."

My anticipation rose but then fell when the grandmother said she had never heard anything about Hiro marrying a foreigner.

Soon Katsuaki's father, a carpenter who had been working on a house nearby, arrived home on his bicycle. We needed him, Katsuaki explained, to give us a proper introduction to the patriarch of the *honke*, the main branch of the family. In traditional Japanese families, the eldest son, as head of the main branch of the family, inherits the family's land and takes care of the ancestral graves.

Just as we were about to enter the *honke* patriarch's house, Yoko handed me the bottle of Chivas I had given to them earlier. "Why don't you give this to the patriarch?" she suggested. I felt awkward taking back the gift, but I was depending on her and Katsuaki to help me navigate the complexities of village life.

The patriarch was an old man with a grizzled beard. When I handed him the Chivas, he gave me a wide smile that showed missing teeth. He welcomed me into his house, which had walls of exposed mud and straw. Massive, crooked beams supported the roof. The house looked as if it could have been three hundred years old, but the old man told me it had been built right after the Great Earthquake of 1923.

As soon as I was seated, the old man went to the small family shrine at the back of the room, and came back with a handful of wooden ancestral tablets and shuffled through them. The tablets were long and narrow, and had kanji painted on them in black brush strokes.

These tablets were representations of the family ancestors, the ancestral gods that would guide and protect the family. The only time I had ever seen such tablets was when I was writing about a Japanese television show that depicted "true stories" of the supernatural. In the show, just as something tragic was about to happen—an old woman possessed by the devil and trying to kill a child, for example—one of these ancestral tablets would fly through the air like some supernatural being and land on the person with the distinct clacking sound of wood on wood just in time to dispel the evil.

The patriarch could not find a tablet with the name of my Great-Great-Grandfather Shichizaemon. I was sure he had already looked before and was only shuffling through the tablets again for my benefit. Then he brought out a neatly folded piece of rice paper. "This is what made us think we might be related to you," he said.

The paper was an "IOU" for a large amount of money that the patriarch's grandfather had borrowed from a man named Komiya Shichizaemon and received back after repaying the loan. "The only reason I can imagine that Shichizaemon would have loaned us so much money is that we were somehow related."

"This IOU shows which pieces of land Shichizaemon held as collateral against the loan," explained Katsuaki's father. "Apparently Shichizaemon also had substantial gambling debts of his own."

If this was Hiro's father, perhaps the debts explained why Shichizaemon had been willing to allow his daughter, Hiro, to work in Yokohama as a maid and had permitted her to marry a foreigner.

The patriarch had another document showing Hiro had contributed an enormous sum at his grandfather's funeral, suggesting she must have been a close relative.

"Come," said the patriarch, "let me show you the grave."

The old man led us down a narrow dirt path past a large farmhouse. Behind the house was a cemetery about the size of a large backyard. It was a stone's throw from the elevated tracks of the bullet train, and periodically we could see the bull-nosed train zip past. Along one side

320

of the cemetery, separating it from the large farmhouse, was a three-foot-high wall made of piled-up gravestones.

"After a few generations, individual graves are not important to the family anymore because those ancestors become gods," Katsuaki said with a laugh. "Maybe your great-great-grandfather's grave is somewhere in that wall."

My eyes opened wide. I was a little shocked at the thought.

The old man led us to a large, relatively new looking gravestone of polished black granite. The first thing I noticed was the prominent design carved into the headstone: two eagle feathers crossed. *Hiro's family crest! This could be it,* I thought. I couldn't stop beaming. Katsuaki had noticed the crest too and smiled at me.

Behind the big headstone was a smaller, much older looking stone the size of a shoebox. "Look here," said the patriarch. He rubbed some of the moss off the stone and began to read. "This stone was laid by Shichizaemon."

We looked more closely at the newer black headstone. Above the two crossed eagle feathers was a series of names showing all the family members whose ashes had been buried there. The oldest family member was Komiya Tojiro. *Tojiro,* I thought to myself. The name sounded familiar. I pulled out my genealogy of Hiro's family. I showed it to Katsuaki. A man named Tojiro had married Hiro's older sister, been adopted into the family, and taken the Komiya name because Hiro had no brothers. He would represent the main branch of the family, the one responsible for maintaining the grave and carrying on the family name.

"Where do Tojiro's descendants live?" I asked Katsuaki.

"They live right there," said Katsuaki, pointing to the big farmhouse beside the cemetery. "They are from one of the oldest families in Yokouchi. There was a Hiro in that family, but they insist that she had no children."

I could feel the tension in the air. Clearly, the two families did not get along. And yet it was probably Tojiro's family to which I was most closely related. As we left the cemetery and walked past the old house, I asked if I could take a few pictures. Katsuaki looked alarmed.

"Go ahead," said the patriarch.

As I was taking pictures, the patriarch went up to the front door of the farmhouse and knocked. A man with jet-black hair that had been greased back and who looked to be in his early forties came to the door.

I later calculated he must have been Tojiro's great-grandson. He had evidently just awoken from an afternoon nap and looked annoyed as he rubbed his eyes. I moved closer to hear what they were saying.

"He came all the way from America," the patriarch said, pointing toward me. "He has pictures and everything. You should see them."

The patriarch pulled from his pocket a clipping of Mukuyoshi's newspaper article. "They wrote all about him in the *Yomiuri Shimbun*," he said, waving the article in the air. "How is it going to look if you refuse to see him now?"

The man took the article from the old man and barely glanced at it. "I know nothing about this article," he said coldly, returning it to the patriarch. Then he looked my way, narrowing his eyes and staring at me for a few seconds before giving me a wary nod. "Well, okay. Come in."

Like the patriarch's house, the walls of this Komiya's house were of mud and straw with large, rough-hewn timbers supporting the high roof. We sat on the tatami mats inside in an order which, I quickly realized, represented a distinct hierarchy. As the invited guest, I was placed to the left of my host in front of the alcove where a brush painting hung. On the right of our young host was the patriarch. Although older, he appeared to be of a somewhat lower status than the Komiya whose home we were in. On my left was Katsuaki's father. Still standing out in the pounded-dirt entryway were the young priest Katsuaki and his wife. They were important people in their respective communities, but in this village, it seemed, they didn't even have enough standing to be invited into the house.

"So what do you want from me?" the other Komiya asked sharply.

"I'm trying to find out about Hiro. She married my great-grandfather, Julius."

"No. Hiro never had any children," he replied firmly, as if he had already checked out the story. He nodded to an old lady who had been waiting in the dark recesses at the back of the room and now came forward to serve us green tea.

"Show him the pictures," the patriarch said.

I pulled out my album and showed him my pictures of Hiro and Julius with their seven children.

"You're talking about things that happened one hundred years ago," said the man. "How should I know if these pictures are real?"

I was taken aback by the vehemence with which he rejected my story.

I took out my genealogy of Hiro's family and proceeded to name Hiro's sisters and the men that they had married, including Tojiro, my host's great-grandfather. The mention of Tojiro seemed to impress the man.

"What do you plan to do with this information?" he asked.

"I am writing a family history."

The young man seemed to relax. Perhaps he thought I wanted a share of his inheritance. He took a crumpled piece of paper out of his pocket. Hiding it behind the palm of his hand, he smirked.

"Well, everything you say is completely wrong. It wasn't Hiro that married a foreigner, it was her sister Fusa," the man said triumphantly.

I didn't know what the man was talking about, but I was excited. He had acknowledged that there was a foreign connection. I started to press him for more information, but Yoko gave me a nod from the doorway.

"We should leave now," she said quietly.

Afterward, I told Katsuaki and Yoko I wanted to check our host's family birth registry at city hall. Now that I had an address, I figured, the research should be easy. Yoko discouraged me, worried that we could get in trouble prying into the affairs of others. When I said I would go on my own, they reluctantly agreed to accompany me.

My request at city hall for the records set off a lot of head scratching. To check the records, I had to be a direct descendant, and the official didn't believe a white man like me could possibly have Japanese ancestors. The supervisor, an efficient-looking woman, however, came by and asked me some questions. Katsuaki and Yoko explained the situation. The officials huddled. Finally, the woman agreed to investigate.

"I'm sorry, I can't find anything," the official said when he returned to the counter half an hour later. Then he looked at the chart again. "Wait a minute." He went back to his boss for another consultation. Another hour passed. My train would be leaving soon, and I was now feeling bad about having dragged Yoko and Katsuaki into this fruitless search.

"Let's forget about this," I said. "I've already caused you so much trouble."

"No, we should wait," said Yoko. "Let's pray."

She put her hands together, closed her eyes and bowed her head. I closed my eyes and put my hands together.

Out of the corner of my eye I could see Katsuaki. He looked calm. I thought of Hiro and then I suddenly felt confused. *To whom am I praying?*

The Shinto gods? Katsuaki had said Shinto was more an embodiment of Japanese history and culture than a religion. *But how much a part of Japanese history and culture was I?*

"If only they would find something," Yoko said, as she put down her hands. There was a new intimacy in her voice that touched me.

When the official came back with a sheaf of papers, he was shaking his head. "This is the *koseki* [birth record] starting with Shichizaemon, but I don't see Hiro's name and I don't see Julius's name. Do you want an official copy anyway? That would be 2,500 yen each."

Katsuaki looked at me. "Might as well," I said.

"We'll get a copy, too," said Yoko. "I've always been curious about this family."

We must have been at the city office for nearly three hours when we finally got the records, returned to the car and headed for the train station. My train was scheduled to leave in ten minutes, so we had to rush. As we drove, Yoko sat in the back quietly going through the papers.

"I found it!" Yoko suddenly shrieked. "It says here Karu Helm."

I could hear the excitement in her voice and it thrilled me that this woman who I had only met that morning was so caught up in my search. I looked at the document she held. Glued to one page was a tiny strip of paper no more than a quarter-inch wide and an inch long with the name Karu Helm written in Japanese. It had been attached to the registry on top of the name of Fusa, Hiro's sister, and marked with a red seal.

At first I was confused. Who was Karu Helm? Then it hit me. Karu, of course, was the Japanese way of pronouncing Karl. That would be Julius and Hiro's oldest son, the one who had taken Japanese citizenship for business reasons and changed his name to Charles to distance himself from his former German nationality. Under Japanese law, a person must be placed in a Japanese family's birth registry before he or she can be recognized as a citizen. Since Hiro was dead by the time Karl discovered that he needed to become a Japanese citizen to register Helm Brothers' many ships, Karl must have arranged to have his name included in the family registry of his mother Hiro's divorced older sister Fusa.

In time I would learn that Hiro's other older sister, the one who married Tojiro, died at a young age. Tojiro, who had by then been adopted into the Komiya family, remarried. Since neither he nor his wife had a biological connection to the Komiyas, he saw no reason to maintain relationships with his former wife's family and no longer welcomed Hiro and her sisters at the house. Hiro stayed instead with her aunts and uncles, relatives of Katsuaki's.

My journey to Egomori, the mountain village, in search of my other Japanese Great-Grandmother Fuku had made me feel connected to Japan. But this was a link that traced me back to my precise Japanese roots. Those birth records made it clear that my Great-Grandmother Hiro had been born and raised right there in the house next to the cemetery. While in the past, I would have avoided being entrapped in the web of mutual obligations that require such a commitment, the connection to Yoko and Katsuaki was one I longed to cultivate for me and for my children.

IN THE SUMMER OF 2004, I decided to take a trip to meet many of the people I had come across in the course of my family search. Then forty-eight, I was about the age Great-Grandfather Julius was in 1885, when he sold his first company in Yokohama and bought his dream plantation in Virginia. I was about the age my father was in 1973 when he sold Helm Brothers and shed us, his family, as if we were burdensome winter clothes, before embarking on a world tour with his new wife. Great-Grandfather Julius and Dad had jettisoned their pasts in their search for a new life—and had been disappointed. I was choosing a different path, one that was taking me back into the past.

That summer, the plan was for me to travel to Japan for a couple of weeks. Marie and the kids would join me later. First, I visited my cousin Tsunemochi Atsushi in Kobe. Atsushi had grown more philosophical over the years. While there is an invisible thread that binds us all, he said, we don't see it until we are ready. He reminded me of the stormy day in 1983 when he had gone to visit my father in Yokohama. Dad had politely listened to the story, but was uninterested in learning more. Atsushi and I, by contrast, had followed every lead in search of our roots.

On one of his recent overseas trips, Atsushi had come across the remains of St. Francis Xavier, a Jesuit who was one of the first Westerners to come to Japan when he arrived in 1549. For Atsushi, a religious man, Xavier's role in bringing the Christian religion to Japan had a powerful meaning. Xavier, I later discovered, was Basque as is my wife Marie. Eric used to find it strange that he, with his Japanese blood, should be celebrating Basque traditions just because Marie's family was Basque. We told him that he was inheriting the culture of both his parents, as every child does. Yet, here was this odd link between the Basques and the Japanese.

I bid the Tsunemochis goodbye and visited the wooded grounds of the elegant Wakayama castle, not far by train, where Julius had trained his peasant soldiers in 1871. The original castle, built in the sixteenth century, had been destroyed by American firebombs during World War II and been rebuilt in the 1960s.

I visited the Wakayama city museum nearby and met the new curator. He took me to the sites where Julius had taught his soldiers to march. We walked under massive old camphor trees that must have been there when Julius lived in Wakayama in 1871 and along the moat where he had taught his men to build pontoon bridges. I thought about how shocked the soldiers had been to discover that the bridge they had built in a few short hours did not collapse when they marched across it. The pontoon bridge, it seems to me now, is symbolic of what the West had brought to Japan: a focus on speed, function and efficiency, often at the cost of aesthetics and tradition.

I had never visited Ise Shrine, the most sacred Shinto shrine in Japan, so I decided to take a detour to see the famous site. The shrine is rebuilt every twenty years on an adjacent lot because the main pillars on which the entire building rests are buried directly into the soil in accordance with ancient designs and would start to rot. The old shrine is dismantled, and its pieces distributed to shrines across Japan. Only a single post is left in the ground covered by a small hut, as if to keep alive that divine connection between the natural world that the earth represents and the sun goddess.

I attached myself to a tour group that traveled slowly through the shrine complex. When we finally reached the top of the stairs to see the shrine, there was only a white curtain that stretched fifty feet across a dirt field. "Where is the shrine?" I asked the guide.

"It is hidden behind the white curtain," he said. "Ordinary people are not allowed to look upon it."

At first, I felt duped and walked away. I had traveled two days for this? I suspected that the curtain, like the one that hid the Wizard of

Oz, concealed a lie. That impression was reinforced when I heard a tour guide explain to his group how exposure to the shrine had helped a bald man grow new hair.

When I returned to look again on that white curtain, I could not shake the feeling that it really did hide something powerful and mysterious. Shinto, with its focus on the daily rituals that bound the people to the earth—the planting and harvesting of rice, of birth and of marriage—had rooted Japanese to their land for millennia. This place of worship modeled after ancient rice granaries was identical in every detail to the original structure built fifteen hundred years ago and yet was only ten years old. It was a powerful metaphor for the paradox of change and continuity that was so much a part of Japanese life. I had always felt that traditions like these, which saw the Japanese race in a special light, excluded people like me with mixed blood. Yet, for the first time I understood Japan's dilemma: How do you maintain this rich and complex culture while at the same time adapting to powerful new currents of technology and society? Would Japan ever totally accept inter-racial marriage, adoption and people of other cultures?

As I traveled across Japan that summer of 2004, I felt as if I were in a twilight zone in which everything was connected. I spent an evening with an English teacher who had received Julius's autobiography from my father's cousin Richard and had become obsessed with the story. The two had met on an Internet site where they both engaged in their hobby of trading license plates. The man intended to travel to Rosow, the birthplace of Great-Grandfather Julius, to find out more about his past.

On my way back to Tokyo, I received e-mail from a collector whose hobby was to track down the "spirit life" of his ancient clocks. One of his clocks had the name of my other great-grandfather, Edmund Stucken, pressed in relief on its copper exterior. We had connected that summer by chance when the collector's son, using the Internet, had come across the Stucken name in a biography of my brother, Chris, who was on the board of the Japanese-American Chamber of Commerce in Seattle. The father had been searching for the proper home for his clock for thirty years. We drank coffee and exchanged stories about our respective journeys into the past. I knew that Atsushi would love the clock and suggested he give it to Atsushi.

A few days later, Marie arrived in Tokyo with our two kids, meeting me at the condo some Japanese friends let us borrow for a week. The next day we went to a fancy shopping district to look for a kimono for Mariko so we could attend a kimono party we had been invited to. "Do I look Japanese?" Mariko turned to me and whispered as we walked along the crowded sidewalk.

I smiled and stepped back a little to give her a good look. Mariko wore a white dress printed with hundreds of tiny purses that looked like tiny slices of watermelons. She was gorgeous with her black hair cut shoulder-length. She walked with her shoulders back, her head held high and a spring in her step. Her face was open and easy to read. The young Japanese people who walked by seemed, by contrast, sullen and unhappy.

"Not really," I said. "You walk different. You wear different clothes." I meant it as a compliment—she seemed more free-spirited than the people walking by—but she did not like what I said. Mariko frowned slightly as if to hide her thoughts, to meld with the crowd.

Only then did I realize how desperately Mariko still wanted to fit into Japanese society. When people in America asked her if she was Japanese American, Mariko had a simple answer. "No. I'm Japanese and American." I had been impressed by that answer. It didn't occur to me that she meant it in a very literal sense.

We took a train to Hiratsuka where we had arranged to meet the Komiyas, our distant Japanese relatives. The Komiyas took us to visit the grave of my great-great-grandfather, Hiro's father, beside the elevated bullet-train tracks. Then we walked to the father's house for tea.

When we had finished our tea, Katsuaki's mother brought out a large box.

"We thought Mariko might enjoy this," she said.

When Mariko opened the box, her eyes lit up. It was a *yukata,* a light cotton summer kimono. The mother helped Mariko put it on. Mariko modeled it for us. She looked radiant clothed in the material of bright reds and blues.

On the way home, Mariko was quiet. She chose to sit on the other side of the train carriage as she often did when she didn't want people staring at us, wondering what her relationship was to us. Back at the condo, she lay on her futon and read a Japanese comic book she had purchased on the way home. I was making a pot of tea and Marie was reading a book.

"I want to find my biological mother," Mariko said suddenly.

I was caught by surprise. As a little girl, she had often asked about her biological mother, but it had been many years since she had shown any interest. Looking back now, it's clear to me that my search for family had re-awakened her interest in her own biological parents.

"I don't know if we would be able to find her. We don't know her address," I said.

"Isn't there somewhere we could go to find out?" she asked.

"We could, but they have a policy against revealing this kind of information." Then I added something I would regret for the rest of my life: "Your biological mother has our address. She could find you if she wanted."

As soon as I spoke, I froze.

"You didn't need to say that," Marie said to me sharply.

Mariko looked at me with tears welling up in her eyes. "I hate you," she said, shaking her head.

I grimaced, as I often did when I was uncomfortable, as my father always did. Mariko thought I was mocking her.

"Nobody hurts me as much as you." She spit the words out at me before turning around and going to her room.

Only now, years later, have I begun to understand that my failure at that moment as a father also reflected my tendency to evade difficult questions of love and human relationships by turning to logic. Mariko had expressed a longing to meet her biological mother and connect with the Japan of her birth. My role as a parent should have been to offer my support, to help her in any way she needed to achieve her heart's desire. Yet instead I had hurt her deeply. I had undermined her confidence by questioning her biological mother's desire to see her.

What I had said to Mariko was not the whole truth. Even if Mariko's biological mother had wanted to establish a relationship with Mariko, she likely would have been reluctant to contact us, believing she would be intruding in our lives.

I should have been better prepared for the question. I knew that earlier generations of Asian children adopted by American families had faced many problems. I had read books about the alienation they felt growing up in white communities cut off from their cultures and from people like themselves, but I had convinced myself that we were different. *We were culturally sensitive,* I told myself. *Our love was unconditional.* I believed it was better to tell the hard truth than to allow my daughter to build up illusions about what her biological mother might be like.

I had not understood that just as I was searching into my past to establish my sense of identity, to come to peace with Japan, Mariko needed to take her own voyage to understand her past, to find her family roots. Yes, she was in our family tree, but somewhere out there, she knew, was another family tree. Now that I had undercut her, it would take Mariko far more courage to do what she had to do.

As I think of that day ten years later, I realize that something else lay behind what I said: I was afraid of sharing my children with a stranger, even if that stranger was her biological mother. That's the truth. When Marie and I started thinking about adoption, I was secretly relieved that Japanese adoption policy did not allow biological mothers the option of continuing to visit their biological children as had become common in the United States. I didn't like the idea of having a third parent involved because of the potential for emotional turmoil in us and in our children.

It always pained me when I read stories of adopted children who left their adoptive parents and latched onto their biological parents as if genetics could trump all the thousands of hours of love and nurturing adoptive parents give. So while I had always resolved to help Mariko find her birth mother when the time came, I had hoped that wouldn't happen until she had grown up. I couldn't accept the possibility that, as adoptive parents, Marie and I couldn't fulfill all the needs of our children.

I have often heard people say that raising children is just a question of loving them. How wrong that is. Love is just the beginning. I should have known. Dad had loved me too, I now understand, but that was not nearly enough.

WE STOOD THERE AT THE bank of the river, my son Eric and I, leaning against the rubber river rafts pulled up on the gravel, while the guide ran through the basics.

"Wedge your feet under the inflated sides of the raft," he said. "That'll keep you from being thrown out of the boat."

We were about to ride the Upper Klamath River as it plunged ten miles from where we were, high in the southern Oregon mountains, down through deep gorges and steep hairpin turns before meandering across the California border. We would pass through forty rapids, including some of the toughest in the Northwest. At one segment, called Hell's Corner, the river would look like a waterfall as it cut through lava beds so sharp they had ripped holes in the bottoms of similar rafts. Other tour organizations, I later learned, required participants to wear wetsuits as protection. We only wore life jackets and helmets.

It was Eric's sixteenth birthday and an opportunity for me to spend some time with my son. He remained a mystery to me in many ways. For years he loved reading encyclopedias about electricity and weather and would even enjoy wading through electronics manuals. I envied him for his self-assurance and his logical mind. Whereas I found manuals confusing and preferred to learn things through trial and error,

Eric patiently learned the inner logic of every device in the same way he learned to navigate complex computer games.

Recently, he had started to show more interest in his Japanese past. He had started using his Japanese birth name as his computer sign on; and I had heard him boast to his friends that he could speak Japanese. When I had tried to talk about our family history, he had responded simply, "They are not my relatives. They have nothing to do with me." I tried to explain to him at the time that families were not only about blood ties. Marie, he and I were all part of the same family even though none of us was related by blood. Eric was not convinced.

That summer he had begun training for football, and his arms and shoulders bulged. When Eric was younger, he and I often locked arms in a sumo stance and pushed against each other on the slippery wood floor of the kitchen. Now on the few occasions when we locked arms, I could hardly budge him. Once, Eric simply lifted me in the air as I had once done to him as a boy. I was embarrassed, but I also felt a moment of joy—in these teenage years, we had so little physical contact. Eric spent most of his time on multiple computers playing games, connecting with friends over Facebook and listening to music on his iPod. There were frequent battles of wills as I tried to get him to help more around the house. I missed the bundle of squealing, laughing joy that Eric had once been. I worried we were drifting apart as my father and I once had.

When the rafting guide came to the end of the talk, we put on our lifejackets and helmets and climbed into the raft together with two other teenage boys and their father.

"Now, we need a leader with some experience. Any volunteers?"

I raised my hand. I hadn't rafted much, but I was confident I could handle it. I hadn't yet heard the story about the woman who had broken her leg falling out of the boat. She had to complete the entire trip on the rapids with a piece of bone sticking out of her leg.

"Okay," the guide said turning to me. "Just make sure everybody responds at the same time when I give a command." I could do that.

As we pushed off, the sun glistened on the water. I felt a charge of energy as I dug my paddle into the water and the current began to carry us along. The waves slapped at our boat playfully, sending spray into our faces. We paddled up to a pillow of water that gathered before a giant boulder and then plunged down a chute to the right.

A momentary panic sent my heart racing, then I felt a wall of water crash over me and I laughed out loud. "Disneyland will never be able to create a ride like this," I shouted to Eric over the roar of the crashing water, and I could see the hint of a smile.

As we shot down the river, we bumped into rocks and saw explosions of water as waves crashed into each other. The sense of danger only added to the thrill. Our boat seemed to have little trouble navigating the rapids; our paddling hardly seemed to matter.

"Right forward," said the guide as we approached the edge of a precipice and shot down. I dug my paddle down but there was no water. The raft had slid up the side of the boulder and my side was in the air. In a flash, I was thrown into a boiling churn of freezing water.

Calm down, I told myself. I leaned back and lifted my legs as the guide had advised, but the river spun me around and tossed me against one boulder after another. Water forced its way through my nose and throat. I couldn't breathe. When the boulders finally gave way, I fell down a waterfall and plunged into a deep pool where an undercurrent pulled me down, holding me under water until I was swallowing water and choking. Just when I thought I could come up for air, the undercurrent pulled me down again. I was drowning.

I'm going to die, I thought. And just as that thought hit me, I was struck by another, even more terrifying thought. *Where's Eric?* I struggled to swim, but I was a ragdoll against the relentless current.

I had to turn back, somehow swim up this river, but the onrush of water was just forcing more water down my throat. Just when I thought my lungs would give out, I saw a blur of orange and an outstretched arm. A hand grabbed my right arm firmly and pulled me in. It was Eric. His dark eyes bathed me with their warm concern. My world turned inside out. I was happy, relieved he was safe. He was alive. He was alive! But I also felt weak and helpless. Wasn't I the one who was supposed to be saving my son?

A thirteen-year-old boy was sobbing loudly beside me. "I want to get off this boat. I want to go home."

"There is nowhere to go," said the guide. "We have to get through this."

The boy curled into a ball and continued to cry.

"Are you okay?" I asked Eric. "Does that hurt?" I pointed to a large scrape along his stomach.

"I'm fine."

"Thanks for helping me," I said. "I thought I was going to drown."

Eric did not respond, and I wondered if I now looked smaller in his eyes.

But there was no time for chit chat. Just as we all got back to our stations, the raft headed toward another sharp drop. "Forward right," said the guide, now speaking more loudly.

We dug in. I felt a pain in my chest. As we went down Branding Iron, I paddled with everything I had, but my strength had left me. Each boulder loomed like a menace. I shuddered at the sight of sleepers, rocks close to the surface that appeared as dark spots on the water surface. The river seemed to boil with fury, tipping the boat sharply from side to side and whipping my face. I shivered with cold while, under my right arm, my rib cage burned with pain. I looked back at Eric, calm and determined. I felt proud of him, and that helped me to swallow my own pride.

"I'm going to have to switch with you," I told Eric after a few minutes. "I don't have the strength. You should be the leader."

Eric took my place and dug his oar powerfully into the water. It was now largely he and the guide powering the boat around the rocks. The rest of us were shivering and tired. We wondered if we would survive another fall. How glad I was that Mariko and Marie were not on this trip. How glad I was that we had come through this. How glad I was ...

Suddenly, the boat stopped: we were wrapped around a rock that rose four feet out of the water. The rushing current pressed the ends of the boat around either side of the rock. I was high above the water on the left side of the rock, and Eric was just below me on the same side. The others were on the front of the boat wrapped around the opposite side of the same rock.

"Let the air out on your side," the guide screamed to me.

"What?" We were stuck on a rock in a raging river and I was supposed to let the air out of the boat?

"Now!" said the guide.

I crawled up to the top of the raft and leaned precariously over the side, trying not to look down at the raging river. I slowly unscrewed the cap. "*Sssssss.*" The boat was collapsing and I would soon fall into the raging river. "More" said the guide. I was afraid but I continued to let the air out.

"Shut it now!" the guide said suddenly. I fumbled, then focused and finally screwed it tight. Without warning, the front of the boat caught a current and the raft was pulled down a chute. I held on to the boat as air suddenly moved to my side of the boat, barely keeping us afloat as we sped down the river.

"Wow, how did that work?" asked Eric.

"Someone told me about that maneuver a long time ago. I always wondered if it would work," said the guide.

I was shaken, but I felt a peace growing inside me. Growing up, my father had always warned me against expecting too much. He once warned me that I would fail in my career if I ever returned to the United States because I wouldn't have the advantage of speaking Japanese. Now I know that Dad just wanted to protect me from the inevitable disappointments, but in doing so he had cut away at my confidence. When I looked at Eric, I could see that he had no such issues. He had a confidence that I never had as a young man. I had helped him become who he was and those choices, in turn, had shaped me. *I had done something right*. That thought filled me with pride. As I thought of that, I realized that Dad, too, must have felt pride in his children during the final years of his life. He had done something right.

The river calmed as the land flattened out. It was clear we would make it. As we drifted across the California border, we spotted a six-point elk sipping water. River otters raised their heads. We didn't speak much on the bus ride home, but I could feel something between us that hadn't been there before. At age fifty-two, I had experienced for the first time in my life, a total loss of control. And Eric had been there for me.

"I'm really proud of you," I said to Eric as we climbed out of the van and headed for our hotel. "But let's not tell Mom too many of the details. She'll only worry."

Eric nodded gravely. We had a pact.

In the months that followed, Eric, in his growing independence, was often impatient with me. I, in my frustration, sometimes lost my temper. Occasionally, there were sharp words. But somehow, since that day, I have known that life would never pull us apart as it had my Dad and me. Eric and I were not connected genetically, but on that summer day, those rapids, wild and uncontrollable, had thrown us together to reveal a bond stronger than any biological code. I knew then that my son and I would always know how much we cared for each other. If, from time to time, we started to slip apart, the memory of white water on that summer day would be there to pull us back together.

THE VIEW FROM
ANOTHER
BLUFF

A T HOME IN SEATTLE, IT sometimes feels that I have the best of both worlds. I live on a bluff with a view of the Puget Sound that a visiting relative said reminded him of the view from Helm Hill in Honmoku before the sea was filled in. As I get older, I find the Japanese in me beginning to reassert itself. More often, now, I prefer the subtle bitterness of green tea to the instant buzz of strong coffee. I find relaxation pruning my pines, red maples and wisteria to give them the distinctive shapes I remember from Japan. I take the salmon, halibut and clams natural to the Northwest and cook them in the Japanese way with sweet sake, soy sauce, ginger, rice vinegar and green onions. And in the four decades since I first left Japan, Japanese culture has so permeated America that there is little from Japan that I cannot find here.

All around my home are the touchstones of my journey into the past: a red lantern used on one of my great-grandfather's barges; the copper handle of a paper door I found on the island paradise my father visited during the Occupation; and the grinding stone in my backyard that I took from the village of the disgraced samurai. Each taps a memory that leads me back into the past. I can feel the shiver of excitement my great-grandfather felt on that bright autumn day in 1869 when he first set foot in Yokohama, a town decked out in bright paper lanterns and colored banners in preparation for the horse races. From that

day, my family's fate has been linked inextricably with Japan's like two parallel strands in a chain of DNA.

A few decades after Julius trained Wakayama peasants in the ways of the Prussian Army, Japan emerged as a military and economic power. Yokohama's development as a prosperous port created the conditions for Helm Brothers' success as a stevedoring and forwarding company. And just as the advanced powers of the West snubbed newly modern Japan, my Grandfather Julie, as a man of mixed blood, also felt the sting of prejudice. The same earthquakes and wars that wounded Japan pulled at the fabric of my family. Dad was drawn back to a defeated Japan as an Occupation soldier; I was drawn back to report on the dark side of the Japanese miracle.

I am still trying to find out who the military men are in the photo of my great-grandfather. His true legacy, however, was his pioneering spirit, the drive that took him away from the comfort of his family and community to build a new life in a new world. Without his decision to venture out, I would lack a dimension of my being that I've come to value. As a father of two children who must find their own way, I am reminded by Julius that there are drawbacks to being part of a close-knit community, just as there are challenges to being an outsider. Life is a little more predictable, but it can also be narrower. As someone who comes from three generations of "in-between" people who faced continuous upheaval, I've learned that we build our communities wherever we are, with whomever we choose. Julius arrived alone in Japan, but he lured five of his siblings from faraway Europe to join him, then married Hiro and created his own tribe. We survive to pass on our own values and establish our own truths. If we are lucky, with each generation these truths become more universal, less insular, a foundation for greater understanding across cultures.

In Seattle, I have found such a community among friends, relatives and colleagues at work.

I continue to visit Japan every couple of years to spend time with my Japanese relatives. On my last visit to Japan, I took Komiya Katsuaki and his wife Yoko to see the grave of my great-grandmother, Hiro Komiya, in the Foreigners' Cemetery overlooking Yokohama harbor. I also showed them the small gravestone of Julius and Hiro's first daughter, Lina, the one who died at birth. When Katsuaki knelt down to look more closely at the grave, he suddenly pointed to a tiny mark on the top left of the grave.

"That's our family crest," he said with excitement. "See the three wisteria blooms?"

I had always wondered whether the baby had been buried in this dark corner of the cemetery out of shame. Now it pleased me that Hiro had honored the baby with her family crest. It remains unclear why the Komiya family's crest was different from the crest with two eagle feathers that had been passed down through our family. Perhaps they represented two branches of the Komiya family. Perhaps Hiro had adopted the crest of the other Komiya family after her brother-in-law had remarried and rejected her. But the gravestone was another connection to the Komiyas.

Afterward, Katsuaki told me that the word in Japan for destiny, *unmei*, originated from the ancient Japanese belief that people at birth were given a certain bounty from God. If you were born with three thousand days' worth of food, that was how long you would live. That was your fate. Lina, evidently, was born with no rice to her name.

When I expressed some skepticism about the notion that so much of life was predetermined, Katsuaki looked at me strangely. "Don't you remember how we met?" he asked. "We don't usually read the back sections of the *Yomiuri* newspaper. What was the chance that Yoko would come across that article about you?"

What, for that matter, was the chance that Marie and I would have ended up with Mariko and Eric? Was that fate too? I wondered. *And what about my cousin Atsushi? He spoke of an invisible thread that binds us all, but that you don't see it unless you are searching for it.*

No. It was not just fate that Marie and I ended up with Eric and Mariko. It was Mariko who won me over with her song about ants and helped overcome my fear and doubts about having Japanese children. It was Marie who snatched the note from the boathouse bulletin board and immediately called the pastor in northern Japan and arranged for us to adopt Eric. And I, I chose to write this book, looking into my family's troubled past and reaching out to distant relatives to better understand myself, to heal old wounds and to seek to be a better father.

Before we left Japan, I took Marie, Mariko and Eric again to see Dad's grave at the Foreigners' Cemetery. While Eric scrubbed the gravestone, Mariko helped me trim the azalea bushes. Marie cleaned out the vase and put fresh flowers in it.

When we were finished, we stood at the foot of the grave and bowed our heads.

Look at how big Mariko and Eric have grown, I told Dad. *You would be impressed by Eric. He is sharp as a tack. And Mariko? Mariko would have found a way to reach you as I never could.*

Now as I think of my two children, I whisper my thanks to the gods and to my mother and my father. I see beyond their battles to remember the evenings when, after my mother had tucked us into bed, my father would come into the room with his ukulele and sing "My Bonnie Lies Over the Ocean" or "Red River Valley." I understand now how Mother fell in love with Dad when she heard him sing in harmony with his two brothers as they were washing the dishes. I imagine Dad looking down at me with that charming smile he once gave me in the sushi bar when he told me the story about Hiro and the samurai. And I chuckle at the thought of my father finding his place among the German and Japanese ancestors he had once spurned, but who are now the collective gods of my family.

Ft Lawton, Washington June 6-11, 1946

Traveling to Ft Lawton Washington under the best of conditions
Marvelous scenery, much excitement with Great Expectations in going to Japan

AFTERWORD

GOING THROUGH OLD PHOTOGRAPHS OF my family with Josh Powell, the designer of this book, I came across a picture of dad leaning against a tree looking out over a body of water that seemed oddly familiar. The caption read, "Fort Lawton," a name that had recently been in the news because the fort was shutting down after serving the nation for more than a century. In the photograph, Dad was in full uniform. He had just completed his studies at the Army Language School in Michigan and was on his way to Japan to serve in the Occupation. The army base where he stayed as he prepared for this strange new venture in Japan, I had discovered for the first time, was in Magnolia, the neighborhood I chose to make my home. How is it that these odd coincidences continue to strike? Or perhaps, as Atsushi once told me, they are not coincidences. Perhaps as we look back at our families, we become just a little more aware of the threads that, woven together, form the narratives of our life.

It is an odd truth that in our branch of the Helm family, the male genetic line has come to an end. Grandfather Julie was much envied when he had three sons. Those three sons, in turn, begat five sons. But none of us five have had biological male children. My three male cousins have no plans to have children. My brother and I both have sons we adopted from Japan.

To my great-grandfather, my grandfather and even my father, not having biological children to carry on the bloodline, to pass on our particular genetic fingerprint, might have been regarded as a curse. For me, it has proved a special gift because it is for this reason my wife and I are blessed with Mariko and Eric.

And although growing up as adopted children in a mixed-race family has sometimes been difficult for them, they have both adapted well. Mariko feels a special mission in life. "When I was young, I would think that it was my fault that people were staring at me; that somehow I had done something wrong. I did not blend in with my family, and those implacable eyes were my punishment," Mariko, at sixteen, wrote to me. "But now I realize that it is us, our family, who have to teach people that it's okay to look different."

Eric looks at his adoption in coldly logical terms. Culture, he says, is not about ethnicity, but about upbringing. Although he is Asian in terms of the way he looks, he understands that many of his cultural values are more Western. He is studying Chinese because his high school does not offer Japanese language classes. I hope that his knowledge of kanji, which are quite similar to Chinese characters, will one day ease the way for him as he rediscovers his Japanese heritage.

As for me, my journey into that past has taught me that my family contains few heroes. Still, I have embraced my family as I have embraced Japan, a culture whose complex tapestry, I now understand, has enriched my life in more ways than I will ever fully grasp. I know that our fates will continue to be inextricably linked, mine and Japan's, for I have taken Japan's children for my own.

I hope my children will adopt this story for their own, but I know now that this will only be a small part of their story. They have their own journeys to take, their own stories to write.

I N WRITING THIS FAMILY MEMOIR, I depended heavily on countless friends, relatives, scholars and strangers. I drew liberally from unpublished reminiscences by Great-grandfather Julius Helm; my Opa, Grandfather Robert Schinzinger; Opa's second wife, Shizuka; my mother, Barbara Helm; and my distant cousin, Tsunemochi Atsushi. I also benefited from the genealogy work by my late aunt Jane Schinzinger and my dad's late cousin, Trudy Webster.

I conducted more than a hundred interviews over the course of my research. Karl Helm's late daughters Trudy, Lillian and Margaret were invaluable. Dad, his two wives Toshiko and Barbara, his two brothers, Ray and Larry, and his cousins Richard Helm and Leo Ellis and their friends, Eileen Charlseworth and Lucille and Michael Apcar, were also a great help. Uncle Ray shared his knowledge and gave me binders full of family photos and letters he had assiduously saved. Dozens of old-timers in Yokohama shared their experiences, and I thank my childhood friend, Mary Corbett, for helping to arrange many of those interviews.

Many Japanese scholars helped me, but I want to give particular thanks to Saito Takio and Nakatake Kanami of the Yokohama Archives of History, Takeuchi Yoshinobu of the Wakayama City Museum, Tsutsumi Yukichi of the city of Kurume and Umetani Noboru, formerly of Osaka University. Former Helm Brothers employees who provided information included Mori Taro, Teshirogi Takao, Joseph Splingaerd and Ozawa Matsuko.

For historical background, I drew from dozens of published sources including: *The Making of Modern Japan,* by Ken Pyle; *The Making of Modern Japan,* by Marius B. Jansen; *Everyday Things in Premodern Japan,* by Susan B. Hanley; *Awakening Japan: The Diary of a German Doctor: Erwin Baelz,* edited by

Toku Baelz; *Oyatoi Gaikokujin*, by Shigehisa Tokutaro; *The German Prisoners-Of-War in Japan, 1914-1920*, by Charles Burdick and Ursula Moessner; *Embracing Defeat*, by John W. Dower; *The Western World and Japan*, by G.B. Sansom; *Yokohama in 1872*, by Paul C. Blum; *The Austro-Prussian War*, by Geoffrey Wawro and *A Historical Guide to Yokohama*, by Burritt Sabin. I also drew from extensive files SCAP (Supreme Commander for the Allied Powers) put together on the Helms and their businesses as it tried to sort out whether the family should be classified as friends or enemy. (See Lesliehelm.com for an annotated bibliography.)

Thanks to the Webster family for sharing their wonderful collection of Helm family photos. Most of the photos from the Occupation were taken by Dad. The woodblock prints of the Customhouse and the "Map of Early Yokohama" are from the collection of the Yokohama Archives of History.

Special thanks to author and aunt, Ella Ellis, who gave me the confidence to embark on this journey; Brenda Peterson, who taught me to bring emotion to my writing, and Chalmers Johnson, who shaped my thinking on Japan. Among the many who read my manuscript and helped me shape it are Dori Jones Yang, John Runyan, Maureen Michelson, Sheldon Garon, Fred Notehelfer, Sheila Johnson, Neil Gross, Colter Mott, Burritt Sabin and, most important of all, my wife, Marie Anchordoguy.

Thanks to Bruce Rutledge, publisher of Chin Music Press, who took a chance on this book. I was blessed to have as my editor, David Jacobson, a man who knows Japan well, is a great wordsmith and showed great patience and understanding as he helped me wrestle down this book and prepare it for publication. A special bouquet to the book designer, Josh Powell, who created a beautiful work of art from an impossible stack of family albums, postcards, stamps, stock certificates and random documents.

My mother, Barbara, and my siblings, Chris, Julie and Andrea, have been a great comfort to me all my life, and I can't thank them enough for always being by my side. As for Dad? I really believe he would have been proud of this book. One thing Dad taught me was that it's important, above all, to tell the truth as you see it, even if it might make a lot of people uncomfortable.

This book is dedicated to my wife, Marie, and our children Mariko and Eric, who have supported and encouraged me along my journey and have filled my life with joy and meaning.

LESLIE HELM IS A VETERAN FOREIGN correspondent. He served eight years in Tokyo for *Business Week* and *The Los Angeles Times*, was bureau chief for *Business Week* in Boston, and has reported from South Korea and India. He is currently executive editor of *Seattle Business*, an award-winning monthly magazine. Helm earned a master's degree in journalism from the Columbia University School of Journalism and in Asian studies from the University of California, Berkeley. He was born and raised in Yokohama, Japan, where his family has lived since 1869. Helm now lives in Seattle with his wife, Marie Anchordoguy, and his children, Mariko and Eric. He enjoys hiking and gardening in the summer and snowshoeing and playing squash in the winter.